**dreams
in double
time**

refiguring american music

A series edited by
Ronald Radano,
Josh Kun, and
Nina Sun Eidsheim

Charles McGovern,
contributing editor

dreams in double time

jonathan leal

on race, freedom, and bebop

DUKE UNIVERSITY PRESS / DURHAM AND LONDON / 2023

© 2023 DUKE UNIVERSITY PRESS
All rights reserved
Project editor: Lisa Lawley
Designed by Matthew Tauch
Typeset in Garamond Premier Pro
by Westchester Publishing Services

Library of Congress Cataloging-in-Publication Data
Names: Leal, Jonathan, [date] author.
Title: Dreams in double time : on race, freedom, and bebop / Jonathan Leal.
Other titles: Refiguring American music.
Description: Durham : Duke University Press, 2023. | Series: Refiguring American music | Includes bibliographical references and index. Identifiers: LCCN 2022045887 (print)
LCCN 2022045888 (ebook)
ISBN 9781478020752 (paperback)
ISBN 9781478019985 (hardcover)
ISBN 9781478024583 (ebook)
Subjects: LCSH: Jazz—History and criticism. | Jazz—Japan—History and criticism. | Bop (Music)—History and criticism. | Jazz—Social aspects—United States—History—20th century. | Music and race—United States—History—20th century. | Araki, James T. | Raúlrsalinas, 1934–2008. | Wing, Harold. | Harlem (New York, NY)—Intellectual life—20th century. | BISAC: MUSIC / Genres & Styles / Jazz | SOCIAL SCIENCE / Ethnic Studies / General Classification: LCC ML3506 .L405 2023 (print) | LCC ML3506 (ebook) | DDC 781.6509—DC23/ENG/20230406
LC record available at https://lccn.loc.gov/2022045887
LC ebook record available at https://lccn.loc.gov/2022045888

Cover art: Dizzy Gillespie plays at Eddie Condon's, circa 1960. Photo by Susan Schiff Faludi / Three Lions / Getty Images.

**for octaviano
y elevinia,
mary y josé**

I didn't like the way he carried himself, loose and dreamlike all the time, and I didn't like his friends, and his music seemed to be merely an excuse for the life he led. It sounded just that weird and disordered.

James Baldwin, "Sonny's Blues" (1957)

contents

Acknowledgments · ix

INTRODUCTION · 1
dreaming otherwise

ONE · 25
after-hours

TWO · 46
layered time

THREE · 74
quartered notes

FOUR · 114
among others

EPILOGUE · 152
affinities

Notes · 161 / Bibliography · 207 / Index · 227

acknowl-edgments

Dear Dreamer,

In some ways, this book began a decade ago: first as joy-filled jam sessions in Denton, Texas; then as a long essay for a seminar led by Walton Muyumba; then as a series of years-long conversations with Walton, Javier Rodriguez, Masood Raja, Ramón Saldívar, José David Saldívar, Anna Schultz, and Charles Kronengold—and then, finally, as the braid before you now.

In that sense, this book is in many ways a record of young adulthood, a record of a decade of formative experiences, musical collaborations, and dream wanderings with poets and musicians, painters and programmers, composers and agriculturalists, scientists and historians, scholars and writers, living and departed. It bears the traces of a world warped by pandemic catastrophe, ecological collapse, political nefariousness, digital voids, astrocapitalist greed, racial violence, heteroblivious policy—and, crucially, also the traces of those who have been working to counter these forces and bring a different world arrangement into being. Each revision and reharmonization of the following pages has been a modest attempt to grapple with grief and promise through sound and story, to grapple with what it means to find oneself through rhythms and melodies half remembered. Each iteration has also helped me grow and grow up, has helped me hear anew the immense weight of human inheritance. Writing transforms a writer, dreams the texture of waking.

Thinking back on some of the journey: in Denton, Walton Muyumba, now a longtime mentor and friend, took me under his wing alongside Javier Rodriguez and Masood Raja, helping me contextualize my efforts as a borderlands musician within a broader story of social struggle and possibility, becoming the spiritual coach I didn't know I needed. Too, Paul and Sandi Rennick, percussionists and composers who have influenced my musical life more than I can articulate, modeled for me the highest forms of care, rigor, and soul in contemporary music education; on and off the stage, I witnessed them stoke performers' unique musical passions and invest in the transformative power of true teamwork, and those moments have never left me. I was fortunate to spend time with them as a younger person, and I'm grateful for their friendship now.

Later, at Stanford, in soft sunlight among the redwoods, a number of generous souls guided me as I refined and pursed the questions that came to animate this book. Ramón Saldívar, José David Saldívar, Anna Schultz, and Charlie Kronengold offered immeasurable support, engaging my ideas, steering my madcap enthusiasms, and genuinely caring for me as a human being. La Maestra Cherríe Moraga opened my eyes to parts of my life I had been too frightened to look at directly; she liberated me from unacknowledged inhibitions and inspired me to dig deeper, to articulate my pieties, and to accept myself such that I might accept and offer love more deeply. And Paula Moya's brilliance, determination, and goodwill served as a constant inspiration throughout my time on the Farm, and I feel exceedingly fortunate to have learned from her.

At Stanford, through the Interdisciplinary PhD Program in Modern Thought and Literature, I also had the great fortune of working in various capacities with Michele Elam, Héctor Hoyos, Jeff Chang, Tom Mullaney, David Palumbo-Liu, Shelly Fisher Fishkin, Yvonne Yarbro-Bejarano, Mark Greif, Vaughn Rasberry, Carol Vernallis, Jennifer DeVere Brody, Elizabeth Kessler, Robert Trujillo, Monica Moore, Rachel Meisels, Amy Potemski, Nancy Child, Heidi López, Rigoberto Marquéz, Jonathan Rosa, Adrian Daub, Margaret Sena, Elvira Prieto, Frances Morales, Chris Gonzalez Clarke, Tim Noakes, Tobias and Catherine Wolff, and many others, all of whom helped me appreciate, through their energies, talents, and interests, how much richness this world holds. Getting to know them all was one of the greatest joys and privileges I was afforded as a graduate student.

Importantly, research support in the form of a graduate fellowship from Stanford's Center for Comparative Studies in Race and Ethnicity, a scholar-in-residence position at El Centro Chicano y Latino, a Creativity in Research Fellowship from the Hasso-Plattner Institute of Design, a Mellon Dissertation Fellowship from Stanford University, an AMS-50 Dissertation Fellowship from the American Musicological Society, an Emerging Critics Fellowship from the National Book Critics Circle, and a postdoctoral fellowship from the Society of Fellows in the Humanities at the University of Southern California all made it possible for me to assemble and process this dreamwork, to practice (re)linking seemingly disparate concepts and conversations, and, crucially, to keep a roof over my head in two of the world's most excruciatingly expensive towns. I'll always be grateful for the stability and community these fellowships afforded.

Like many books, too, *Dreams* is a record of camaraderie. My interlocutors and fellow graduate student travelers—Maria Cichosz, Calvin Cheung-Miaw, Max Suechting, Jeremiah Lockwood, Tysen Dauer, Gabriela Salvidea, Gabriel Ellis, Ioanida Costache, Juliana Nalerio, Thao Nguyen, Rebecca Wilbanks, Cameron Awkward-Rich, Chris Suh, So-Rim Lee, Michiko Theurer, Annie Atura, Michael Kinney, Courtney Peña, Imán Muñiz, Luz Jimenez Ruvalcaba, Karina Gutierrez, Cristopher Vásquez, Melanie León, Kristin Wilson, Long Le-Khac, Annika Butler-Wall, David Stentiford, Katja Schwaller, Alberto Quintero, Mitch Therieau, Henry Washington Jr., Miguel Samano, Chiara Giovanni, and many others—all provided support as I drafted portions of what became this book by way of writing groups, feedback sessions, late-night ravings, Spotify playlists, caffeine binges, read-a-thons, zany recountings, and creative practices. As our paths have diverged in recent years, these folks have continued to inspire many by bringing their whole selves to their artistic and scholarly practices. Their work is and is of the future.

After Stanford, midpandemic, I moved to Los Angeles, tenderfooted yet hopeful, and I'll always be grateful for how readily and warmly I was welcomed by my new colleagues at the University of Southern California. I feel an immense sense of gratitude for Josh Kun, especially—an inspiring mentor, gifted teacher, and brother in sound and spirit—who was central to this life transition and has been to my thinking about musical possibility since I first wandered into a lecture of his a decade ago. Major thanks, too, to all of my colleagues in the Society of Fellows in the Humanities and the Department of American Studies and Ethnicity, which offered me home bases during my postdoctoral years. My colleagues in these spaces—including Daniela Bleichmar, Hilary Schor, Luísa Reis-Castro, Ruthie Ezra, Jessica Varner, Diane Oliva, Ella Klik, Ajay Batra, Meredith Hall, Alice Echols, Nitin Govil, Jennifer Petersen, Elda Maria Román, Jenny Chio, Cavan Concannon, Mike Ananny, Alice Baumgartner, Lydia Moudileno,

Ashanti Shih, Peter Redfield, Isaac Blacksin, John Carlos Rowe, Juan de Lara, and Natalia Molina—were endlessly inspiring and kind as I worked and learned and wondered.

I offer my deep thanks, too, to all of my new colleagues in the Department of English at the University of Southern California, who have offered much support and encouragement as I've worked, written, listened, and sounded across fields and joined the team officially. A very special thanks to my brilliant faculty cohort mates, Sarah Kessler and Corrine Collins, who inspire many daily through their writing and examples and have encouraged me personally through some deeply difficult trials; warmth and gratitude, as well, to David St. John, David Román, Karen Tongson, Devin Griffiths, Zakiyyah Iman Jackson, Dana Johnson, Danzy Senna, Elda Maria Román, Ashley Cohen, Aaron Winslow, Alice Gambrell, Melissa Daniels-Rauterkus, Geoff Dyer, and David Ulin for helping me acclimate to a new academic home in a vast, luminous city.

Huge thanks, too, to my partners in time and praxis at the University of Southern California—the inimitable Adrian De Leon, Jackie Wang, Nate Sloan, Joan Flores-Villalobos, Fiori Berhane, Neftalie Williams, and A. E. Stevenson—for the consistent realness, spiritual grounding, and head-clearing conversations. Thanks, too, to the many friends and creative collaborators who have offered gentle nudging and endless inspiration these past few years, including Charlie Vela, Michiko Theurer, Erin Lynch, Fidel Martinez, Brandon Guerra, Matt Penland, Akira Robles, K. J. Stafford, Kevin Raab, Kathleen Montes, Amos Magliocco, Lindsay McClintock, Liza Black, Jonathan Maiocco, Alison Konicek, Alysse Padilla, Jesus Sanchez, and many others I hold dear. Much gratitude, as well, to Kenji Okubo, for offering essential research assistance from Japan; to Marcus Clayton, who offered invaluable help with the final preparations of the manuscript; and to my agent, Akin Akinwumi, at Willenfield Literary Agency, who has helped me envision new creative possibilities for myself and my work and offered much encouragement and patience.

Major thanks to everyone at Duke University Press, including Ken Wissoker, Ryan Kendall, and the series editors of Refiguring American Music—Josh Kun, Ronald Radano, and Nina Sun Eidsheim—as well as the anonymous peer reviewers of the book manuscript, whose generous and generative feedback helped this project become itself. *Dreams* wouldn't have been possible without the support, insight, guidance, and encouragement of this mighty editorial village, and I'll always be grateful for their wise words and good humor.

Special thanks, too, to the many people who helped me complete research for this project, including Barbara Kukla, for speaking with me about Harold Wing and Newark's many jazz histories; Tad Hershorn for guiding me through the archives at the Institute of Jazz Studies at Rutgers University; Tokiko Bazzell and the archivists at the University of Hawai'i at Mānoa for research assistance related to James Araki; Dale Araki, for talking with me from Japan about his father's music; Linda Moody for speaking with me about bebop, race, gender, and her late husband, bebop multi-instrumentalist James Moody; Malee Wing for chatting with me about her father's many musical contributions; Eugene "Goldie" Goldston for laying things out for me in downtown Newark; Tim Noakes and Robert Trujillo for the ample help with the Raúl R. Salinas Papers at Stanford; and the many, many others who gifted me leads, clues, and generosity.

Last: my deepest thanks to my kin and close family, without whom none of this would have been possible—Susan Leal, Danny Leal, Sonya Garza, and Alyssa Jalomo, who have encouraged me from the beginning; C. Starlin Lemons, for sharing wondrous years of light and love; and my grandparents, José and Mary, Elevinia and Octaviano, who set such positive examples and loved their families and communities dearly. I dedicate this book to them; to James Araki, Raúl Salinas, Harold Wing, and their families; as well as to everyone the numerous musicians mentioned in this book inspired. Following their stories and listening for their dreams has helped me hear my own life, family, and world differently. For this and much more, I'll always be grateful.

With much love to you and yours,
Jonathan

Tano's saxophone. Source: Author's personal collection.

intro.
dreaming otherwise

When I quiet my mind and rest my eyes and grant my memory space, I can still recall the saxophone in my late grandfather's home—there in San Juan, Texas, at the edge of two nations and the center of more histories—the metal and plastic variably reflective when naked in the blistering sunlight, tarnished slightly near the bell but otherwise gleaming and inviting, as if still just arrived from the Sears Roebuck catalog in the sheen of the early 1950s. It would have come by mail, just after World War II, just before my grandfather's military service in the US Army, just before his studies as a music student, just before the birth of his and his wife's first child. From that saxophone, once housed in a modest hard-shell case lined with soft blue fabric, the sounds of varied worlds once emerged with regularity, at times in the company of other instruments and musicians, though most often in the humid dark of South Texan solitude. From its curves once bloomed laconic wind band pieces, local upbeat Tejano classics, buttoned-up swing favorites—and, notably, energetic, earnest attempts at conversing with an iconoclastic Black sound forged after-hours in Harlem nightclubs thousands of miles from the heat mirages of the Rio Grande, made local through ink and vinyl and rumor and report, rendered audible through records pressed and sold and spun and later stored away: *Charlie Parker with Strings*, Charlie Parker and Machito's *Afro-Cuban Jazz Suite*, Charlie Parker and Dizzy Gillespie's *Bird and Diz*.

"I loved music from the beginning," my grandfather told me when I once asked him about these things, reticent as I was about prying into his inner life. As he recalled:

Aquí en el Valle it was all by ear. There was no sheet music for me, so I learned how to play that way. Then I went to high school, and I learned how to read music, and then I went to college and was a music major and played with the guys who were in the One O'Clock Lab Dance Band at North Texas State College, and those guys could really play. I learned about modern jazz. Everyone was way ahead of me, writing their own music. It was challenging, but I still enjoyed it. I learned so much from listening and playing, and for years and years I played, especially when I came home to the Valley.

My recollections of my grandfather's saxophonic musicianship are spare; he had all but stopped performing by the time I joined the cosmos. But as I—distant now from our shared homeland—have reflected these past few years on the records he most loved and the artists he most admired, I have felt his tastes steering my questions, his memory guiding my ears. As time has passed and this world has smoldered, remembering my grandfather's musical dreams and harmonious sensibilities has offered me a shelter, a refuge that, today, finds its form as this offering, *Dreams in Double Time*—a work that in part explores gaps and overlaps in my and my grandfather's generational experiences as well as meditates on the questions I am left with in the wake of his death. This book, that is—through its loops and syncopations, its measured longings and layered stories—focuses on a music that inspired my grandfather and a great many others in his generational cohort, as well as a great deal more over the course of the past eighty years (and counting): bebop, an underground Black achievement with a woefully "inadequate" name.[1]

In the pages that follow, I listen for and alongside musicians like my grandfather and sustain a cluster of questions grounded in relational cultural study: Why was a radical avant-garde music, a wartime idiom created after-hours by Black experimentalists in 1940s Harlem jam sessions, so generative for young, differently racialized nonwhite listeners during the global realignments of the postwar years? How is it that the dreams encoded in bebop, specific to African American experiences, came to transform the lives of differently racialized listeners as they dealt daily with the violences of state and national power? What might a focus on the "other colors" of American undergrounds teach artists and scholars about the pasts and potentials of postnational American dreaming? What kinds of futures can relational histories of musical engagement create?

To begin offering answers to these questions, this book entwines my own scenes of remembrance and consideration with three stories, three arcs, three multitemporal, (audio)biographical narratives that, much like my grandfather's own style of storytelling, loop and intersect, overlap and interweave.[2] Each story, one flowing into the next, follows one member of what I'm calling a trio of loosely linked, differently racialized listeners—and, in effect, their respective music scenes, contexts, and communities.[3] My grandfather didn't know these three figures, never played with them or listened to their music, but I would like to think that they would have gotten along, would have bonded over their shared sounds and mutual interests. Together, their stories, distinct yet inseparable, evoke a dense interplay, a polyrhythmic relation, a sense of a moment greater than the sum of its parts.

The first figure, James T. Araki, was a Nisei multi-instrumentalist, soldier-translator, and eventual literature and folklore scholar credited with helping introduce bebop to Japan during the Allied Occupation, not long after his internment at the Gila River War Relocation Center. The second, Raúl R. Salinas, was a Mexican American poet, jazz critic, and longtime activist who endured the US carceral system for over a decade and whose investments in jazz from behind and beyond bars helped document East Austin's rich music histories and instantiate a bebop-inflected Xicanindio literary idiom. And the third, Harold Wing, was an Afro-Chinese American drummer, pianist, and songwriter who performed with bebop's pioneers—including Charlie Parker, Dizzy Gillespie, Erroll Garner, Miles Davis, Bud Powell, and Babs Gonzales, as well as singers including Ella Fitzgerald, Shirley Horn, and Etta James—before eventually taking the lessons of the music to his work as a public servant in Newark's City Hall after the uprisings of the late 1960s. By following these figures through their communities during the postwar decades, *Dreams in Double Time* expands bebop's narratives, recording the reach and importance of Harlem's Black experimental musicians among differently positioned and marginalized listeners of color across (and beyond) the United States—audiences newly driven to disrupt the standard logics of racial democracy through their insistent, dissonant dreaming. Working against a backdrop of studies devoted to jazz masters, this book attends to listeners for whom the Black-centered musical revolution of bebop proposed new ways of being in the world, for whom it became an affectively and intellectually powerful force, for whom it offered a symbolic language critical of the larger forces of governmental, state-sanctioned imperialism, for whom it challenged the totalizing singularity of whiteness during the second half of the twentieth century, for whom it offered opportunities to imagine new critical-artistic forms of confrontation with a racially supremacist, imperial nation emboldened during and after World War II. *Dreams in Double Time*'s stories, in effect, shed light on the lasting need for relational antiracist thought, aesthetics, and coalition building—a matter crucial even before there was a United States, a concern vital amid the wartime nationalism of the so-called short-lived American century, and a notion pressing for all of us now, amid the layered crises, looming precarities, and nationalist viralities of the 2020s.

* * *

It's no secret that in the United States, the 1940s were years of widespread tension and acceleration.[4] Domestic migrations, shifting class dynamics, cultural mediatizations, and racial tensions grew increasingly intense, spurred by the boots of a martial economy. Also accelerating were efforts to maintain the definition of social divisions under the guise of order and renewed security: Jim Crow segregation laws cleaved domestic communities and military units during the war; the Bracero program instrumentalized migrant laborers while denying them long-term securities; Executive Order 9066, issued on the basis of pursuing "every possible protection against espionage and against sabotage to national-defense material," resulted in the xenophobic internment of Japanese immigrants.[5] Disorganized and paranoiac, these measures were generated from an all-too-familiar defensive position: when met with the real martial and ideological crises that accompany states of war, American government leaders doubled down on the corrosive hierarchies propping up the mainstream national fantasy.

That recalcitrant fantasy remains a cruel mirage, a monocultural siren song built on white supremacist fictions, a corrosive myth protected by what Vaughn Rasberry has called a "racial democracy," or a "regiment of governance" "in which the rights, principles, and affective dimensions of citizenship are distributed to or withheld from citizens on the basis of race"—and in which the regime is upheld by a "network of disciplinary, punitive, and terroristic measures meted out to racial subjects by state and non-state actors alike."[6] The national fantasy during that crucial period of global conflict became a deafening rallying cry, an unsettling chorus demanding univocality.[7] And amid its numbing drone, a new, iconoclastic approach to musicking emerged from Harlem's underground—an approach that fused Black migrant aspirations, Harlem's unique magnetisms, and deeper theoretical critiques of power and hegemony: what came to be known, "most inadequate[ly]," as bebop.⁸

Before this music was incorporated into postcard narratives of American improvisatory freedom, unsurprisingly, many listeners heard it as simply a new form of Black "noise": the work of "loose and dreamlike" walkers, the stuff of "disorder, the unthought, the unplanned, the unwelcome, marked by the apparent absence of the human capacity for reason."⁹ As Vijay Iyer explains it, this "ejection" of Black music "from the category of music [itself] align[ed] directly with the historic and ongoing dehumanization of Black people"—the very dehumanization that those in service of global capitalism have for "the past half millennium" used "to rationalize and justify enslavement, imperialism, plunder, and genocide."¹⁰ This world-imposing hearing of Black musicking as noise is precisely what makes me so interested in the ways differently racialized nonwhite people engaged with it, lived with its attendant myths, heard in its angularities and complexities a route to dreaming together, with and across difference.

Although Mexican Americans, Japanese Americans, Afro-Asian Americans, and many other racialized groups were already intimately aware of the horrors of midcentury racial democracy in the United States before bebop traveled beyond Harlem's underground, for some young listeners and practitioners, this music was a revelation that disrupted racial democracy's divide-and-conquer logics and fostered new understandings of social connection. Hearing this mode of Black musical dreaming that unsettled and affirmed—that blurred boundaries, challenged fixities, invited new modes of being, and rearticulated the force and presence of Black countermodernity—was a transformative encounter, a "meeting of worlds and meanings."¹¹ The improvisatory, dialogical, embodied, and situational "mode[s] of relation" this musicking insisted on called into question a racial capitalist logic that "incentivize[d] minority groups to claim whatever advantages they [could] instead of recognizing shared struggles with other minority groups."¹² To listen to and study Black radical musicking—whether as a formerly interned Japanese American newly enlisted in the US Army, or as a Mexican American prison poet recalling the sounds of his East Austin upbringing, or as an Afro-Chinese American negotiating his biracialization and cultural influences while aspiring to a musical career in Newark, or, like my grandfather, as a borderlands proto-Chicano learning modern jazz through recordings and rehearsals and jam sessions—was to begin to understand one's relationship to others, to rebellion and racialization, to a nation over which one had little immediate control. It was to start dreaming of new worlds beyond the logics of white supremacy, to begin "fus[ing]" that "dream world to the world of ordinary things," and, in effect, to start bending the real itself.[13]

* * *

As a concept, dreaming has come not only to signify the literal neural processes that texture sleep, entwine with memory, and disrupt logic and temporality but also—particularly in the United States, amid the radical legacies and neoconservative co-options of civil rights movement discourse—to connote the metaphorical language of individual and communal aspiration, of social and political possibility, of national fantasy and utopian longing.[14]

While this book isn't strictly about the former—it offers neither psychoanalytic readings of cultural productions nor intensive "dream ethnographies" descriptive of a historical unconscious—it does learn from the associative, multitemporal progressions of dream experience, bringing the fractious, contradictory, and remembered to bear on more traditionally linear presentations of theory, history, relation, interiority, affinity, solidarity, and musicking.[15] Here I treat dreams as a shorthand for the interfaces between internal and external, imagined and real, remembered and forgotten, self and other, in order to offer a new way of theorizing creative worldmaking, political activity, sonic invention, and the larger historical fields in and through which such praxes connect and resonate. For just as the forces of history are filled with contradiction and demand multiscalar and multitemporal attention, so, too, do the structures of our literal and figurative dreams outpace our extant modes of description, narration, and theorization—and, much like music, inspire new attempts, new languages altogether.

Connecting this idea of dreaming to radical musicking—or, better, considering radical musicking as a form of dreaming, hearing dreams as a kind of radical music—links this book's differing yet related stories. To dream in and as music, through and with sound—to listen for and learn with the limits of one's self, community, and surroundings; to stretch the invisible threads lining the fabrics of the everyday; to dissolve inherited boundaries between processes, objects, phenomena, and people; to think and live in a realm beyond routine expression, beyond the normal limits of articulacy—is, as I understand it, to improvise at the edge of form, to create from and layer atop the strangeness of the quotidian, to act on its insistent surreality in the service of a different vision.

This approach of course isn't new in itself, nor imposed on this book's individuals and communities from some distant theoretical perch, but instead is part of a long tradition of artistic-intellectual praxes generated not only in response to but *despite* the devastating cruelties of "modernity's crucible."[16] Elizabeth Alexander, for instance, thinks in her work through physical and conceptual spaces of and for Black art by way of a dreamlike "black interior," a liberated realm for abstract thought with real-world import, an "unfettered dream space" in which "social identity" "need not be seen as a constraint but rather as a way of imagining the self unfettered, racialized but not delimited."[17] Robin D. G. Kelley, in his landmark *Freedom Dreams*, focuses on the intimate relationships between "revelatory dreams" and "political engagement," following generations of activists and surrealists alike to emphasize that "in the poetics of struggle and lived experience, in the utterances of ordinary folk . . . we discover the many different cognitive maps of the future, of the world not yet born."[18] And Daphne Brooks, in her watershed Black sonic feminist *Liner Notes for the Revolution*, writes of "radical dreaming, rehearsals of the what-might-be, the what-could-have-been, the conditional exploration of elusive histories that remain outside of our discreet group that may yet still be conjured and examined through creative manifestations."[19] From Frantz Fanon to Aimé Césaire, Toni Morrison to Fred Moten, Richard Iton to Saidiya Hartman, Esperanza Spalding to Tyshawn Sorey, Matana Roberts to Camae Ayewa, the figure of dreams as signifying aspiration though not reducing to it, as conjuring new worlds but not reifying them, has been a key motif in antiracist Black study and theory for generations and has gained new urgency and momentum as this world's maladies have intensified.

As a Chicano scholar and musician raised in and by the US-Mexico borderlands, I entered this strand of Black relational, antiracist worldmaking, like those of the primary subjects of this book, sonically, socially, proximally, relationally. Like my late grandfather—a lifelong borderlands Tejano, amateur saxophonist, bebop-loving listener, and local community builder in the post–World War II years and beyond—and like many others of his generational cohort, I, too, am compelled by the conditions of social possibility that avant-garde, racialized musical practices create. To echo Ronald Radano: I'm interested in the "hyperreal, dream-like aspect of music that so remarkably and continually draws our attention," in that guiding vibrational energy that "incites passion, prompts deep philosophical reflections, and inspires glorious rhapsodies of poetry and prose."[20] Keeping that dreamlike quality in the mind's ear, and all it might inspire, is at once a spiritual, social, and scholarly goal of this work.

* * *

For many radical musicians and listeners during that pivotal postwar moment in the mid-twentieth century, organized sound was not a static object to be handled and analyzed, not a product or document to be fetishized, but rather a means of indexing and fostering new social relations—and thus an important analytic-theoretical medium in its own right. In this book, as a practitioner myself, I emphasize this approach; rather than pursue new theories *of* or *about* music, I aim to understand music itself (more broadly, sound; more accurately, musicking; more directly, "human action: the sounds of bodies in motion") as a medium for dreaming, speculating, theorizing, connecting, and relating.[21] As an improvising musician actively bringing formal musical training, improvisation, composition, production, and performance research experience to bear on various modes of theoretical praxis and cultural historical study, I work here to understand musicking as a densely signifying cultural practice just as capable of generative insights about the personal, social, and historical as more traditionally representational visual and textual media forms and practices.[22] As I write, I aspire to render and pursue musical theorizing as dreamlike *activity*—much less a noun than a verb—while at the same time attending to Theory as historically conceived within Western academic pathways and philosophical genealogies, reading it in critical relation to the work of ostensibly "minor" figures, activities, and communities.[23] Most directly, by relying on this intentionally open-ended, context- and medium-specific understanding of *theory as action*, I work here to draw attention back to marginalized, differently racialized individuals and communities who have been repeatedly denied opportunities for their own self-articulation, let alone due recognition for intellectual output with a critical distance from things "Eurological," to borrow George Lewis's term.[24] I work here to draw attention back to theorist-musicians and musical theorists who have largely been understood as such by legitimating institutions only in retrospect, where the underlying project is not one of radical recognition but rather of neutralization by incorporation.

As theorists, as dreamers, bebop's musicians were asserting Black intellectualism as undeniable and in the process participating in a larger struggle for basic human dignity that, crucially, didn't overlook racial difference in the pursuit of any re-enlightenment aspirations to universalism, to amnesiac responses to modernity's ills.[25] Part of this effort was an approach to the historical that was shaped by the legacy of forced removal, dehumanization, slavery, and rebellion.[26] In their work was an approach to the scrap, the fragment, made concrete by the allusion, the melodic burst, that was generative and subversive, tethered all the while to real-world reference.²⁷ This intramusical grounding is ultimately part of what made it such a deeply powerful (counter)modernist repertoire: contrary to detractors' claims, bebop musicians on the whole weren't anarchic nor nihilistic but rather invested in the immediate relevance of past traces for the present and the future. The musicians, demonstrably invested in blending the blues idiom so constitutive of past Black musical expression with contemporary pop and European classical gestures—and often with an air of playfulness and mischief, evincing critique in varying affective modalities—brought a new, fervent articulation of circumstance to a moment needing to hear itself.²⁸ "There was a message in our music," drummer Kenny Clarke once recalled. "Whatever you go into, go into it *intelligently*. As simple as that."²⁹

Emerging from after-hours jam sessions in Harlem, as chronicled in this book's first chapter, bebop's stylized contours and sonic gestures expressed "minor-key sensibilities," as Richard Iton once wrote, "generated from the experiences of the underground, the vagabond, and those constituencies marked as deviant—notions of being that are inevitably aligned within, in conversation with, against, and articulated beyond the boundaries of the modern."³⁰ At the style's aesthetic and political core was a fundamental resistance to the racism and anti-Blackness the US nation-state was founded on, a refutation of "the state-sanctioned or extralegal production and exploitation of group-differentiated vulnerability to premature death."³¹ The qualities of these musical expressions—coming when they did, sounding as they did, disrupting what they did—cracked open new universes for listeners not only from coast to coast, lingering with memories of live sets and hovering over record players and jukeboxes, but also well beyond the continental United States, across a world reeling from war.³² In that postwar moment, bebop's dense and layered soundworld created opportunities for variously marginalized listeners to find themselves in relation to others, to imagine new connections and interpret their own local experiences anew, to draft new modes of pleasurable opposition (or oppositional pleasure) by dreaming their own new dreams.

This is indeed the central story of *Dreams in Double Time*: Black bebop musicians' radicalities and complexities; the palpable distances between racially coded sights, sounds, and narratives in the mainstream press; and the very idea of a musical idiom as a midcentury signifier of race, aesthetics, rebellion, and an unapologetically radical Blackness all made it possible for distant yet linked listeners grappling daily with the violences of state and nationalist power to hear the world anew—to hear across the rifts of the 1940s via imaginative, past-informed, and future-oriented responses to the value systems of Eurological musics and their attendant industries. As Black theorists, as critical dreamers, bebop musicians' objects and processes of focus were largely intra- and intermusical, political, historical, social, and individual. In this way, local instances of musical rebellion—the minutiae, interiorities, and contradictions of improvised performance—for many other listeners modeled an improvisatory mode of communion that in disrupting older musical systems and their attendant histories proved generative at the levels of both aesthetic and social possibility.[33] As a form of revelatory improvisation—as a means of creating soundworlds that, in drawing from the past and imagining the future, revealed qualities of the present—bebop musicians both enacted and inspired critiques of taken-for-granted assumptions about Black masculinity and musicality, personality and community, abstraction and beauty, gone and not yet. "Everything we stood for," writes Gillespie, found form in sound: "intelligence, sensitivity, creativity, change, wisdom, joy, courage, peace, togetherness, and integrity."[34]

So here I explore the notion of sonic dreaming in this postwar moment by way of the "otherwise possibilities" created by Black musicking, doing so by attending to how some of those possibilities became manifest for nonwhite youth coming of age amid the perils of unprecedented global war. I take seriously the fact that the "*Black speculative musicalities*" Iyer has described as "sonically disruptive practices that posit new ways of becoming musical, otherwise possibilities for Black life and Black subjectivities, and radical futurities for the 'philosophy of the human being'" have always emerged in relation to other proximate communal imaginaries, lived experiences, and dream geographies; such musicalities have repeatedly inspired new visions, relations, and projects, and it's among the goals of this book to find new ways of describing how this relationality has been experienced.[35]

* * *

Today, at the edges of my own wakefulness, adrift midmorning in downtown Los Angeles as police sirens scream and car horns morph into half-remembered melodies, a track called "Move" echoes in my mind's ear—a bright piece performed and recorded in mid-1950s Hollywood while a world rebuilt itself and my grandfather, all of twenty, tried his hand with jazz musicians in the cool reprieve of the southern fall. Recorded by Clifford Brown's All Stars as part of a jam session, "Move" moves, sears; the take is a minor miracle of physical endurance, particularly for the rhythm section—drummer Max Roach, bassist George Morrow, and pianist Richie Powell—each sprinting in lockstep for over fourteen minutes, their efforts coalescing into a shimmering ground for soloists to stand on and wail. I've loved the record since I was a boy, and I knew of it only because it was among the many in my grandfather's home. When I listen to it these days, and especially when I spin my grandfather's copy, I can still hear, amid the rush and din of the living, the soft tap of his right shoe.

Thinking of my grandfather being moved by a recording like "Move," of him loving the Clifford Brown All Stars' *Jam Session* LP (1955) on which it appears as much as he did classics by artists including Vicente Fernandez and Lydia Mendoza, has brought me comfort and strength as the years have passed and I have learned more about this world's entanglements and shortcomings. Additionally, thinking of listeners like my grandfather, once proximate in time and sentiment, if not space, to the midcentury clubs of New York and the after-hours studios of Los Angeles, has pushed me as a musician and writer increasingly toward methods of sounding, telling, and listening that make space for the unexpected, the contradictory, the shifts in the story—toward ways, that is, of learning from those edges of our own wakefulness, from those strange and associative logics estranging the mundane; toward ways of hearing the seemingly incongruous sounds and stories of our daily living as not only deeply interconnected but also revealing of the limits of our categories, our musical templates, our means of making sense.

Methodologically, then, I work in this book to find form for that nebulous space between archive and repertoire, event and memory, fact and legend, remembered and forgotten, ultimately listening for antecedent geographies by listening across a compartmentalized present. Approaching musical and cultural histories as "bundle[s] of silences," I read across multiple archives for "minor" materials previously excluded from historical narratives, effectively rendered mute, forgettable, and unnecessary, and then I read those materials in relation to each other.[36] In this regard, I follow Brent Hayes Edwards, who has argued that to approach any archive critically "is to read it in concert with another," "supplementing the blind spots and biases of one repository with the additional and differently classified documents in another."[37] Even though the material resulting from that cross-pollination never produces "complete" stories, it yields insights only available through comparison and layering, through juxtaposed objects and ideas "that make [productive] trouble for one another."[38]

One result of this approach is that this book offers a different route through music in the postwar decades precisely *because* it relies almost entirely on these "minor materials": the scraps, the surplus, the forgotten, the incomplete, the inscrutable, the irreducible, the ghost notes. In this book many "minor" sources, characters, theories, and analytic techniques rub elbows for the first time, and I seek to show that this isn't a haphazard mix nor a quixotic pastiche but rather a natural weave: a recovering and recombining of stories and materials often omitted within disciplinary academic space for the sake of local clarities. The larger goal of these recoveries, for me and hopefully for others, is more adept structural analysis, more patient and relational critique.

In that spirit: what I don't wish to do here is present the three primary subjects of this book as "major" figures, significant as they were to their local scenes; instead, by following their activities, I want to highlight the institutional and disciplinary systems that have contributed to their and others' minoritization.[39] This work aligns with that of writers including Saidiya Hartman, Cathy Park Hong, and Alex Woloch, who, theorizing from their different critical coordinates, remind us that calling something "minor" means interpolating it into a structure, a system, a narrative; it means identifying or assigning a function, a position in a hierarchy. It signals a position of power, as well as that power's perpetuation. To "minor" or "minoritize" is to subordinate, to set one thing aside to emphasize something else, to put one thing in service of something else. And as many have long known, some painfully so: an attention to minor figures can say major things.

This leads to at least two observations, one more practical than the other. The more practical is that actively seeking out material categorized in various discourses as minor is a demonstrable path to new perspectives on extant narratives—a way of uncovering stories that can only be told when attention is shifted to people, feelings, processes, and works subordinated in existing materials. The less practical—and perhaps more candid—is that it's clear we need better representational forms, tools from a future where the master's house no longer stands.[40]

Many theorists have long been on this track. On the jazz front, Ben Ratliff once wrote in a *New York Times* op-ed that one remedy for jazz history's "hard shell of cliché" might well be "the study of the nonfamous"—a mode of presenting jazz "the way musicians have talked about it, not as a matter of schools and eras but as a slow-boiling stew of experience."[41] Too, scholars and writers including Ingrid Monson, Nichole Rustin-Paschal, Farah Jasmine Griffin, Sasha Geffen, Daphne Brooks, Karen Tongson, and others have, again, counteracted the corrosive macroproject of heteropatriarchy by focusing on how gender and sexuality shape all parts of American music and how women, trans, and nonbinary performers, writers, composers, leaders, business owners, and all else have been not only routinely and systematically overlooked but in fact actively repressed. All of this work underscores a deep need to foster a recuperative relationship to that which has been left behind—that which has been relegated to pure function, that which has been omitted and discarded. As I understand it today, we need to embrace the B sides of our tangled histories, as they have the potential to reveal far more about our worlds and shared fates than many of us are led to expect.[42]

* * *

While the core of this book consists of three stories, three loosely linked (audio)biographical narratives, entwined with each other and with my own memories and "time[s] of consideration," the arguments here don't rest solely at the level of individual experience.[43] Rather, through an (audio)biographical mode, I work to organize structural and historical arguments, engagements, and relations—to focus on the idea that "however singular a person's life may be, the value of examining it lies in how it [might serve] as an allegory for the culture as a whole."[44] While this book closely follows James Araki, Raúl Salinas, and Harold Wing's lives and works as well as draws on my own embodied experience and recollections of my grandfather's musical life, individual biographies are less my ultimate focus than the intimacies of the messy structures and systems that living, listening, and dreaming reveal.

I also don't claim to present authoritative life narratives of the listeners I follow, nor necessarily celebrate them as heroic, unsung geniuses. Instead, I suggest that what I've learned of their varying engagements with a Black radical music of the postwar years not only reveals on-the-ground machinations of racial democracy but also specific, improvisatory attempts at musically informed new worlds, at new, "unfettered dream space." I emphasize this as a formal and theoretical point throughout the book—the idea that the individual narrative is not a terminus, though perhaps an end—because race and racism, though experienced and expressed personally, supersede individual experience, constitutive as racial ideas are to social institutions, political bodies, economic arrangements, and regional geographies. Rather than fetishize the individual as the primary unit of social inquiry—a fetishization with deep roots in many Western epistemologies, a shortcoming at the heart of the American mythos, an obsession central to rhetorics of stardom, celebrity, and troubled genius under capitalism—this book instead works to present senses of people and praxes *in relation*, as expressive of interlinked scales, forces, and pressures. Contrary to both nationalist mantras and atomistic historiographies, *Dreams in Double Time* resists the narrative templates of heroism, reaching instead for ways of representing personal experiences as inseparable from other lives and broader stories.[45]

And like all stories, the stories in this book are gendered. *Dreams in Double Time* is as much about music as it is about racialized masculinities, as much about the illumination of shared fates as the negotiation of gender identities "tenuously constituted in time, instituted in . . . exterior space through a stylized repetition of acts."[46] As I follow this book's trio through varying scenes and situations, I thus consider the colonial systems of classification and hierarchization that perpetuate violent social cycles across the gender spectrum. I also think through long-circulated stereotypes that have, at every turn, produced real-world effects: Latino men as "macho, hypersexual, lazy, drug addicts and dealers"; Asian men as "hypo-masculine," "passive, shy"; Black men as "angry," "violent," "unintelligent," and "aggressive."[47] I take seriously the gender axis of theorist Sylvia Wynter's argument that a "Western bourgeois" "conception of the human," "Man," has long "overrepresent[ed] itself as if it were the human itself," resulting in a human classificatory logic built on subjects' distances from an arbitrary ideal.[48]

As I've tracked engagements with bebop as a mode of Black radical dreaming, particularly by way of the three figures whose (audio)biographies anchor my structural analyses, I've remained attuned to the fact that bebop's angularities and attendant cultural narratives have as much to do with aesthetics as they do with a nation-state built in part on the systematic traumatization of young nonwhite men. I've considered how this musicking can't be separated from these psychic geographies, how its musical and social features can't be dissociated from relational crises of racialized masculinities, how its multisite emergences and institutionalized retellings have always been steeped, consciously or otherwise, in the experiential densities of gendered life. I've tracked how gender negotiations are everywhere in this music born of a Black interior, this music absorbed by variously (dis)affected young men who, as James Baldwin writes in his classic bebop fiction, "Sonny's Blues," knew "two darknesses" most intimately: "the darkness of their lives, which was now closing in on them, and the darkness of the movies," against which they "dreamed."[49]

Following feminist and queer-of-color arts and culture scholars, I write mindful of the ways that corrosive masculinities have warped art practice and scholarship (and certainly music and music history).[50] I have also kept in mind that "spaces and places are not only themselves gendered but, in their being so, both reflect and affect the ways in which gender is constructed and understood."[51] Using individuals' stories as windows into larger structural situations, I keep in mind how every location, zone, and scene this book's listeners were part of—the jazz club, the recording studio, the army base, the prison cell, the bandstand, the neighborhood street—was shaped by both racializing and masculinist codes, each code shaping in more and less conscious ways each figure's engagements with sound, space, and other people. The result of this work is a book that invites and aspires toward newly relational questions, toward newly liberated dreaming.

* * *

Again, concerning issues of race, this book is fundamentally relational. Across its case studies, I pay close attention to each artist's site- and time-specific racializations, their engagements with racial difference (and Blackness specifically), and the coconstitutions of their racial identities. I track race as a mode of classification and resource allocation with roots in colonialism and thus the modern world-system; as a logic perpetuated by continuously circulated multimedia representations with immense determinative power; and as a force kept dynamic through ever-changing racial formations.[52] In effect, this book attends to the specific racial and ethnic categories that listeners like Araki, Salinas, and Wing dealt with as they learned with and from Black radical music: Nisei, Japanese American, and Asian American; Mexican American and Chicano; mixed-race, Chinese American, and Afro-Asian American; and, to be sure, whiteness and Blackness as embedded in the national category of American.[53]

Race, as a concept, is a sedimentary, location-specific inheritance, a set of differentiating, classificatory logics and practices inseparable from colonial annihilation and communal striving; its expressions form the basis of contemporary capitalisms and necropolitical procedures, constitute the conceptual grounds for onto-epistemologies of the human, shape the ethics and economies of daily living on an ailing planet. Race's presence at virtually all levels of human relation makes it a primary analytic for examining and explaining shifting, unequal distributions of resources—as well as for appreciating the avenues people take not only to become conscious of personal biases but also to become acquainted with the experiences and histories of others.[54]

And in the American context specifically, race is a distinct colonial echo.[55] The overvalued new world built from the genocides of the colonial encounter was one of systematized, enforced social hierarchy, constructed via the essentialization and taxonomization of phenotypical and cultural difference. This violent sorting was related to a palpable desire to create new wealth rapidly, a desire acted on via the horrific erasure of indigenous peoples and knowledges and a routinized denigration of Blackness and its eventual nightmarish coupling with chattel slavery. Today the world still owes much of its shape to that imperial belligerence; today the legacies of the colonial enterprise live as necropolitical, climatological, and interpersonal scars on a global scale, beyond the relationship between Europe and the Americas, and whatever futures are pursued will have some relationship to this blood story.

With this colonial history in mind—and the hierarchizing approach to difference it inscribed in the institutions it built (the modern versions of which abound)—this book strives to perform a key operation: a methodological decentering of whiteness in order to grapple with minoritized people in relation to one another rather than in a defensive posture vis-à-vis specters of whiteness, white supremacy, and white people. As has been written about and certainly experienced, racial formation in the United States (via whiteness as an institutional ideal and Blackness as an "ontological plasticity") tends to encourage and reward competition, with groups compelled to position themselves in relation to Blackness and Black people well before formal emancipation.[56] George Lipsitz puts it this way: for hundreds of years now, "the power of whiteness [has] depended not only on white hegemony over separate racialized groups but also on manipulating racial outsiders to fight against one another, to compete for white approval, and to seek the rewards and privileges of whiteness for themselves. Aggrieved communities of color have often sought to curry favor with whites in order to make gains at each other's expense."[57] And "yet while every racialized minority group has sometimes sought the rewards of whiteness, those groups have also been able to form interethnic antiracist alliances."[58]

Local instances of solidarity, difference appreciation, and togetherness among people of color are thus an important, radical thing. This is part of what's important to me about Araki, Salinas, Wing, and many others' resonant investments in Black radical music and their related understandings of proximate rebellions: their lives and works evinced artistic engagements that didn't deracinate the music from its makers (which has been and is still so often the case), that didn't seek to transform Black musicking from verb to noun, as Amiri Baraka memorably described it, but rather sought to understand better, with increased emotional and experiential clarity, the world as it was for others who shared similar, though distinct, experiences.

Considering differently racialized individuals, communities, and their respective histories *in relation* by centering music making as a form of subversive, alter-American dreaming thus informs this book's central contributions on race in and beyond the United States. Building on relational approaches developed by sociologists, cultural theorists, and arts critics, in this book I approach racialization and racism as context specific, and racial categories as interlinked, inseparable as these concept-metaphors are from the messy, real-world intersections of differently positioned people in inexhaustibly complex locations. Approaching race in this way involves breaking from traditional comparatist efforts to pursue social analyses based on "one-at-a-time relationships with whiteness for each aggrieved group," efforts that effectively recenter whiteness and occlude "polylateral relations among aggrieved communities of color."[59] Instead, I place each inquiry and conclusion in conversation with seemingly contradictory communal archives, reaching beyond not only traditional disciplinary norms but also extant narrative templates operative in many cultural histories and criticisms. The central motivation, to draw on Frantz Fanon, is to fight to recover stories of individuals and communities finding strength in one another, and to present those stories in a way that participates in the fight for "the birth of a human world," "a world of reciprocal recognitions."[60] To pursue idioms, that is, that might capture our entangled pasts and, with luck, help us pursue futures premised on mutual concern and coinvestment.

To consider improvisation in this relational racial context—to consider, in particular, the kinds of musical improvisation linked to Black musics and especially to bebop—is to understand improvisation, as Iyer puts it, as *"movement in relation,"* as a maintaining of specificity and difference in pursuit of closeness, safety, and the future tense inherent in survival.[61] Drawing on a conversation between Manthia Diawara and Édouard Glissant—a conversation in which Glissant remarks that "Relation is made up of all the differences in the world and . . . we shouldn't forget a single one of them, even the smallest. If you forget the tiniest difference in the world, well, Relation is no longer Relation. Now, what do we do when we believe this? We call into question, in a formal manner, the idea of the universal"—Iyer points out that truly relational thought and activity is that which maps "movement in relation to power," freedom in relation to "histories of enslavement and domination," and thus dreams in relation to one another.[62]

By turning to bebop as it was heard and responded to by differently racialized individuals, this book treats as vitally important those instances of knowing coinvestment in others' strife and creativity that this Black music afforded as a planet smoldered and an episteme shattered. It treats as important the stories of three individuals coming to a form of situational (and, eventually, historical) consciousness in part through their relationship with a new sound and its makers. This matters because it helps us understand why some white, conservative US listeners during World War II were so afraid of Harlem's new sounds; it's also important amid our disconcerting present conjuncture, filled with so much of the same, unchanging.

* * *

This project's title, *Dreams in Double Time*, evokes the layered speeds, densities, and dissonances that characterized bebop performance and the utopian aspirations of many radical ethnic American artists, committed as they were to exposing and signifying on the United States' racial fantasies, familiar as they were with the layered temporalities undergirding every note, phrase, and set they played and absorbed. Methodologically and formally, then, this book is thus a dreamlike braid, a work in and of double time: improvisational and essayistic, "carefully undisciplined," guided by formal loops and interruptions, temporal bends and overlays. I adopt this form to capture something of the interconnected, multiscalar temporalities of the musical structures and lived experiences of the midcentury conjuncture, to argue for the necessity of multitemporal forms to communicate new truths about dreaming under duress.[63]

To explain more fully: in many creative music circles, the phrase *double time* often indicates a music compositional gesture in which a key musical element, typically the melody during a solo, is doubled in speed "while the accompanying instruments remain [steady] at the slower tempo."[64] (In some cases, as in the memorable oscillatory theme of Thelonious Monk's "Brilliant Corners," "all the instruments [double] the tempo together.")[65] A rhythmic device common to ballads, given their typically slower tempos and longer melodic lines, the simultaneity of slow and fast times offered by many double-time phrases creates a sense of rhythmic contrast and relation—a sense of interconnected, multiscalar processes generated by at least two intimately related musical ideas unfolding at different rates of speed, all within the same musical frame. In *Dreams in Double Time*, I've worked to make this musical device significant to the project's narrative form and content by braiding interrelated stories and memories that unfold at different rates of speed. The intention is to create a sense of generative contrasts, temporal interconnections, avenues for historical defamiliarization.

In each of the following chapters of this book—"After-Hours," "Layered Time," "Quartered Notes," "Among Others," and the epilogue, "Affinities"—the narrative discourse thus shuttles between slower, dilated scenes of improvisatory musicking and faster, compressed prehistories of that musicking and the agents involved. Drawing on traditions of braided narrative fiction and rhythm-driven music composition, the work aspires to a narrative modality of thick time, of stacked and polyrhythmic temporalities, in order to translate some of the layers of historical sediment present in radical ethnic American musicking into a compound story, "loose and dreamlike," that resists monotemporal linearity, encouraging a different sense of historical passage.[66]

To accomplish this, I draw on my praxes as a musician, writer, and interdisciplinary humanist to synthesize a variety of differently constructed primary materials, "evidences of *dreams manifest in sound*," into narrative-driven units.[67] At times, I work with audio recordings, liner notes, concert and album reviews, and solo transcriptions; at others, with cover art, personal letters, short stories, poems, unpublished fragments, news articles, and personal interviews. As I handle these materials, I actively work to cross-pollinate: I approach each written text, for instance, as akin to a vinyl record containing traces of listening practices, musical affinities, and sound environments ready to be unlocked and amplified with the right interpretive needle.[68] I also work to bring a literary critical sensibility to musicological practice, treating each solo, riff, and tune as a way of reaching for new "language"—for, as Baldwin once put it, a new system or "vocabulary" that might for a moment "bear the weight of reality."[69] Through interviews, I get a sense for how other musicians and listeners understood the issues at stake; through musical transcription and performance practice, I bring an embodied music research perspective to this historical work—not to claim any exclusive knowledge of the past but instead to map temporal gaps and affective registers at the level of my own musicking body, to shuttle between historical artifacts and contextualized muscle memory in pursuit of hidden questions.[70]

* * *

Chapter 1, "After-Hours," situates readers in this layered narrative, providing context by engaging the history of bebop's emergence in Harlem and its subsequent spread across the United States. Bicoastal in its geography and polytemporal in its telling, the chapter tracks the music and its culture both as the local work of young Black experimentalists and as a critical, transformative aesthetic force that dramatically altered not only the jazz narrative in the United States but also the country's intellectual history writ large. Drawing on archival research, literary writing, and interviews I conducted with musicians and historians, this chapter tracks the role of race in bebop's initial production and reception, moves critical bebop discourse away from a strictly Black-white binary narrative, and projects outward into an understanding of the relationship among race, musical dreaming, and shared fate. Doing so, I argue, allows us to hear bebop's histories and resonances relationally, in ways that defamiliarize primarily Black-white historicizations of the music and its makers.

Chapter 2, "Layered Time," then engages the life, music, and writing of Nisei jazz multi-instrumentalist and literary scholar James Araki. Like "After-Hours," it utilizes a dreamlike, polytemporal structure, finding form in an essayistic oscillation between recording sessions for a transformative (yet largely unknown in the United States) Japanese American jazz album, *Jazz Beat: Midnight Jazz Session* (1959)—one of the earlier jazz records to utilize studio overdubbing—and the musical and transnational circulations that shaped Araki's life. Bringing together archival research, narrative-driven close listenings, oral histories, personal interviews, newspaper clippings from Japanese and US publications, literary writings, cultural analysis and jazz criticism written by Araki, and albums from late 1940s Japan, the chapter contextualizes a single individual's intimate musical dreaming to illumine broader social and historical systems of subjection. It also provides the first extended interdisciplinary musical and cultural analyses of the primary materials discussed, contributing not only to foundational journalism on Araki in Japan as well as short-form historical vignettes in the United States but also to studies of Asian American jazz more broadly.[71]

Chapter 3, "Quartered Notes," continues the looped narrative thread of "Layered Time" and engages the life, writing, and musical imagination of Raúl Salinas. Like the preceding chapters, it, too, utilizes a structure involving braided times, blending narrativized close listenings of archival material as well as jazz poetry records Salinas recorded in the early 2000s (with Mexican American alto saxophonist Tomás Ramírez and Chinese American saxophonist and writer Fred Ho) with Salinas's bebop-informed Xicanindio poetry and journalism of the 1950s–70s, written while enduring the racist cruelties of the American carceral system. Synthesizing archival research, analytic and narrative engagements with Salinas's three jazz poetry albums, close readings of Salinas's printed and performed jazz writings, and a musical and literary critical engagement with Salinas's first live public performance of his most famous poem, "A Trip through the Mind Jail," this chapter illuminates the naked injustices of the American criminal justice system, engages the relationship between literary writing and improvisatory music making, moves beyond a Black-white discourse about jazz writing (and, by extension, the Beats), contributes theorizations of carceral aurality to contemporary abolitionist scholarship, and offers the first avowedly musical study of Salinas's Xicanindio jazz writing and life to the foundational Latinx literary scholarship on his poetics and politics.

Chapter 4, "Among Others," continues the threads of the preceding chapters and engages the life and work of Harold "Chink" Wing. Like the pages that precede it, "Among Others" creates loops and overlays through its essayistic construction, finding unifying form through a close engagement with a historic photograph and through personal interviews I conducted with Newark musicians and historians, particularly with a former musical mentee of Wing's, Eugene "Goldie" Goldston. Drawing on archival research at the Institute of Jazz Studies, a personal collection of albums on which Wing plays, newspaper clippings, literary writings, and narrative close listenings, this chapter troubles the heroic individualism of hegemonic American fantasies (and masculinist bebop discourses) by focusing on communal virtuosities, collective temporalities, and accompanimental ethics.[72] It thinks through the relationship among race, music, discrimination, and community by following an Afro-Asian American's reclaiming of a pejorative nickname and his collaborations with primarily Black artists; unpacks the granular musical details of group improvisation; and contributes the first scholarly engagement with Wing's work.

The epilogue, "Affinities," brings the book's themes and figures back together to reiterate the primary themes of the project as a whole. As in a musical reprise, "Affinities" returns to the sense of relation that motivates the form and content of the study, connecting Araki, Salinas, and Wing to one another as well as to other Mexican American, Japanese American, and Afro-Asian Americans who shared similar musical affinities, including my late grandfather, whose spirit animates my questions. Equal parts elegy and summation, this final piece concludes in part by considering my grandfather's engagements with Charlie Parker's music while living in the Rio Grande Valley, the US-Mexico border region my family and I call home; there, at the edge of nation-states, relational, postbinary improvisations on American identity acquire a special charge—race, interiority, and musical praxis converge in heightened, locally specific ways, and, as many musicians have long modeled, in such spaces the thick chords of solidarity often reveal more just futures.

Among these chapters' key interventions are their interdisciplinary analyses of improvisation and composition across media; their attention to underground networks of music circulation, creation, and documentation in and beyond the United States; their focus on music and racialized masculinities; their investment in "histories from below" that highlight minor figures and materials; and their relational (decolonial) commitment to the study of race and ethnicity. Taken as a whole, *Dreams in Double Time* thus aspires to a relational scholarly-artistic discourse that interweaves figures, sites, materials, and histories often considered in isolation—not to resolve their inevitable tensions in a tidy appeal to a universal but instead to sit with them, listening for their chords.

* * *

As in private and communal dreams, in this book juxtaposed media, memories, archives, and analytic research methods reveal unsung stories. As the chapters unfold, those new stories in turn reveal a larger narrative of how a Black radical music invited differently racialized thinkers of color to critique American racial democracy. As I reiterate throughout, bebop, Harlem's "new sound," helped young audiences hear and in some cases disrupt processes of racial subject formation in the United States; an aesthetic revolution initially forged by Black musicians became a remarkable social force for a greater population of racialized Americans, many of them oppressed and economically poor; in its diverse immediacies of expression, it gathered a formidable social significance, one ironically enabled by its circulation within the ideological discursive networks of midcentury commercial markets. This music became a medium for a remarkable social energy; the very *idea* of nonwhite musicians frustrating traditional economies of aesthetic prestige through an undeniably sophisticated communal idiom opened up surprising avenues for differently racialized and positioned listeners of color in their respective communities, listeners pursuing new modes of belonging amid domestic strife and global war. At the heart of this social opening was an underground's radical experimental ethos: What happens if we play *this* melody over *these* chords? What happens if we invert this pop song's shape and mood? What happens if we play this phrase twice as fast? What happens if?

For the figures mentioned in this book and the scenes and communities to which they contributed, answering these questions involved engaging defiant, joyous Black musicking, dealing intimately with the logics of localized racializations, and pursuing relational projects in decades marked by profound changes on the local and international levels. Asking "What if?" encouraged the creation of dynamic models—overlays, simultaneities, creative maps—that provided building blocks for innovative approaches to problems in different domains and, importantly, for ways of being American otherwise, for thinking beyond a violent monoculture. For Araki, what emerged was an intimate understanding of multiplicity that relied on transoceanic experiences, ethnography, historical research, literary criticism, military service, multi-instrumentalism, and overdubbed studio recording; as I argue in chapter 2, "Layered Time," the lifelong challenge of finding suitable ways to translate incongruous materials and histories into locally meaningful forms unified his experimentalisms across diverse fields and circumstances. For Salinas, what emerged was an understanding of poetic technique and political inquiry linked to the new sound and its aftermath in the jazz milieu; as I argue in chapter 3, "Quartered Notes," the challenge of finding language for the social and historical forces that bebop was linked to helped Salinas find the voice that would make him a hallmark Chicano poet. And for Wing, what emerged was a sense of creative practice rooted in accompaniment, shaping his musicianship, multi-instrumentality, and composition not around ideals of "heroic virtuosity" but around a communal virtuosity of shared experimentation and mutual development; as I argue in chapter 4, "Among Others," Wing's experiences with the new sound—its musical content and its initial creators, as he performed with many of them in Harlem and Newark—ultimately shaped his approach to the relationship between art practice and community building. Each of these individuals, contributing to their local jazz circles as performers and avid listeners, found in the music an interpretive code for their varying American experiences; each of them found in it "some key," as Ellison once put it, "to a fuller freedom of self-realization."[73]

In isolation, the chapters and figures of this book illumine matters important to Chicanx, African American, and Asian American aesthetic and political histories, but when considered together, they produce a surplus revealing of deeper postwar thought and feeling, as well as an intimate prehistory of revolutionary coalitional struggles for social justice in the 1960s and 1970s. These stories, indicative of and connected to many more, offer readers a chance to hear and feel bebop differently—not as a mythic symbol of hip inscrutability nor an apex of contemporary jazz neoclassicism but rather as an invitation to relational, antiracist worldmaking. Through its fragments, interruptions, episodes, loops, riffs, and overlays, this book offers readers a chance to hear the ways young Black musicians in wartime Harlem laid the foundations for different senses of American citizenship beyond a Black-white binary in the postwar years—how their music unlocked new ways of thinking and hearing among youth of color across the United States, how their creativities opened up new worlds of sonic and social possibility for folks just like my own grandfather. This idea, threaded through each of the interlocking chapters, is one of this book's more global takeaways.

As I argue throughout, at times linearly though more often elliptically: for listeners whose full inclusion in the American body politic remained a dream endlessly deferred, the spirit and substance of this midcentury Black radical musicking was a route into an alternative America: an emergent riff-space, a harmonic hyperplane, a corrective convalescence. To listen for a future in it—beyond the drone of white supremacy, beyond the grip of postwar anxiety—was to embrace a vital, shared inscrutability in a hostile, harrying world. It was to hear a world otherwise—to dream jaggedly, feverishly, in the insurgent space of double time.

one.
after-
hours

Among the CDs and long-playing records in my late grandfather's personal music collection, eclectic and piecemeal as it was, there once lived a crisp reissue of *Bird and Pres: Jazz at the Philharmonic*, a Norman Granz production recorded in 1946 nearly two thousand miles from my grandfather's home, nearly three thousand from Harlem, there, in the late-night glamour of a storied auditorium that once marked a heart of Los Angeles. I am listening to this recording now, seated on a metal bench in Pershing Square, a stone's throw away from where that concert took place, baking in midday autumn warmth. Laser disc spinning, headphones ablaze, my mind drifts between layers of sedimented time, retracing routes of musical travel and noting, amid the din of overhead helicopters and the twists of Charlie "Bird" Parker's solo on "Lady Be Good," the energies linking generations, the sounds drawing memory close.

Listen: on "Lady," after the opening applause, after Arnold Ross's loping piano introduction, after the first portion of Charlie Parker's blues-shaped solo, after he clicks seamlessly into double time against Billy Hadnott's walking bass line, note the nested microrhythms blooming against the established pulse, every downbeat cracked and shimmering like broken glass in lamplight; note how Parker's infectious rhythmic sensibility nudges the accompanying musicians ahead slightly, energizing them into a forward lean; note the gap that immediately follows the solo's end, filled by a bass feature, tenor sax giant Lester Young reluctant to follow Parker's choruses; note Young's eventual step out, his buttery tone, his contrasts with Parker's style, and yet his resonance with it.

The second Jazz at the Philharmonic (JATP) concert, of which this moment was part, marked one of the earliest major West Coast performances of what was by then known as bebop. It featured a now-storied lineup of musicians, including Charlie Parker and Dizzy Gillespie, who had traveled westward a few months after the war's end, eager to see what new dimensions of their insurgent musical vocabulary they might hone, what successes they might enjoy. Today, for me, the recording of this concert does not serve only as a link to my grandfather's life, an invitation to try to listen through his ears, nor only as a new connection to this lettered, coastal city, long its own dream factory, its own site of radical intervention, but also as an entry point into some of the awakenings this East Coast vocabulary made possible, as well as an invitation to ask, once again, how bebop came to be.[1]

This chapter thus engages the storied history of this once-new mode of insurgent musicking in relation to race and resistance, interiority and community, experience and mediation, travel and performance, memory and meaning. It does so while interpreting the music in two ways: as the work of young experimentalists drawn to Harlem and one another, and as a radical intellectual style that disrupted extant stories about Blackness and modernist aesthetics in the United States and beyond. As this chapter's story progresses, it asks some fundamentals: Who made this music, and why? How was it produced and received? How did music critics, the vast majority of whom were white men, write about what they heard? How did race and gender shape this music as a practice, as well as factor into its uptake by distant listeners? Where and how did this music travel? And what might following those vectors teach us about affinity, solidarity, and shared fate?[2]

* * *

As the story goes: Minton's Playhouse on 118th Street in Harlem served as bebop's physical epicenter. Founded in 1938 by owner, musician, and American Federation of Musicians delegate Henry Minton, the club quickly became the go-to location for improvising musicians to experiment free of industry sanction. In 1940 Minton hired manager and pianist Teddy Hill to run the Playhouse, granting him programming responsibilities, and shortly thereafter, a house band was put in place, making it logistically feasible to feature jam sessions in the club's regular performance scheduling.[3] The house band's members—Kenny Clarke (drums), Nick Fenton (bass), Joe Guy (trumpet), and Thelonious Monk (piano)—effectively became primary voices in the new sound's formation.[4]

Together, these and the other musicians frequenting Minton's and its companion club, Monroe's Uptown, pursued new musical stylings during lengthy, after-hours Monday-night meetups that afforded participants the institutional and imaginative elbow room to push one another into new sonic terrain. Drummers Kenny Clarke and Max Roach reimagined the flow of musical time by shifting the drum set's timekeeping function from the bass drum to the cymbals, freeing up the kick for surprising, syncopated "bomb" beats and solidifying the ride cymbal patterns now synonymous with jazz drum set performance.[5] Bassists including Jimmy Blanton and Oscar Pettiford explored more complicated accompanimental lines, often pulling closer to improvising soloists and thus reenvisioning what musical support could sound and feel like. Bud Powell, Mary Lou Williams, and Thelonious Monk sketched out new and idiosyncratic possibilities on piano, expanding harmonic and rhythmic horizons while reimagining traditional right- and left-hand roles. Players like Charlie Christian, J. J. Johnson, Stan Getz, and especially Dizzy Gillespie and Charlie Parker developed bombastic new soloistic vocabularies that made productive use of melodic saturation, rhythmic complexity, timbral exploration, and harmonic surprise (e.g., tritone substitutions). Vocalists like Sarah Vaughan showed through virtuosic scat improvisations and nuanced song interpretations that this new, modern style was not solely the domain of male instrumentalists. And through the form of the small combo, a performance unit more economically and logistically pragmatic than a large ensemble, these musicians were able to augment the rhythmic, melodic, and harmonic palettes of blues-informed popular music with new colors, tensions, and moods, emphasizing extended solos that flouted the logistical, performance, and market strictures of the traditional bandstand.

"What we were doing at Minton's," recalls Gillespie in his autobiography, "was playing, seriously, creating a new dialogue among ourselves, blending our ideas into a new style of music."[6] At this style's core was a new density of form and feeling, geometrically exact and spiritually inspired, propelled by hidden linkages and interplays, allusions and reharmonizations, newly sketched movements "from one note to the other."[7] "We invented our own way of getting from one place to the next," Gillespie says. "Musically, we were changing the way that we spoke, to reflect the way that we felt. New phrasing came in with the new accent. Our music had a new accent."[8]

The musical practices Gillespie mentions transformed sites like Minton's and Monroe's into spaces of alternative American possibility, spaces of Black joy and trial that existed at once within and beyond the harsh realities of the American waking world—spaces where risk, experimentation, and the pursuit of new knowledges coexisted with exuberance, laughter, and sweat.[9] Newcomers and interlopers to these sites were often thrown headfirst into the fire by regulars and their unforgiving new sound; uncompromising, impatient, and mischievous, the regulars worked at every turn to preserve a momentarily liberating insularity and to affirm, through their performances, "that old formulas were no longer good enough"—that "the morass of clichés" that had come to dominate many bandstand solo improvisations was outmoded and that what was needed was instead a more searing vocabulary, "a new articulation."[10] The jam session, as escape, as ground zero, as utopic underground, became a site of personal and communal transformation, of formal and technical radicality—a space in which convivial, audaciously re-inventive musical thinking lent form to frustration and glee and thus began to reshape social possibility in a city beset by racial violence and a world engulfed by war. What emerged was an encounter point, an aural meeting place in which a vast range of musical styles became raw material for an emergent, energetic, and deeply personal musical radicalism—"New Orleans syncopation, Ellingtonia, southwestern swing, rags, gospel, Broadway show tunes, popular songs," "contemporary classical music," the blues, as well as Afro-Cuban musical concepts.[11] Through their experiments these musicians conjured new realities, sounding them out in local code; as pianist Mary Lou Williams once recalled, they "worked out a music that was hard to steal."[12]

Too, Harlem's specificities, its particulars "as a site of both adjacency to death and alternative practices of freedom," enabled the unique swirl of joys, urgencies, and local Black experimental traditions across the arts that made bebop what it became, aesthetically, conceptually, and sonically. "Long an ideal site through which to imagine black community within and beyond the United States," Anthony Reed reminds us, "Harlem sits at the crossroads of a nation and world, past and anticipated future."[13] Amid the surrealities of war, racial violence, and resource scarcity, Harlem, as a site of safety and danger, as a nexus of not yet, too long, and right here, enabled the creation of "a sonic order that challenged white containments" and, by extension, mitigated pressures to accede to their power.[14]

Those white containments, at once conceptual and corporeal, grew in strength and insistence during the war years, as well as in their aftermath. Fears of domestic destruction and foreign encroachment ushered in a gradual homogenization of whiteness as a racial formation and categorical descriptor, bolstered by shifting boundaries and new "possessive investments," by a strategic, selective, and differential de-ethnicizing of historically harassed communities—Italian, Irish, Jewish, and others—which effectively hardened an anti-Blackness constitutive of the United States historically and the West generally. In the context of increasing wartime nationalist pressures to conform to an American patriotic ideal, to a national template synonymous with midcentury whiteness, then, interethnic alignments with Black artistry and experiential relation that then translated into divestments from whiteness as a structural aspiration were, and remain, at once transformative and necessary—part of what plenty of radical musicking both emerges from and helps make possible. For a time, that is, and for select listeners, siding with Black cultural forms and Black artists meant resisting the inducements of assimilation and hazarding altogether new "dream[s] of American form."[15] It meant converging, however briefly, on a new language for rebellion.

* * *

Audio recordings of bebop's early days are relatively spare, in large part because of material and labor issues during the early 1940s. In June 1942, specifically, when the music was still congealing, James Petrillo, president of the American Federation of Musicians (of which Minton was still a delegate), announced a recording strike in an effort to funnel money from music companies to working musicians, a strike that lasted until November 1944.[16] During this stretch, while some musicians were able to complete a few recordings, most notably the V-Discs of the Billy Eckstine Orchestra, none were sold en masse, leaving a significant archival gap that continues to shape how this music is remembered and reanimated. At around the same time, bebop had also become coterminous with wartime unification efforts that were at best soothing a jittery populace and at worst sacrificing its members without qualms. Many of the familiar hierarchies of class, race, market, and gender were becoming newly suspect; Black male musicians who had been "asked to die for a democracy that declined to treat them as full citizens" began to exercise "a rare opportunity to act freely," to step out of line, to imagine otherwise.[17] As Eric Porter writes, "Bebop emerged during a period when other musicians and observers increasingly saw jazz as a vehicle for African American political activism. The federal government's enlistment of black musicians to perform at USO shows, make V-disc recordings for troops, and appear in jazz-themed films with patriotic messages afforded these musicians and their supporters the opportunity to engage in Double-V activism, in which they linked support for the war with a demand for African American rights within and outside the music industry."[18] This merger of bebop with overt political activism highlighted a color line that routinely suffocated "men who had been prepared to risk their lives for their country in combat abroad," as Paul Gilroy once put it, "but who were still denied basic human and civil rights in the land of their birth."[19] For musicians, fans, and detractors alike, Harlem's iconoclastic new improvisations rhymed with political urgency; for many, radical musicking meant demanding change, denying comfort, and sounding an alarm.

This demand for political change, social justice, and racial equality eventually found explosive form in the 1943 uprisings in Harlem, Detroit, Los Angeles, Texas, and Alabama—conflicts that overlapped with the start of the United States' Japanese and Japanese American internment period.[20] Across the country, differently racialized nonwhite citizens were enduring wartime nationalist crackdowns, flattening and Manichean propaganda campaigns, and stiff, multifold reinforcements of American hegemony. And as the United States ramped up its martial efforts abroad, debates about which communities should shoulder the heaviest burdens—and which could be seen as loyal, as trustworthy, as invested in preserving the nation-state's material and ideological stability—dovetailed and intensified.[21] In this stifling environment, naturally, many young people resisted, finding strength and comfort in one another by converging in public spaces, listening to the latest musical projects, experimenting with the latest dances and hottest fashions, and effectively challenging the norms of a segregationist, imperfect union.[22] As Luis Alvarez argues convincingly, this "world of wartime youth culture included a matrix of Afro-Latino-Asian connections and influences," connections and influences that effectively served as "a dress rehearsal for more overtly politicized social movements in later years."[23] Understandably, music, and specifically the musicking of bebop's architects, was central to this; as bandleader Roy Porter once put it, pointedly, "What these red-neck cops didn't realize was the bebop and jazz that the black musicians were playing was bringing the races closer together."[24]

* * *

By 1945, with an Allied victory in Europe becoming ever more likely (though the atomic means to achieve it in the Pacific were still unimaginable for the general public), mainstream audiences were catching wind of the new sound.[25] Through new performance opportunities, bebop had traveled from uptown to downtown, setting up camp on Fifty-Second Street; too, industry recording had resumed. At the start of the year (January 9, 1945), Gillespie recorded, among other tunes, the octave-leaping "Salt Peanuts," one of the most popular and recognizable bebop recordings ever created.[26] Near the end of the year (November 26, 1945), Parker recorded the blistering "Ko-Ko," a reworking of Ray Noble's 1938 "Cherokee," which became Parker's signature and a hallmark of the idiom.[27] Soon thereafter, with the help of disc jockeys and word-of-mouth networks, these and other recordings of the moment helped bebop acquire a small but notable place in the recorded-music market, thus introducing it to new listeners in and beyond New York.[28]

Coincident with the emergence of bebop recordings were at least three converging forces that complicated public engagement with the music and made activists' political demands difficult to process. The public bravado of musicians like Gillespie and Parker, the emerging potential for record companies to profit off of bebop, and the occasionally positive coverage by some trade publications (especially *Metronome*) were for the moment coalescing into a condescending sense of the music not as an insurgent and joyous practice but instead as a still-raw mode of invention in need of direction.[29] The oppositional energies of this music for a time succumbed to a cultural logocentrism; jazz critics and publicists, endowed with far more institutional power to construct media narratives than musicians alone, capitalized on the fact that bebop, primarily an instrumental style, was largely *wordless*, its rebellions and references encoded in a different, more mesmeric semiotic tongue. As a result, the press ascribed meanings and narratives to the music that proved commercially expedient, aligning and shifting aesthetic and social evaluations with the public's buying power.[30]

As bebop's notoriety increased, that is, many listeners attempted to pin it down, to define it by critical excoriation, unstudied imitation, or straight encomium; as the story goes, the proliferating definitions reproduced the process of commodification that had only years before cooled swing from verb to noun.[31] This shift, systematic and precedented, was the process by which a related musical idiom had lost its immediate context and relevance, had become nominally contained, squeezed for profit. That process entailed, per Nathaniel Mackey, "the erasure of black inventiveness by white appropriation."[32] It meant, "on the aesthetic level, a less dynamic, less improvisatory, less blues-inflected music and, on the political level, a containment of black mobility, a containment of the economic and social advances that might accrue to black artistic innovation."[33] It reiterated that which the word *jazz* has long indexed: a set of "relations to music," "sites of conflict," "multiple vectors of desire," and "narrative and tropological tendencies" that not only establish "the conditions for hear(d)ing the music" but also sort the people creating it and profit as rapidly and completely as possible off their lives and memories.[34]

This process of cultural plunder, of experiential theft, of erasing Black inventiveness, was, again, not anything new. In fact, it was something key musicians in the scene originally accounted for. As pianist Mary Lou Williams recalls of the early days at Minton's:

> I went to Minton's every night. When the thing started, Thelonious Monk and the others had a little band going. They were afraid to come out because they were afraid the commercial world would steal what they had created. So they stayed in Harlem, at Minton's and the downtowners began to come up, writing their notes on their little pieces of paper and everything.... [Later] I heard some of the guys speak about not wanting to play downtown or play in the open so everybody could take it from them. Because you know the black creators of the music have never gotten recognition for creating anything.... I don't think anybody is looking for any big applause or anything about what they've created. But after a while, you get kinda really disgusted and dried out because everything you create is taken from you, and somebody else is given recognition for it. But the music is so great, I think half of them could care less, except they have to eat and sleep, you know.[35]

With Williams's words in mind, the recordings, concerts, and news articles of the mid-1940s speak differently. (Listen, for instance, to the juxtaposition of emcee "Symphony" Sid Torin's awkward crowd addresses on the live recording of the June 22, 1945, Town Hall concert in New York and the intimate onstage banter among the members of Gillespie's quintet featuring Parker.) What began as an after-hours practice, a mode of invention that would be "hard to steal," had entered the local market space in a pronounced way: "Once it got inside the marketplace, our style was subverted by the press and music industry."[36] What began as an unnamed convergence of forces and opportunities—as drummer Kenny Clarke once recalled, "The music wasn't called bop at Minton's. In fact we had no name for the music. We called ourselves modern"—had become a market's genre category, a fashion, a stereotype.[37] And as many have long been painfully aware: to name is to claim.[38]

* * *

Here, in contemporary downtown Los Angeles, as my grandfather's CD reissue of JATP '46 arrives at "After You've Gone," as the old palms in Pershing Square stand sentinel in the afternoon air, my ear works to follow Parker through his up-tempo element, Gillespie as he reaches into the upper corners of his range amid the intensity of the sonic sprinting, Lester Young as he works through the speedy chord changes. Courting a sunburn near a cluster of chess players and an elderly man with a sketch pad, listening through a wash of revving motorcycles and a distant, wailing car alarm, I find myself wondering what might still be learned from such artifacts of jubilant immediacy, what lessons these crackling recordings might still offer a world that has in many ways moved past them, what echoes of the older forces structuring the night of that concert nearly a century ago still have a presence in this world, this time. Asking myself these questions, I remember Kareem Abdul-Jabbar's foreword to *Chasin' the Bird*, a graphic novel published midpandemic to mark Parker's centenary:

> For Bird, hell was being black in America. I'm tempted to say things were worse in the 35 years he lived between 1920 and 1955, with open segregation and aggressive Jim Crow laws. But as I write this, black men and women are vigorously protesting in cities across the country after the police killing of George Floyd, who choked out a plea of "I can't breathe," while a white cop kneeled for nine minutes on his neck. We're also in the middle of a nationwide quarantine due to COVID-19, which is killing blacks at three times the rate of whites.... 65 years after Bird died, hell is still being black in America. But for Bird, music was the ideal of heaven and while we listened we could experience what heaven might be: intense, carnal, miraculous, celebratory—but fleeting. Ending with the last note. Like life.[39]

Layered atop the physicality of my late grandfather's disc, the audible traces of this Los Angeles concert, and the Harlem jam sessions it built on is the thickness of the present Abdul-Jabbar describes, the legacies of the still-unfolding pandemic and the ongoing movement for Black life, the echoes of urgent protests and the (necro)politics of aspiration, of breathing itself. I think of this as I note my surroundings and reflect on what I've learned of Parker and Gillespie's midcentury visit to this city of love and quartz—initially for "a two-month residency at Billy Berg's Hollywood jazz club," though, in Parker's case, extended by the psychological and substance-abuse issues he was dealing with, which eventually resulted in his institutionalization at the Camarillo State Hospital just a few months after the recorded concert performance I've been listening to on repeat.

"Unlike [in] New York," writer Matthew Duersten notes, wartime and postwar Los Angeles "was segregated, and black musicians were expected to be entertainers, not serious artist-musicians."[40] This negatively affected the immediate reception of this music on the West Coast. While there were of course a number of listeners and performers enamored with the new sound—among them the regulars of the vibrant Central Avenue scene and musician-entrepreneurs like Norman Granz, who established the JATP concert series and believed in bebop's energies—on the whole, the rejection of the music by the city's powerful had profound effects that spanned the country and lasted for decades. It not only negatively impacted Parker, for one, but also fueled subsequent negative portrayals of the music and its makers in the press; one Los Angeles radio station, KMPC, even banned bebop recordings altogether: "The currently popular style of Bebop music is degenerate, a contributing factor to juvenile delinquency. It is suggestive and nothing short of dirty!"[41] While history has proved these claims uninformed, racist, and fear soaked, their half-lives have been long, and their resonances with today's struggles loud and undeniable. I keep this in mind as I absorb my surroundings, noting who is eyed near me, fled from.

* * *

"Around 1946," Gillespie once recalled, "jive-ass stories about 'beboppers' circulated and began popping up in the news. Generally, I felt happy for the publicity, but I found it disturbing to have modern jazz musicians and their followers characterized in a way that was often sinister and downright vicious. . . . Stereotypes, which exploited whatever weaknesses might be, emerged. Suable things were said, but nothing about the good we were doing and our contributions to music."[42]

Among those stereotypes, most of which propelled a general media narrative of delinquency, was the modern jazz musician as a drug junkie. In March 1946, for instance, a divisive *Time* magazine article, "Be-Bop Bebopped," represented this new music and the people associated with it as inscrutable, delinquent, reckless, and hopelessly strung out; bebop was "overheated, with overdone lyrics full of bawdiness, references to narcotics, and doubletalk."[43] In such a media context, musicians struggling with patterns of substance abuse were at once condemned and fetishized, reified into narrative figurations to be variously trafficked and refuted in musicians' biographies, family histories, film narratives, and literary representations—Elliott

Grennard's short story "Sparrow's Last Jump" (1947), for instance, or Julio Cortázar's fiction "El Perseguidor" ("The Pursuer") (1959), or Ross Russell's novel *The Sound* (1961). Many of these representations were extrapolations from and exaggerations of Parker's drug struggles. From the 1940s until his death in 1955, this deeply troubled Parker; he lamented that reporters linked his hard-won musical proficiency to drug use in the wider public imagination, as the association not only distorted the music and the young people making it but also gave the wrong ideas to scores of aspiring, impressionable performers. "Any musician who says he is playing better either on tea, the needle, or when he is juiced," Parker once said, "is a plain, straight liar. When I get too much to drink, I can't even finger well, let alone play decent ideas.... Some of these smart kids who think you have to be completely knocked out to be a good horseman are just plain crazy. It isn't true. I know, believe me."[44] That Parker loved reading and discussing "politics and philosophy," Ingrid Monson notes, "was less interesting to the press and his imitators than his drug abuse, time spent in a state mental hospital in Camarillo, California, sexual excess, and apparently magical, unmediated ability to coax entrancing sounds out of an alto saxophone."[45] To listen for Parker through this representational fog, to become acquainted with the machinery of fantasy, to intuit narrative gaps and sensationalist discontinuities in the process of (re)routing recorded sounds through personal, local particulars, was thus to learn something of the underlying structural pressures that, for many artists and listeners, made dope feel like a salve. As James Baldwin explores it in "Sonny's Blues," it was to take steps toward becoming vulnerable and proximate enough to hear the sounds of others in pain, of others seeking connection, and, crucially, to link those longings to one's own.

Too, through figures like Gillespie, bebop's visual mythography became solidified in the press, reified through repetition: Gillespie's curved stance, his fluffy goatee, his long suits, his styled beret.[46] One illustration, similar to another by William Gottlieb and circulated in an infamous *Metronome* article in 1947, seems to anticipate Ralph Ellison's invisible man by rendering Gillespie (and, crucially, his Blackness) literally invisible; all that remains in the frame are his fashion identifiers, bebop's de facto visual trademarks (see figure 1.1).[47] In the same article, jazz critic Barry Ulanov largely panned the then-recent work of Gillespie's orchestra—a big band experiment that brought bebop's musical language to a larger ensemble—on the grounds that it was, among the handful of contemporaneous jazz modernisms (Lennie Tristano's on one end, Stan Kenton's on the other), the most ill-formed (read: the least white, European avant-garde), full of "bitter[ness]," "frantic clowning," "endless quotations of trivia," and "senseless screams."[48] (Interestingly enough: that same year *Metronome* also gave Gillespie two prestigious awards: "They named me as best trumpet of the year, and my orchestra was listed as Band of the Year in 1947.")[49] These coexisting, contradictory representations—visual abstraction (that is, removal), critical reprimanding, and institutional rewarding—along with the stereotype of the jazz junkie, all converged to solidify, as Ellison once wrote, this music's "most inadequate" name in the American public imagination.[50] As defined by a predominantly white male media infrastructure, bebop meant everything and nothing—it was situationally and definitionally plastic, as Zakiyyah Iman Jackson writes of Blackness more broadly in the history of Western epistemologies, in the sense that the new music could satisfy whatever functions it needed to in any given moment in order to preserve extant myths of white musical and social superiority.[51] For many listeners, these new sounds were simply *too much*—too boisterous, too modern, too unoriginal, too dangerous, too unrefined to be taken on their own terms. The adjectives many writers chose in their descriptions of it merely mapped the extent of a deep-set white anxiety over the sound of Black joy and intellect.[52] The music, for many, was noise: unwanted sound by unwanted people.[53] And the musicians making it, coded, as their ancestors had been, as "savage, irrational, subrational, pathological, and effectively mad," were routinely swept aside—"called 'crazy,'" as Amiri Baraka (LeRoi Jones) writes, or "'dishonest frauds,'" or, "in that slick, noble, patronizing tone that marks the liberal mind: 'merely misguided.'"[54]

Too, there were also many listeners—some of them precursors to the white hipsters who, in the moment of the Beats, stood apart from the codes of American normalcy *by choice* rather than by force—who evangelized the new sound, chasing the ways of leading musicians, contributing to their rising celebrity. Again: Gillespie, press friendly, was occasionally lauded by those who were more conservative; Parker, unpredictable, was initially imitated by musicians and fans alike (especially at the level of his heroin and alcohol use, which, again, Parker himself lamented as a staunch advocate for education and disciplined practice: "Do as I say, not as I do").[55] In most cases, however, Black musicians themselves were often not taken seriously as the music's spokespeople in the mainstream press; theirs was a creation that, *somehow*, for *some reason*, required explanation by others, definition by emboldened "authorities"—a shift from verb to noun.

Yet despite efforts to quell this Black experimentalism, the musicians kept their work alive by relying on one another, by pushing one another through collaboration and cutting sessions, just as they had done in the early days at

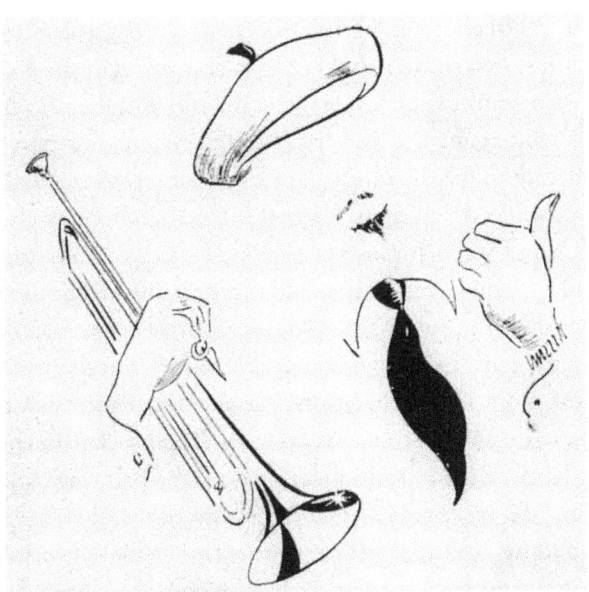

FIGURE 1.1 Dizzy Gillespie's Blackness rendered invisible in the pages of *Metronome Magazine*. Source: Stanford University Music Library Archive.

Minton's and Monroe's. For in those early jam sessions, with the development of a new imaginative and discursive idiom, bebop provided a plane on which to invent while uninhibited, to push one another free of white constrictions.[56] The new sound had effectively afforded an experimentalism that stood apart from an imaginatively insular mainstream, had extended a legacy of subversive and liberatory invention that, as La Marr Jurelle Bruce puts it, "imagine[d], manifest[ed], and practic[ed] otherwise ways of doing and being—all while confounding dominant logics, subverting normative aesthetics, and eroding oppressive structures of power and feeling."[57] This, without doubt, was a pursuit worth protecting, a modality worth extending, a spirit worth keeping alive.

* * *

And yet, by the late 1940s, magazines were beginning to pronounce bebop's death.[58] Out here on the West Coast, writer Dave Dexter, for one, wrote in 1947 that any "bands and musicians planning to come to Hollywood" should be aware that there are "no be-boppers wanted! . . . Beboppers attract attention . . . by running six thousand notes a minute, bad notes, good notes, in between notes, just so they're notes, regardless of the chords." Shortly thereafter, similar slights began appearing in the East Coast music press, with many columnists eager to brush off the music as a short-lived fad.[59]

But as anyone who has endured systematic oppression would confirm, dreams don't die easily. In fact, it's safe to assume that a pronouncement of a dream's death is just a signal that it's made camp elsewhere.[60] Within the United States, for instance, beyond avid listeners and amateur practitioners like my own grandfather and more established professionals like Rene Sandoval in the South Texas borderlands, there were many differently racialized musicians thinking through this music in multicultural ensembles, taking the music in new directions, carving out unanticipated possibilities.[61] There was, for instance, Hawaiian-born Filipino–Japanese American jazz savant Gabriel Ruiz Hiroshi Baltazar Jr. (Gabe Baltazar), who met Charlie Parker in 1948, explored his own extensions of bebop's vocabularies on records including *The Paul Togawa Quartet* (1957), played with Stan Kenton's groups, and, years later, became close with one James Araki, who had embarked on his own similar, parallel journey. There were Los Angeles–based Mexican American musicians like Anthony Ortega, who picked up the bebop idiom and took it in new directions, as is evident on mid-1950s releases like *A Man and His Horns* (1956), particularly "Birdwatcher," one of that album's up-tempo tunes.[62] There were the dense big band modernisms of arranger Johnny Richards (born Juan Cascales), on display in maximalist through-composed works like *Annotations of the Muses* (1955) and *Something Else by Johnny Richards* (1956).[63] There was alto saxophonist Frank Morgan, a Central Avenue virtuoso who, alongside musicians including Howard McGhee, Dexter Gordon, Hampton Hawes, and many others, localized bebop in a West Coast atmosphere tending toward "cool." There were folks throughout the Pacific Northwest, including alto saxophonist and flutist Roscoe Weathers, the "Charlie Parker of Seattle," largely overlooked by major labels, whose music has only just recently been rereleased by way of a compilation entitled *I'll Remember* (2020).[64] There were musicians who never made recordings, musicians who never toured, musicians who never notated their originals and yet were beloved by their local communities, musicians who trusted in the energy of this music born of Black struggle and radical creativity. And, of course, the listeners who helped make all that musicking meaningful.

Beyond the United States, too, the music enjoyed an expansive global reach in the postwar years, as has been written about extensively elsewhere, resonating across Latin America, Europe, South Africa, the USSR, and East Germany, becoming in different ways an extension of the "noise uprising"

Michael Denning has tracked through the early twentieth century.⁶⁵ In the greater Afro-Caribbean, there were the foundational collaborations between Gillespie and Chano Pozo, which were key to the development of bebop and what came to be called "Latin jazz." In the Soviet Occupation Zone of postwar Germany, there were big band groups like Melodia Rhythmiker that, as Helma Kaldewey describes them, were working to fuse Stan Kenton's bombast with what they heard of bebop, once playing a bop-driven encore to "over a thousand young people [who] demanded more bebop" at Berlin's Steintor Variety Theater.⁶⁶ In apartheid South Africa, there were the Jazz Epistles, a key Black bebop ensemble whose *Jazz Epistle Verse 1* (1960) proved a vital release and featured, among its storied lineup, Kippie Moeketsi, "South Africa's Charlie Parker." Around the world, for locally specific yet globally entangled reasons, bebop found new resonances, new listeners, new reach across a shell-shocked planet undergoing multifold social transformations. This was what ultimately proved most unsettling to those who dubbed bebop Black noise in the United States and abroad; as Eric Porter put it, building on David Stowe, "Bebop's interracial audience was more threatening to white society than [even] the music's role as a symbol of race pride."⁶⁷ Its challenges, deep and immediate, helped a generation hear itself.

* * *

"For a generation of Americans and young people around the world, who reached maturity during the 1940s," writes Gillespie in his autobiography, "bebop symbolized a rebellion against the rigidities of the old order, an outcry for change in almost every field, especially in music. The bopper wanted to impress the world with a new stamp, the uniquely modern design of a new generation coming of age."⁶⁸ As is evident with the three listeners I'd like to start following now—James Araki, Raúl Salinas, and Harold Wing—the fire sparked by bebop traveled well beyond Harlem in long arcs from Austin to Los Angeles, Newark to Tokyo, spread by the circulation of performers and records, mobilized by the contingencies of history, evocative of new, unanticipated "rebellion[s] against the rigidities of the old order."

Araki, a Japanese American interned at the Gila River War Relocation Center under Executive Order 9066, was, again, a prodigious multi-instrumentalist and composer who as a young man found inspiration in the pioneers of Harlem's new sound. Shortly after hearing bebop musicians perform in the mid-1940s, he traveled to a war-ravaged, newly occupied Japan as a soldier-translator with the US Army. By day, he translated government documents between English and Japanese; by night, he played jazz for American soldiers seeking entertainment along the Ginza in Tokyo. Latching onto the complexities of the new sound's architextures, Araki incorporated its features into his playing; in effect, he is now credited by Japanese jazz historians as having helped spread bebop to Japan.[69]

When Araki returned to the United States from Japan in the 1950s, he enrolled in college at the University of California, Los Angeles, under the GI Bill, completing studies in Japanese literature, folklore, and translation while performing and recording with other professional musicians active in Southern California's energizing scenes, including Lionel Hampton. Also active in those scenes was a young Raúl Salinas: a Mexican American hipster raised in East Austin and working seasonally in California with his family. After being arrested for drug distribution—and, as it happens, after being detained in a Los Angeles County facility at the same time as famed tenor saxophonist Dexter Gordon—Salinas began a prison odyssey that lasted through the 1960s, penning poems from behind bars that would ultimately yield a new, intermedial mode of Xicanindio literary expression, a mode infused with an improvisatory sensibility distinct from most Beats, finding form in work he produced throughout the rest of his writing life, including a shelved collection of jazz writings called "Jazz Jaunts."[70]

When Salinas set down "Jazz Jaunts" in the 1970s, he dedicated it to an Afro-Chinese American named Harold Wing—or, as he introduced himself to Salinas in the 1950s, "Chink Williams." Based largely in Newark, New Jersey, Wing, again, was a drummer, pianist, and songwriter who, as a young man, collaborated with a number of bebop's architects, including Parker, Gillespie, Powell, Miles Davis, Erroll Garner, Babs Gonzales, James Moody, Sarah Vaughan, and international star Ella Fitzgerald. Wing, a consummate modernist and an evident pragmatist, worked to find ways to wed the radical and the practical in his music, experimenting through his song arrangements, his drumming, and eventually his work in Newark's City Hall with ways to make communal change happen.

When we listen across these stories for bebop as a mode of radical, alter-American dreaming, we can hear the ways an underground's spirit was modulated across disparate scenes and nonwhite communities, the ways it afforded a generation of young people new opportunities to challenge "the racial norms of the wartime United States" by embracing a unity in difference, a mode of connecting in relation.[71] Following Araki's, Salinas's, and Wing's activities within and across their various communities illumines this in ways still relevant to contemporary art practice and activist struggle.

From the end of World War II through the end of the long 1960s (approximately 1973), these individuals' works and travels cut across many of the defining features of the postwar realignment (or what some writers, following Henry Luce's coinage in 1941, have understood as a brief "American century" because of the country's new economic dominance and, relatedly, cultural influence).[72] In the weeks following the United States' atomic bombings of Hiroshima and Nagasaki and Japan's subsequent surrender, Allied forces began a military occupation that lasted the better part of a decade (1945–1952). This occupation signaled not only the end of the war but also the beginning of an American ideological and military dominance that would define the coming years. Many of the servicemen participating in this occupation—including Mexican American intellectual Américo Paredes, Black jazz pianist Hampton Hawes, and, of course, Araki himself—were doing double work: on the one hand contributing, via their presence, to a new American imperialism and on the other hand subverting the official narratives of an idyllic American democratic system by bringing their own experiences of domestic marginalization to their work.[73] Araki's experiences as a Nisei internee shortly before his arrival in Japan, combined with his uncommon musical abilities and early appreciation for what Harlem's new sound could express, ultimately converged in that occupation moment; bebop became something of a cognitive map, a stabilizing guide through the complications and pressures of a life between worlds.[74]

When Araki returned from Japan in the early 1950s, joining a large cohort of American servicemen pursuing higher education via the GI Bill, he returned to a different world. In full swing, via the Korean War and soon the Vietnam War (and, indeed, the Cold War), was a new phase of the battle between democratic and communist world futures. The latest scent of American jingoism hung foul in the air; Levittown niceties and unjust zoning were transforming the country into its latest racio-economic configuration. And amid these changes, the music Araki still loved, performed, and recorded was a guiding force: dynamic and transformative, grounding and inspiring. As a graduate student, he augmented his study of Japanese literature, folklore, and history with performances and collaborations in the evolving jazz scenes of Los Angeles and Berkeley, accompanying stars including Lionel Hampton and Buddy Rich in studio recording sessions. The contrast was palpable: where a decade earlier he had been attending high school in a war relocation center, he was now working professionally as a jazz musician and literary scholar, linking histories through his art and study that others had been attempting to erase.

Meanwhile, Salinas, who had spent his youth in East Austin, visiting Black establishments on the Chitlin' Circuit, including Victory Grill, had experienced firsthand the difficulties and opportunities of life as a Mexican American in Jim Crow–era Texas. His hardships and relationships—coupled with a youthful awe for the new Black sounds from Harlem, brought to him by way of live performances, recordings of musicians like Parker, and trade publications like *Down Beat* and *Metronome*—made the new sound, for him (just as for Araki and many others), a strong organizing force, a guide through the complexities of American life that he was ultimately on a path to help articulate. Salinas also knew, because of his travels to California in the early 1950s, the difficulties of manual farm labor as a Mexican American citizen as well as the overlaps and discontinuities of life for Mexican Americans in California as compared to in Texas. He was able, at a young age, to get not only a broad picture of life as a Mexican American in different parts of the Southwest but also a comparative sense of youth cultures, and in particular of the jazz scenes in those areas. In these Californian jazz environments, frequented by Araki as well as a number of other musicians too seldom mentioned, Salinas started to understand how some of the pieces of this postwar moment fit together.

It was also at one of these performances that Salinas would meet Wing, who toured in the 1950s with the Benny Goodman Orchestra as well as the Erroll Garner Trio. Wing, then a young man trying to establish himself as a professional musician in Newark and New York, was constantly threading the needle between newness and familiarity; the music he was writing and recording was by then being distributed in the United States and Europe, and he was still working to figure out the relationship among his artistic practice, his geographic location, his racial identity, and the histories of and evolving relationships between the new sound of Harlem and the avant-garde of Newark. He brought to the table a sense of how the new sound had progressed on the United States' East Coast even after the "death of bebop" had been pronounced by the magazines (and after the narrative remains of that music culture had been effectively co-opted by the Beats, who had turned it into a figure that, while itself revealing of an American countercultural energy, was notably different from the energies and expressions that had begun after-hours at Minton's).

The movements of these people and sounds coincided with the changing nature of US foreign relations. In 1956 the US State Department began its jazz-ambassador tours, funded by President Dwight Eisenhower's Special International Program; the tours, as Penny Von Eschen notes, were part of an ideological and cultural productive campaign against perceived communist threats and were used to counteract naked "illustrations of American apartheid."[75] The new sound, which had been "vilified by white jazz critics and black dance audiences in the 1940s and early 1950s as the anti-melodic, 'undanceable' music of crazy Negroes, junkies, and hipsters, had become part of the government's Cold War strategy," and this was achieved in no small part by Eisenhower's hiring of Gillespie, one of bebop's original, clarion voices, as one of the key faces of this international effort.[76] It was an effort to recast bebop's narratives—to transform the music from an inscrutable idea into an American celebration, to alchemize it from an energetic youth culture into the soundtrack of ambassadorship.[77]

This image of American democratic idealism was at odds with the lived experience of most people of color in the United States during the 1950s. While some people were able to take advantage of the fact that "wartime shortages of consumer goods and spare parts" had largely ended, many were not so lucky.[78] As Baraka reminds us, violence and uprisings appeared "as directly related to the psychological tenor of [the] time," and in many ways the new sound (which, by then, with the experiments of Thelonious Monk, the maturation of a young Miles Davis, the meteoric rise of tenor saxophonist John Coltrane, and the pedal-point pioneering of Art Blakey's various Messengers, had become even newer) had helped name the new anxiety, just as it had in the preceding years.[79]

At this time, Araki was completing graduate school and trying to decide whether to pursue a career as a professional musician or a literature scholar; for him, the larger cultural anxieties of the postwar years expressed themselves in his own efforts to excavate, preserve, and translate performance knowledges and traditions at risk of total loss.[80] Salinas, meanwhile, had turned to drug distribution, which must have seemed like a salve for a young person seeking a foothold; when he lost his balance, he ended up a Mexican American man in a carceral system notorious for its brutal treatment of nonwhite people. And Wing, meanwhile, was working through his own drug use and artistic dissatisfactions, difficulties that contributed to a period away from routine recording and performance.

And yet this was not the end of any of their stories. Where the 1950s were for many characterized by anxiety and rebellion—from domestic struggles for social justice to more distant fights for decolonization—the work that that period sparked, the trajectories that it established, created for a great many the opportunities for lasting change. That is: in the long 1960s, each of these artists I've mentioned, then older and more experienced, continued their projects with greater clarity and focus. Araki, while completing ethnographic-historical research in Japan, produced *Midnight Jazz Session*, one of the understudied jazz treasures of 1959; he also, shortly thereafter, produced a monograph on a form of classical Japanese balladry that articulated new understandings of his *own* sense of sedimented time.[81] Salinas, while working through his prison years, found his poetic and critical voice while writing about jazz, producing not only a number of jazz poems and critical articles (the latter were circulated in the *Huntsville Echo* as a column entitled "Quartered Notes") but also a distinctive Xicanindio poetics that today bears the formal and experiential lessons of what was once modern jazz. And Wing, in the aftermath of the Newark rebellion, found a way to merge his knowledge of dynamic structures and his compositional impulse into new avenues for others while working as a public servant in his home city, striving among others for social equity. Through these and a variety of other efforts, amid a period marked by ideological tussles, an arms race reminding all of a near-paralyzing nuclear sublime, and prolonged fighting overseas that ultimately funneled unifying energies into simultaneous (but not always synchronous) struggles for social justice, a large number of people (of which these individuals are but a sample) were developing their own new sound.

For these individuals, the difficulties and complexities of the sound that, after developing in Harlem, had transformed each of their lives and projects made plain that difficulty, struggle, and complexity, mixed always with doses of mirth, could offer lessons worth carrying forward. This was also the case for many others across the United States and the world who heard in bebop an invitation to remake, to overturn, to connect through and across difference.

* * *

Rehearsing these stories for myself today, nodding off in Pershing Square as the sinking sun reddens, I can no longer tell how many times I've listened to my grandfather's old JATP '46 recording, how many times "Lady Be Good" has competed with waves of traffic for my ear's attention, how many times "I Can't Get Started" has sent me into a gentle rock and sway, how many times the bombastic set closer, "After You've Gone," has jolted me awake. I can't say, either, what my grandfather would have thought of this park had he been able to visit—the skyscrapers framing the perimeter, the buskers echoing in the distance, the coppered sunbeams bouncing off a thousand mirrored surfaces, rendering the area's prim flora a hypernatural gold. I realize, though, that what I can get a sense of, here in this manicured setting, are some of the social and imaginative forces that have traveled through this place, that have made of it a site of resonant phrases, of layered time.

Seated now in shadows cast by luxury high-rises, my eyelids growing heavy, I think again of what it is our dreams can do, what they can encapsulate. In my notebook I jot down a thought: just as the literal dreams experienced in sleep "can tell the subject something about the truth concealed by its days," so, too, can the wakeful, figurative dreams and aspirations so entwined with histories of American mythmaking—those theories, speculations, and aspirations revealing of the structures of the everyday.[82] In this once-distant place, with my grandfather's personal copy of a live, local album grounding me, the stories of others of his generation inspiring me, I trust in this fully. To ask, repeatedly, as a racialized, minoritized subject, during late-night concerts and midnight jam sessions, Where is our "unfettered dream space," our imaginative plane in which "social identity" "need not be seen as a constraint but rather as a way of imagining the self unfettered, racialized but not delimited"? is, in its own way, to conjure unforeseen openings: to turn one's ears to worlds of (non)sense, to deliver evaluations and speculations in sound, to find "one's dream in the very act of seeking it."[83]

In the coming chapters, I continue in this spirit, following listeners who sought their own dreams through Black radical sound, listeners who explored the boundaries of forms, categories, media, and communities, listeners who developed an awareness of these boundaries and learned to improvise across them. One of my arguments is that music can serve as an entry point into critical, improvisatory, boundary-crossing ways of knowing, acting, and dreaming under American racial democracy. For many young men of color coming of age in the 1940s and 1950s, Black radical music, in particular, moved beyond the productive local insularities of Harlem and revealed a new lexicon for thinking through national shortcomings, for conceiving of shared fate, for breathing among others. Modified across media, space, tradition, repertoire, and circumstance, bebop's shape and feeling offered "a dynamic sense of freedom to its listeners—a barbed challenge as well as the most exhilarating of invitations."[84] At once invitation and excoriation, transformative intervention and underground experiment, bebop once captured and catalyzed dreams of living otherwise. If we follow memory's threads, perhaps it can do so still.

two.
layered time

Night has fallen. I am sitting in my apartment, the west windows open to hazy moonbeams and orange streetlights, blaring sirens and chirping crickets; near me, on a counter, a small block of incense sends warm braids of sweet smoke high into the cool air; nearby, a tower of books leans precariously against a south-facing wall as if weary, or aloof; before me, in a boom box roughly as old as my bones, a disc spins, mailed to me from a musician in Hyōgo, an ocean away—a disc that like a number of my grandfather's old recordings is a reissue of an older vinyl release, in this case a 1959 album led by a man I never met. Listening now, some miles from where he used to perform and just blocks from his grave site at the Los Angeles National Cemetery, I'm struck by a piano ballad, a lush rendition of Duke Ellington's "Day Dream," delivered by one James Araki.[1]

Listen: after the plaintive piano introduction, amid the subtle frontsidedness of drummer George Kawaguchi's brushwork, the round tones of bassist Mitsuro Ono's walking line, the extended harmonies explored and intensified as the song progresses, note Araki's expansive rhythmic palette, the ways his nested tuplets and surprising runs occasionally approach a quadruple time against the ballad's slow heartbeat, his twists and runs across the keyboard impressionist in their shape and bluesy in their tonality. Note the densities and lyricisms of the trio, brought forward by recording engineer Etsuzo Yoshida's clear mixing; note the resonances with and departures from saxophonist Johnny Hodges's well-known version of the tune, which a number of Harlem's bebop musicians knew by heart. "Day Dream," wistful and serene, has lyrics I can't help but hear in my head as Araki outlines its curved melody—lyrics that speak of lovelorn dazes and "castle[s]" "on air," of the places one yearns for in half-conscious, fragile "reverie." As I listen to the recording, my thoughts drifting as Araki's arabesque solo folds on itself, I think of how these sounds have traveled, how this recording was assembled, and under what circumstances. I lean forward, listening a little harder.

As I've learned since first hearing this record some years ago: back in 1959, while Araki was in Japan conducting doctoral research on a form of Japanese folk balladry, his experiences of the Allied Occupation of postwar Japan and the US internment of Japanese residents and Japanese American citizens colliding with his growing knowledge of an ancestral cultural history, he walked into a recording studio with old friends to construct an album that would capture something of the densities of their youths and the textures of their affinities. That project, *Jazz Beat: Midnight Jazz Session*, became a record of Japanese American musical crossings and one of the earliest in the jazz tradition to foreground overdubbing as a creative and radically experimental practice—an example of Nisei sonic innovation; a relational text that troubled the boundaries between nations, people, communities, traditions, and events; and a compelling sign of bebop's reach. As a work that plays productively with the distinctions between recorded objects and live performances, between memory and presence, it articulates a set of revealing confluences, meeting points between aesthetic inheritances and experimental procedures, individual actors and technological extensions, polished compositions and spontaneous creativities, locational specificities and transnational flows. The experiences forming the historical and (audio)biographical background of this record—unjust incarceration, occupational complexity, transnational translation, jazz-shaped musical praxes—converge, for me, into an attempt at a new idiom, a new articulation, a newly unfettered dream.

Here I want to treat Araki's only full-length album as an invitation to contemplate the forces, lives, and dreams structuring it, motivating it. I want to think through this album's twists alongside the contours of Araki's musical life; to listen for an interplay of race, nation, and sound; to follow some of the ways Black radical musicking became a powerful force among differently marginalized youth in hostile settings across a smoldering world. I want to take seriously, too, the "disjuncts between the time of composition, the time of dissemination, and the time of consideration," listening and writing at a few different levels—through my own scene of listening, through the mediations of audio technologies and modes of musical transcription, through this particular album's constitutive deployment of overdubbing and multitrack recording in pursuit of relational form and sedimented time—in order to highlight, again, what such records of a past that's "not even past" might still teach us about present predicaments and potential futures.[2]

Some of the questions and tensions that emerge from all of this include: What possibilities come about when overdubbing becomes part of the creative palette for a jazz soloist, for an improvising group? What happens when verticality, when a multitude of voices, takes audible form, displacing stricter notions of an instrumentalist's "signature sound" as unfolding horizontally, as a single voice over time? What new relational possibilities emerge from these technological, transnational, cross-cultural extensions of the Black radical musicking tradition? In what ways does the use of overdubbing productively disrupt the familiar "heroic virtuosities" of bebop? When one articulates a new "unfettered dream space," as Elizabeth Alexander put it—a new liberatory space at the border of on-the-spot improvisation and through-composed performance—what new expressions and concepts become possible?[3]

In posing these questions, I'm reminded of long-standing (and overplayed) debates about improvisation and composition, authenticity and artificiality—concepts differently linked to Eurological and Afrological musical cosmologies, to binaries that tend to be less revealing of creative praxes than of systems of social value, enforcements of racial hierarchy, and expressions of institutional power. Rather than wade deeply into matters others have already covered extensively, here I pose the questions I do to try and trace some of their implications for relational approaches to race, media, and movement, to try and think beyond ostensibly constitutive binaries, particularly when it comes to categories including Asian, Black, white, American, Japanese, and music. I try here to extend the work of American music scholars, including Kevin Fellezs, who has argued that "the construction of Asian Americans as exoticized aliens" . . . "reduces the chance that they will be heard as 'real Americans,' particularly when they are involved with a music that has been constructed within a racialized binary that excludes them."[4] I'm interested here, that is, in thinking relationally, in listening for the ways differently categorized Beings, entangled structurally, linked experientially, and proximate aesthetically, have resisted their categorizations, have experimented toward distinct yet related ends, and have tried to make sense of a world so frequently flooded with rage.

* * *

> I want to utilize recording technology to make a record of five saxophone voices played by one person.
> —JAMES ARAKI, quoted in liner notes for *Jazz Beat: Midnight Jazz Session* (1959)

The idea came to Araki in the midst of his doctoral study and after-hours jazz gigs, and the challenge of pulling it off was considerable. After meticulous planning and limited rehearsal, the album's trio, alongside engineer Etsuzo Yoshida of Mainichi Broadcasting Systems, completed a marathon recording session together in June 1959, staying up two nights to record and assemble the music, laboring over small details, clipped phrases, and false starts. Yoshida, reflecting on the experience, wrote in the album's liner notes, "Immediately after finishing the two days of recording, I was dazed, as I had not worked on such a physically and psychologically exhausting recording session in a while." He continued, "As a mixing engineer, I was moved when I saw the great enthusiasm of the three friends. It provoked me and kept me motivated. I do believe that recording an ideal record depends on the trust between the mixing engineers and the performers, and how their work is perfectly linked together. However, in a situation like this, where Jimmy plays three or four roles, the project requires more patience and effort than usual."[5]

The recording feat was among the most advanced of its moment, evocative of unfolding transformations taking place in the recording arts. As Jason Stanyek and Benjamin Piekut have written, "The arrival of multitrack technology in audio recording of the 1950s effected a major shift in the aesthetics and ontologies of musical production. Individual instruments or voices could now be isolated, moved around, and equalized separately—the sonic text was conceptualized in layers."[6] Araki, Ono, Kawaguchi, and Yoshida relied on and played with this new additive, palimpsestic approach to musicking, to "decorating time."[7] As Yoshida recalls, "In the spacious studio, we recorded using a composite recording technique: Jimmy listened to the recording he had just made while playing and recording the next phrase. It was a process similar to brick laying; if Jimmy or I lost patience, the effort we'd made up until that point would be lost. Especially on the second night, we pushed each other along and did not allow for lapses in quality. . . . If there was something wrong with the performance or the mixing . . . we had to do it all over again."[8] In a way that rhymes, for me, with the Black musical radicalisms of the early 1940s, this record, pursued

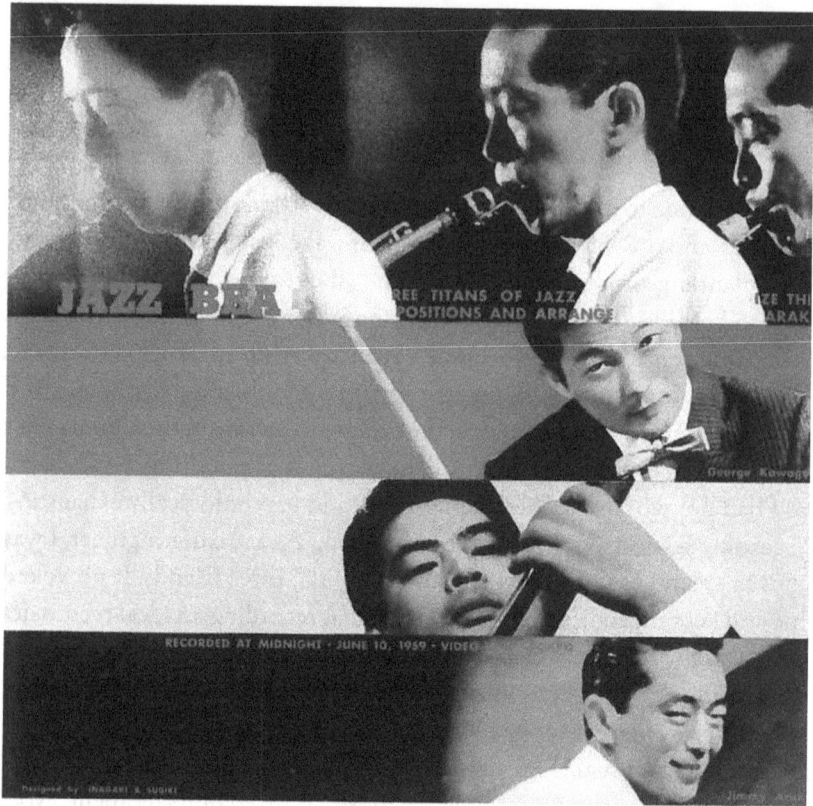

FIGURE 2.1 Layers and overlays on the cover of the Jimmy Araki Trio's 1959 *Jazz Beat: Midnight Jazz Session*. Source: Jimmy Araki Trio. *Jazz Beat: Midnight Jazz Session*, Nippon Victor jv-5006, 1959, LP.

after-hours in a space removed from the listening ear of global whiteness, was a test of endurance and vision, an exercise in pushing the limits of mental, material, physical, and conceptual possibility, an effort to arrive at a new enunciation, an emergent form.[9] It was its own transnational, Japanese American extension of a Black experimental musical tradition as well as a useful disruption of established norms—a hyperreal work that went against the grain of older celebrations of virtuoso "great men" by investing in the more forgiving creative experience of sculpting tracks in a studio; a work of profound technological mediation that pushed against the ironic midcentury staging of bebop as at once the apotheosis of the modern, the sound of racial degeneracy, and the soundtrack of American postwar rebranding.

These days, when I listen to the record, I'm impressed by how directly the project bundles its layers and times across its thirteen songs, the swing and blues influences prominent, the bebop flashes clear and unmistakable, the production seams audible and homey. (The cover alone tells a story; see figure 2.1.) The record is far from flawless in execution and design, whatever *flawless* might mean, but its ambition is persuasive and moving—less a masculinist pursuit of totalizing mastery than an exploration of a new way of musicking in relation, of building time together.

As a practicing musician and producer myself, I'm also familiar with at least some of the logistical and technical difficulties that can and often do accompany album production. So as I listen to Araki's 1959 project, bumpy and lo-fi as it sounds to my present-situated ears, I'm invariably impressed by it, knowing all that had to go right for it to even be completed, let alone distributed and playable today, over six decades later, thousands of miles from its place(s) of origin. Beyond scheduling logistics and budgetary concerns, again, one of the most difficult aspects of its category-bending form was its recording process, one for which there wasn't much precedent—and, for what little existed, much that was controversial.[10]

In 1956, for instance, pianist Lennie Tristano's eponymous, overdub-utilizing record was met with purist venom by critics; songs like "Turkish Mambo," virtually unplayable live without performance modifications, were, for some, controversial when *presented* as spontaneous improvisations.[11] In fact, Tristano's record was experimental enough to warrant surprisingly strident liner notes from critic Barry Ulanov, who came to Tristano's defense: "This is jazz, no mistaking it for anything else. It meets all the requirements: it is improvised, brilliantly adding ideas to ideas all the way through; it swings, rapturously, whether up or middling-up or slow in tempo; it offers . . . that delicate internal tension, that collective creativity which is the special identifying mark of the real thing in this music."[12] In Ulanov's estimation, the "jockeying of tapes and changing of speeds and multiplication of piano lines in Lennie's solo tracks" finds explanation, as if it needed any, in his "personality differences."[13]

Years later, with *Conversations with Myself* (1963), a stunning record that won a Grammy for Best Instrumental Jazz Performance, pianist Bill Evans utilized the same overdubbing approach, layering multiple piano tracks and panning the audio across the stereo channel, creating a fictive acoustic space. Evans—notably part of the (post)bop moment and interestingly positioned within its scenes, given that he was a white male artist and heroin addict divested from white supremacy—writes of *Conversations*:

> I remember that in recording the selections, as I listened to the first track while playing the second, and the first two while playing the third, the process involved was an artificial duplication of simultaneous performance in that each track represented a musical mind responding to another musical mind or minds. The argument that the same mind was involved in all three performances could be advanced, but I feel that this is not quite true. The functions of each track are different, and as one in speech feels a different state of mind making statements than in responding to statements or commenting on the exchange involved in the first two, so I feel that the music here has more the quality of a "trio" than a solo effort. . . .
>
> Looking at this album in reference to the preceding paragraphs, it would be difficult or impossible to place it solidly in either the group or solo category. For me, the unique and enjoyable experience of recording it was answer enough, and as is always so the music contained therein is or is not the positive evidence of its genuine quality.[14]

Araki's own push to experiment with overdubbing four years prior to Evans's was of the same spirit: to reveal and respond to one's multitudes, to write from the space between "group" and "solo categor[ies]," and to do so in relation to others. The effect, to my ear, was an experimental sonic fiction that, at formal, medial, aesthetic, and geographic levels, emerged from the interstices of stage and studio, jazz and not, here and there, Japanese and American, individual and group, piano and saxophone, and all beyond a mononational Black-white binary.

As with Evans, that process also enabled Araki to explore a new relationship to musical time—to explore a multi-instrumentality that he had cultivated over the years, stacking voices atop one another and chopping up different takes; to improve and comp in a different temporal mode, anticipating what he might play in a layer to come, responding to what he and his bandmates had just recorded moments before. As Etsuzo Yoshida recounts, "I didn't realize how much labor and energy would be required to record a session with Jimmy tripling and quadrupling as a musician. On several numbers, Jim alone dubbed four saxophone parts as well as the piano part. Only because tape-recording has become technically advanced were we able to produce a multiple-dubbed recording album. On some of the numbers, only after making five recordings of the same tune could we know if it had turned out all right."[15] This process, begetting a different relationship to improvisatory musicking than live stage performance, an altogether different mode of "double time" experience, in effect invites reconsideration of the still-prevalent discourse around musicians' "signature sounds," linked as "sounds" often are, particularly in jazz discourses, with notions of live, heroic virtuosity and distinctive personal identities, inseparable as they are, too, from commodification, from market value. Often interpreted as an audible expression of self or selfhood, a "sound," as George Lewis has put it, is for many "a carrier for history and cultural identity," particularly "in the context of improvised musics that exhibit strong influences from African-American ways of music-making." "'Sound' becomes identifiable with the expression of personality," an "assumption of responsibility and an encounter with history, memory, and identity."[16] Understandings of such sounds, however—amalgams that they are of physicality, equipment, vocabulary, community, and context—are often premised on the temporality of live events, as well as on mono-instrumental practice, on having an instrumental specialty and sticking to it. "Sound" concepts are also often tacitly premised on fixity, reified through discussion, debate, and music pedagogy; as James Gordon Williams writes, "Young improvisers are often taught that developing one's signature sound on one's instrument is among the most important accomplishments for a musician. It's a sign of reaching a certain level of creative maturity: once you have found your individual sound, you have arrived. [But as Billy Higgins put it] . . . 'the sound keeps changing. Once you "arrive," it's all over. You've got to keep evolving from day one till the time you leave the planet. It's a process.'"[17] What to make, then, of sounds crafted across a range of horns, keys, and strings? What happens to conceptions of sounds when we consider musicians whose sounds aren't yoked to any single instrument but instead exist somewhere between distinct voices, proximate personalities, even layered takes?

To my mind, part of what happens is productive destabilization. To explore a "sound" concept across multiple instruments and through layered, overdubbed recordings is, consciously or otherwise, to foreground difference, development, and relation. It's to explore a "sound," as Gregory Alan Campbell writes of multi-instrumentality (following Lewis's important work with the Association for the Advancement of Creative Musicians), as an exploration of "timbral diversity"—an exploration with a long trajectory in jazz and African diasporic performance "that values multi-valence rather than fixity, and which allows for and even expects the constant renegotiation of performer roles and identity, including an openness in options of physical stage appearance, physical movement, sound textures, and the use of musical sounds and structures."[18] Through this renegotiation, openness, and exploration of "multi-valence" over "fixity," a player's sound emerges as distributed across instrumental, timbral, and even medial "fields" rather than strictly compressed into single instrumental "points." A sound, while remaining personal, in this way becomes something less essentialist and more evocative of widening apertures; it becomes about an increased regularity of encounter with difference and constraint in pursuit of individual revelation and communal definition. As a result, the ideas a sound indexes also open up: "history," "cultural identity," "the expression of personality," "the assumption of responsibility," the "encounter" with "memory." "Creating a sound on one's instrument," writes Williams, thus becomes "a regenerative process of renewing energy": it becomes about "the hearing of one's sound in relation to other vocalists or instrumentalists—the materialization of a spatialized community of sounds through the deep, genealogical study of sonic innovation in sound as an improviser."[19]

Listening to *Midnight Jazz Session*, picking apart its layers, looking over my transcriptions of licks and solos, I'm struck by the ways its contours ask for a different conversation around sound, technology, virtuosity, race, and nation. Listening to the group's rendition of "Take the A Train," for instance—low-key, playful, created by Japanese and Japanese American musicians finding and renewing each other through Black American music—I also think about the layers behind the layers, the inaudible but vital personal backdrop to the sounds being created, the ways voices and histories are being stacked, flipped, transposed, reworked.

* * *

Listening to *Midnight Jazz Session* in the 2020s, amid the innumerable injustices and precarities increasingly woven into the fabric of everyday experience, and especially amid waves of anti-Asian violences linked directly to pandemic-era nativism, I find it alienating and undesirable to dissociate the "time of composition" from the "time of consideration," as in many existing methodological conventions, as well as to detach the album's complexities from the lives, times, forces, and vectors that support and antedate it, to abstract the record from what stories remain of its transnational foundations and principal architect. As "Mangetsu" comes on, Ono's bass solos bouncing from my speakers and around my living space, I reflect on the stories Araki once shared in an oral history, thinking, bleary-eyed, about their import, hearing them as a backdrop for the music animating the air I breathe.

"A day or two after Pearl Harbor," "my dad" "began making crates." "This was a curious thing to do, I thought, but he said, 'We are going to be put into camps.'... He predicted this for all Japanese." "He had experienced discrimination against the Japanese in Seattle and other cities, and he saw how the Germans were treated in Montana during World War One." "I explained our constitutional rights. But he got the last laugh. Four months later, we were being bussed into Santa Anita Assembly Center."[20]

Araki's confidence in his family's "constitutional rights" and the ultimate betrayal of that confidence evokes what his childhood friend and fellow internee, Michi Weglyn, would later describe as "America's betrayal of [Nisei youths'] adolescent dreams and idealism."[21] By the mid-1940s, the US government had forcibly displaced some 120,000 civilians, incarcerating them in so-called relocation centers spread mostly across the Southwest and overseen by the newly created War Relocation Authority.[22] All of these centers—from Tule Lake in California to Heart Mountain in Wyoming to Rowher in Arkansas—were a testament to a country's moral failings. As Matthew Briones has stated powerfully, "Not for the first or last time, America most publicly and unashamedly prioritized the paranoia of internal security over the principle of civil liberty in the 1940s, at the same time that it capitulated to a nearly unimaginable politics of fear, constructing a nationwide apparatus of domestic fascism based on racism while hypocritically claiming to abhor and dismantle the grotesque of international fascism."[23] This hypocrisy, felt acutely by the Issei and Nisei (first- and second-generation Japanese immigrants, respectively), was a defining characteristic of a government bending toward democracy for the few: as expressed in the final report of General John Dewitt, one of the architects of the internment, "The continued presence of a larger, unassimilated, tightly knit racial group, bound to an enemy nation by strong ties of race, culture, custom and religion along a frontier vulnerable to attack constituted a *menace* which had to be dealt with."[24]

Palpable in Dewitt's xenophobic pronouncement isn't just a whiplash response to the horror of Pearl Harbor—an attack that many, including Dewitt, used as justification for the immoral imprisonment of innocent civilians—but also a long-standing "tradition of enmity," as Kandice Chuh has put it, "against Asian-raced populations in the United States," and often "around one Asian-raced group at a time."[25] Japanese and Japanese Americans bore the weight of this enmity in the 1940s United States: residents, citizens, and their families were subjected to racism in the streets and, after Executive Order 9066, to the cruelties and embarrassments of the camps—poor food, unsuitable lodging, loyalty questionnaires. The winds of race, nation, and wartime sentiment created an unyielding storm for many Japanese immigrants and Japanese Americans, a Manichean vortex that promoted unnecessary personal sacrifice, including individuals' renouncement of Japanese citizenship to keep their families together as well as leaders' creation of Japanese American combat units to broadcast token loyalties to the United States' conservative publics. "Concentration camps and wholesale contempt for individual rights and lawful procedure," as Weglyn summarized it, "are not the exclusive province of corrupt tyrannies and maniacal dictatorships."[26]

Where the legal strictures of this internment today highlight the acidities and slippages of American racisms in the mid-twentieth century, the lived experiences of camp—the pains suffered and the activities that made everyday life, in some limited senses, bearable—fill out the picture further. In Araki's case, in April 1942, not long after President Franklin Delano Roosevelt's executive order, he and his family were sent to the Santa Anita Racetrack in Greater Los Angeles, where they and thousands of others were forced to reside in overcrowded horse stalls and stomach spoiled food and repulsive false promises (the latter relayed especially in the *Santa Anita Pacemaker*, the detention camp newsletter).[27] Eventually, Araki and his family, like many others, were transferred to the Gila River War Relocation Center in Arizona, which posed still more challenges: opened in July 1942, in the middle of a brutal Arizona summer, the camp housed upward of thirteen thousand people stripped of their homes, forced into confinement, left to wonder at their present and potential circumstances, and left, again, to swelter in the sun. ("Most inmates," writes Karen Leong, "dug beneath their barracks to find escape from the heat.")[28]

Amid the chaos of this experience, the War Relocation Authority's distribution of the English- and Japanese-language *Gila News-Courier*, a "free" press publication entangled with the US military, worked to cast a spell of normalcy over an obviously disenchanting situation by running local stories on school functions and sports matches alongside updates on war developments and camp policies.[29] For many, though, a sense of relative normalcy instead came from creative outlets, from the freedoms they afforded and the confinements they suspended.

For youths like Araki, that creative outlet was music. As he tells it:

> I saved my money and ordered a $29 clarinet from the Sears-Roebuck Mail Catalog.... With it, I got a book with Hardy Shaw's photograph on the cover. With it, I taught myself how to play the clarinet. It was all very logical. Then, I discovered that the fingerings were quite similar to those on the saxophone. I borrowed an alto sax from the high school.

There was also a very kind reverend named John Yamasaki, Jr., whose chapel was on the next block. That chapel had a piano. He gave me free access to it. That's where I began playing melodies and arrangements that I memorized from records.[30]

To his credit (in my view), Araki was modest about his uncommon musicianship. (As Araki's son, Dale, once told me, "He wasn't one to brag.")[31] In his oral history, he spoke of his capacities only when repeatedly prompted by his interviewer:

> GEORGE AKITA: So you're also a self-taught pianist?
> JAMES ARAKI: Yes.
> AKITA: And you're also an arranger of music by this time, in a sense?
> ARAKI: Yes, arranging my own piano pieces.
> AKITA: Your mind must be wired differently. You're able to see all these things in your head, I'm sure.
> ARAKI: I hear them [the arrangements] in my head. Then it's transferable to the piano keyboard very logically. I would listen to big band arrangements—say, by Harry James, and then I would play them on the piano. There were also sheets of piano music lying around, so I learned to decipher notation. I think the first piece I learned how to play was a prelude by Rachmaninoff.... In high school, after I bought that clarinet and started playing the piano, shortly thereafter, I joined the Gila River Dance Band on alto sax. I've been listening to records since about 1939. I know most of the songs that were recorded over those years and perhaps nearly every song that was popular, I would say up to 1952 or 1953. That became my basic repertory of songs.
> AKITA: So, you can just pick up the music you're hearing on the records, without looking at sheet music, and play it?
> ARAKI: Yes, in most instances, yes.
> AKITA: And improvise?
> ARAKI: Yes.[32]

His fluencies notwithstanding, Araki, like many other Nisei youth throughout the camps, was participating in what Marta Robertson has described as a dual affiliative practice, taking part in the ways many interned Nisei were "employ[ing] sound and movement to create a socially cohesive community, assert their bicultural affiliations and contest sociopolitical identities forced on them."³³ The tumultuous experience of unjust internment was introducing Nisei youth to a nation-state's inner workings all too intimately: government-sanctioned racism, wartime nationalism, widespread fearmongering. And all the while, and for years afterward, the contours of popular music and Black sonic experimentalism were also affording many an understanding of community founded on interethnic affiliation and entanglement. For many, as Loren Kajikawa has written, Black musicking was not "simply a voice from the margins but rather a set of deeply embedded cultural forms that pervade[d] a variety of racialized contexts."³⁴ That the music Nisei youth like Araki came to love in the camps, the music that many found freedom in despite their confinements, was a Black improvisatory music recoded in the internment context as American popular music is significant, evocative of some of the emergent postwar racial formations and affinity networks that would shape the coming decades' struggles for social justice. And while listening on its own didn't produce radical politics in any linear, causal ways, it did offer new entry points into the imaginative, critical work of building community beyond old fealties.

For Araki, this listening was significant, too, because like other young men in his situation, he was eventually forced to grapple with his relationships to race, culture, and nation as a nonwhite subject in a military uniform. "I was drafted," Araki recalls, "in the Spring of 1944, as soon as I graduated [from Butte] High School at the Gila River Relocation Center.... I did not want to volunteer for the Armed Services, having been incarcerated as a Japanese American, but when Congress decided that Japanese Americans would be drafted, I'd just happened to have graduated from high school. I was included in the first wave of Nisei draftees."³⁵ After a brief relocation to Chicago and basic training at Fort Douglas in Utah, he was transferred to the Military Intelligence Service Language School at Fort Snelling in Minnesota, where he completed his language studies and eventually taught his own courses.³⁶ He also played with the Fort Snelling Dance Band, soon becoming its bandleader.³⁷ And in the spring of 1945, just after completing his course of study, as the conflict between the Allied and Axis forces was reaching new intensities in the Pacific Theater, Araki heard a new music being performed by Black radical artists—and like so many others of his generational and situational cohort, coming of age in such a difficult historical conjuncture, he worked to make some sense of what this all meant, what it could mean, how he might respond.³⁸ Like others forced to grow up too soon, and others for whom a "prolonged innocence between childhood and adulthood" didn't exist, the complexities of dense, transgressive, and sophisticated Black musicking created a way to begin finding new language for specific experiences of midcentury calamity.[39]

As many musicians and critics have long articulated, those who came to be known in the United States as bebop musicians devoted their time and sweat to critiquing racist fantasy, economic exploitation, and political invisibility in the midst of a global war in which African American soldiers, paying tribute to a country in blood and trauma, were seeing no return on their compulsory investments. Musicians like Max Roach, Kenny Clarke, Joe Guy, and others, tired of their various exploitations, signified on "the music" itself, creating new invitations to communal awareness while at the same time enjoying the inimitable and contradictory pleasures of musicking together. Like a great many across the borders and bar lines of race and nation, Araki got to practicing and joined this rich fold.

* * *

In June 1946, after a long journey on a slow ship, a voyage itself filled with improvisatory musical encounters beyond the color line—as Araki recalled, "There was a huge contingent of black troops headed for the Kobe area, and we used to have delightful jam sessions onboard"—Araki and his shipmates arrived in Tokyo.[40] Upon arrival, Araki and his fellow soldiers were suddenly plunged into a feverish and complicated postwar scene, its actors on edge and its melodies newly swung. During this period, jazz, that so-called American classical music, that new symbol of American military dominance, became in Tokyo a musical lingua franca, traveling everywhere Allied troops did. Whereas in the United States it was knotty, divisive, and extraordinarily popular, in postwar Japan it was a complex interface between ideologically distant actors, a soundtrack of intercultural encounter. As E. Taylor Atkins relays, during the postwar period, radio shows like "*Gems of Jazz* and *Honshu Hayride* hit the airwaves along with shows starring Kid Ory, Harry James, and Frank Sinatra. Countless jazz aficionados began their personal narratives with the epiphany of hearing jazz for the first time on WVTR or NHK."[41] Too, in late 1945, local disc jockeys and jazz musicians like Matsumoto Shin began using radio programs like *New Pacific Hour* to merge "music with American-style optimism and democratic ideals," creating a "sonic backdrop for life in the ruins."[42] This active merging of jazz with the visibility of military dominance and the gospel of American democracy created an environment in which listening to the music meant not only hearing (or, in many cases, avoiding) its Blackness but also grappling with the United States as a newly defining presence in Japanese social life.

And the music sounded constantly. As Atkins writes, "Jazz blared from Occupation-controlled media and from the entertainment districts set up for the American troops. The Japanese government, on behalf of SCAP, hired hundreds of Japanese entertainers to perform for American troops and for 'democratic propaganda' on the airwaves. Perhaps . . . there *was* no escaping jazz. But the music proved seductive enough that millions of Japanese did not object."[43] That all of this would constitute a sonic front of the Occupation—that the soundtrack for a democratic idealism would find form in a music born of Black Americans who, as Baldwin put it, had "pledged allegiance to a flag" that "pledged no allegiance" to them—underscores the cultural complexities of the postwar scene Nisei soldiers like Araki became part of, to say nothing of the conceptual and practical limits of the nation-state as a means of liberation.[44] As was made apparent by the musical landscapes of Japan during the postwar period, understanding "democracy" occurred not only through abstract political discourse but also on the ground levels of art and entertainment. The ubiquity of jazz in Japan during this period, coupled with the confusion of rapid cultural upheaval and the creation of hardly precedented solidarities between some ethnic American troops and Japanese citizens, created a complicated, sonically saturated context. For many, jazz symbolized "the cultural power of the victor": what was in one part of the world a fervent articulation of Black intellectual practice—an articulation, again, that had gone from verb to noun—was, in another, a sonic scar of Japan's defeat.[45] What in the United States was a fast-moving current containing a wealth of possibilities and contradictions—a current pooling, by way of storied sessions at Minton's Playhouse in Harlem and Central Avenue jam sessions in Los Angeles, into the celebrations of technical ferocity and expressive fervor called bebop—was, in Japan, by way of once-underground players and newly reopened clubs, a quickly evolving cluster of scenes informed by local stars and inflected by visiting foreign musicians. Jazz, in that postwar moment, was the soundtrack of hegemony *and* countermodernity at once; how one interpreted it depended, as always, on who was playing and who was listening.[46]

Araki joined others in contributing to this postwar music scene directly. In 1947 he began a recording stretch with a group of musicians performing under the name the Victor Hot Club. One of the group's early singles, "A.P.O. 500," became notably successful among a swath of young people excited about the newness blooming in a rapidly changing national landscape.[47] After completing his daily assignments as a translator in the "Interpreter Section of General Headquarters," Araki would study "bebop theory and performance techniques," practicing on various instruments, arranging standards, composing originals, and sitting in with local outfits.[48] As he recalls it, "[I remember] playing with one such group at the Club Esquire. It was the most expensive night club in Tokyo at that time. . . . Definitely off-limits to soldiers. . . . This was dangerous, I could have been court-martialed because I was an officer and I would discard my uniform and go there disguised as a civilian. That's a double offense. . . . I used to disguise myself and take my horn and sit in either on alto sax or on piano. . . . This was considered the best group in Japan at that time."[49] After months of similar after-hours performances and translation work, he completed his military obligations and was discharged from the army in 1948, though he elected to continue translating for ATIS (the Allied Translator and Interpreter Section) as a civilian for a year. In 1949 he recorded four new original songs—two sparser, more intimate tracks with Jimmy's Trio and two denser, more populous tunes with Victor Gay Bop—which in many ways evince Araki's attempts to work out the relationship between the swing he grew up with on the radio and the bebop he was working to learn.[50]

Among those four tunes was "Jimmy's Bop," perhaps the only surviving recording of Araki during this period in which he performs the style for which he became known in Japan. Recorded in 1949, "Jimmy's Bop" stands out for its speed and titular invocation. Fast yet not frenetic, the piece features Araki on alto sax alongside seven other skilled performers, and its contours highlight a generative idiomatic tension between swing and bebop techniques.[51] The song's main melody is sequential, jumpy, and off-kilter, yet also smoothly delivered, tonally and harmonically calm (see example 2.1). (This main melody aligns with what Guthrie Ramsey Jr. writes of typical bebop arrangements: "Bebop melodies generally covered large ranges and did not depend on the even antecedent-consequent (question-and-answer) phrase structure of popular songs. They were generally not as singable as other styles of popular music, although their innate musicality, together with the sheer virtuosity that it took to perform them at top speed, astounded listeners.")[52]

Harmonically, Araki's solo, transcribed here, has a poetics rooted in the space between broken, arpeggiated chords and smooth chromatic lines.[53] It follows the song's chord structure in a more traditional way than, say, Charlie Parker or Bud Powell might have, committed as they and others in the Harlem scene were to exploring chord extensions and the overtone series, to creating dissonances unexpectedly suited to the harmonic moment. And yet Araki's solo also features the rhythmic intensity of musicians like

EXAMPLE 2.1 Densities and explorations in James Araki's solo on "Jimmy's Bop." Transcription by author.

Parker and Powell, dense flourishes and embellishments that distinguish it from the swing musicians Araki heard on the radio at Gila River. It also features a direct reference to Parker by way of quotation—a signature lick Parker played across a range of his recordings, including in "Billy's Bounce" (at 1:11), "Dexterity" (at 1:00), "Anthropology" (at 1:08), the *Afro-Cuban Jazz Suite* (at 4:20), and more (see example 2.2). I mention this not just because it highlights Araki's close study of bebop possibility as a performer but also because it draws attention to the proximities and distances between Parker's and Araki's styles. Where Parker's approach to time and harmony was by comparison more radical and angular, Araki's work, evocative as it undoubtedly is of a cadre of performers who laid the groundwork in the 1930s for Parker's and others' radicalisms, was transgressive in its con-

EXAMPLE 2.2 A classic Charlie Parker lick, which James Araki quoted often. Transcription by author.

text, indicative of a youthful desire to experiment, admire, emulate, even speculate. Taken together, the two approaches paint a wider picture of a dense cultural moment: a Bird lick, born of Kansas City living and wartime Harlem magnetisms, finds a home in a solo by a formerly interned Nisei musician and then-veteran performing and recording tunes after-hours in Occupation-era Japan.

As a whole, I think "Jimmy's Bop" balances the disjunctive with the streamlined. I hear it as an attempt to balance bebop's energies and structural complexities with the more familiar gestures and palates of swing, creating a distinguishable style that helped invite Japanese collaborators into the new bebop idiom. The tune, like others, creates "improvisational space by layering generous chord sequences over angular, second-line bomb beats or pedal point or walking bass lines," the staple of the jam sessions that begot the bebop Araki was exposed to as an upstart at twenty.[54] In its stylings and its title, it aligns itself with a Black music born of a distinct yet related urgency; it's as much a form of (audio)biography, of sonic autopoiesis—sound self-writing, riting, righting—as it is an experimentalist aspiration and a swung departure from the verb-to-noun shuffle, or, as novelist Salvador Plascencia once put it, the "commodification of sadness."[55]

Thinking now about the significance of all these details, I'm reminded again of Atkins, who writes that "jazz *occupied* an ambiguous cultural space that Japanese found both irresistibly fascinating yet undeniably frightening. The tensions that tore at modern Japanese society—nativism vs. cosmopolitanism, purity vs. hybridity, social stability vs. upheaval, and aesthetic edification vs. degradation—were acted out on the dance floors, on the bandstands, and in vigorous 'jazz debates.'"[56] These same tensions rippled outward, as we notice in Araki's work, finding form in all manner of media and locations. In art and writing of that time, that place, we see the frictions captured in and enabled by the cultural forms of the moment, the incredible complexities of urban war ruin, of audible and material reconstruction, of a deracinated music compelled into occupational employment, of the emaciations caused by the stress of coming invasion, and ultimately the continued subjugation of peoples and their bodies through the still-unchallenged logic of beat or be beaten, "conquer the conquerers."[57] In this mix were pressing questions: What did victory mean, and for whom? What would the future hold? What would it sound like? Why? Araki's relationship to these questions casts the "victorious end" of "an unhappy war" in a somber light and again highlights the palpable contradictions he and his collaborators embodied as they connected with one another by fusing swing with bebop in occupied territory.[58]

As singular as his experiences were, though, Araki was also like many others who found in music a set of tools for dreaming amid the postwar conjuncture—for navigating large-scale uncertainties at the level of local utterance and collaborative exploration. Like others, he found solace in an avowedly complex music that took as a major concern the limits of articulability, the margins of US political enfranchisement, and the always already transcultural, transnational reach of Black aesthetic practice.[59] If we subscribe to the idea that bebop offered critical commentary on the popular—as defined by the victorious, populated by the subjugated, and pilfered from the aggrieved—then we might say that for a generation of young listeners and practitioners, this Black musicking was a future that flashed up in a moment of danger.[60]

When I listen to Araki's work of this postwar period, I think of what it might have meant to study this Black radical musicking as a formerly interned Nisei soldier stationed near a site of atomic horror; to hear, in one's early twenties, some "unspeakable" though not "inexpressible" truths in Black musicians' solos; to conceptualize them in relation to one's own racialized experiences; to weave that insight into one's aesthetic hypotheses. This, to me, feels like a vital, complicated relational praxis—a means of running not into the arms of American supremacy or away from a compulsory future but rather toward a present, maybe even a tomorrow, of coimplication and "response-ability."[61] It feels to me, as a listener, like groundwork laid, whether knowingly or unknowingly, for important solidarities and their figural reconstitutions; it feels to me like riffing atop rubble, hazarding hope on a scarred planet.[62]

With this in mind, I think Araki's music invites us to renew, though not resolve, the now-anthemic line of inquiry Paul Gilroy lays out in *Small Acts*: To what degree can musics and their histories present "analog[ies] for comprehending the lines of affiliation and association which take the idea of the diaspora beyond its symbolic status as the fragmentary opposite of an imputed racial essence?"[63] I think it invites us to consider the role of Black radical music in historical narratives of postwar Nisei experience, the roles of Nisei musicians in historical narratives of jazz development, and, as Gabriel Solis puts it, the importance of both in the narrativizing and theorizing of "Black Pacific" flows and eddies.[64] I think Araki's music helps us understand, through clarity and complexity of example, not only how solos cross oceans, not only how they capture, brilliantly and often, the speed and sentiment of modern life, but also how they remind us of that vital, relational commonplace: that one's self-concept, one's (audio)biography, is always built in collaboration with others, through close listening, in layered time.

*　*　*

Like the spaces and resultant sounds of Henry Minton's and Clark Monroe's clubs in Harlem, bebop's birthplaces, the layered time and stacked sounds pursued by Araki and his collaborators, both in the postwar Japan of the late 1940s and in that recording studio in 1959, decentered a whiteness that, for many, as Deborah Wong writes, has most often been "present yet rendered invisible by ideologies that create marked and unmarked categories."[65] For many differently racialized nonwhite people, "to be an American and to think about race" meant "engaging with Whiteness and all its performances."[66] For Araki and his recording mates, though, just as for many Black musicians in Harlem, the idea was to disrupt that white-centered logic and to create new imaginative avenues, new modes of collective and, at least in Araki's case, transnational American dreaming.

Across that *Midnight Jazz Session* of 1959, Araki and his bandmates explore this via overdubbing, as I've mentioned, but also through unique treatments of bebop's musical idiom, particularly in swing-heavy musical contexts. Araki's rhythms, especially, are worth listening for—bursts of density that cut through in the context of more linear solos and arrangements, reminiscent of work by postwar swing holdouts like saxophonists Paul Desmond, Lee Konitz, and Warne Marsh, and, pragmatically, more achievable with the constraints and ambitions of the recording project. Such bursts of rhythmic density and complexity were, as Steve Coleman has put it, actually "by far the most dramatic feature of Bird's musical language"—"his phrasing and timing," as well as his playing "in combination with [other] dynamic players."[67] For an improvising musician, approaching longer melodic phrases by exploring smaller rhythmic cells, by utilizing micro-subdivisions and nested temporalities, can change a listener's sense of temporal ebb and flow. In a bebop musician's hands, a flowing melody, like a pane of glass under stress, can fracture into a thousand glinting shards, then be reassembled, recollected with a difference.[68] Araki's overdubbed solos explore that insight, revealing how the two sonic and symbolic worlds of swing and bebop can coexist in a single form.[69]

The bop flourishes on *Midnight Jazz Session* draw special attention to themselves given the prominence of the project's swing and blues energies. Consider three standout moments: first, the 2:56 mark in a very nonbop version of "Almost Like Being in Love," which involves Araki, on alto sax, ending a restatement of the song's temperate main melody by darting up and down the instrument (example 2.3); second, the 2:45 mark in "Day Dream," which involves Araki, on piano, soaring swiftly above contemplative chord changes, filling the otherwise subdued ballad with unexpected rhythmic and melodic density (example 2.4); and, third, the 1:45 mark in "Two Brothers," which involves Araki, again on alto sax, providing a rapid elaboration of a musical idea (example 2.5).

The most overt bebop experiment on *Midnight Jazz Session*, though, is the group's breakneck "Broken Rhythm"—a track informed in spirit and structure by the "conflicting changes, sudden nuances, sharp and impudent interjections" and "broken rhythms" Langston Hughes memorably wrote of in his bebop-focused Harlem portrait, "Montage of a Dream Deferred."[70] Written as a gift for Araki's old friend, drummer George Kawaguchi, "Broken Rhythm," like the rest of the album, foregrounds intricate rhythmic interplay among the instrumentalists, formal quirks and stylistic citations that at once provoke listener reflection and enable performer excitement, and overdubbed solos that display in their arcs a fascination with instrumental possibility, truth telling, and temporal multiplicity. In Araki's "Broken Rhythm," one finds the compression, simultaneity, and sedimentation specific to music as a conceptual and figural apparatus: a gathering of layers and sequences, a thick and dreamlike unfolding.[71]

Take a listen: at the core of "Broken Rhythm" is a relational, percussive interplay between Araki and Kawaguchi (see figure 2.2). Structurally, the song emphasizes collaboration over competition, and when it does feature its soloists, their improvisations are dialogical.[72] The nature of this interplay is named by the invocation of a driving mambo (and a related invocation of Afro-Cuban jazz) in the tune's B section.[73] The stylistic citation gives form to the tension produced by the smoothness and density of the rhythmic interplay mixed with the stylistic imperative to invent in relation to a group concept. Socially and musically, the tune emphasizes a subtle truth of musical ethics: only a thin line ever separates a duel from a duet.

EXAMPLE 2.3 Dense offbeat flurries in James Araki's version of "Almost Like Being in Love." Transcription by author.

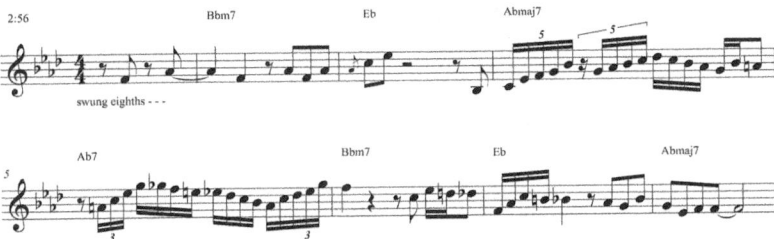

EXAMPLE 2.4 Dense, lyrical cascades in James Araki's version of "Day Dream." Transcription by author.

EXAMPLE 2.5 Rapid shifts of rhythmic feel in James Araki's "Two Brothers." Transcription by author.

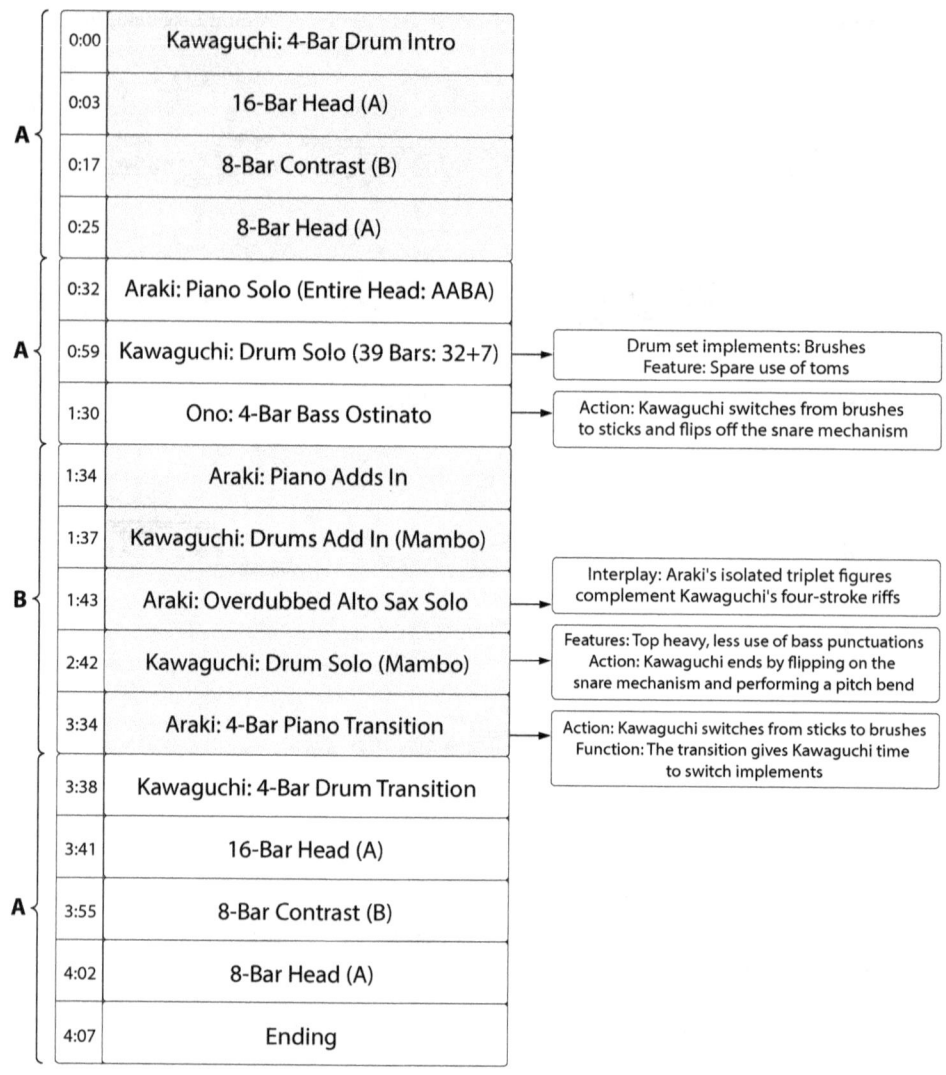

FIGURE 2.2 Loops, overlays, and relational structures in the musical form of James Araki's "Broken Rhythm." Image by author.

A thin strip of tape also created an unprecedented improvisatory dynamic for the group—Araki accompanying on piano while soloing on alto sax, Kawaguchi providing the ceaseless propulsion, and Ono the grounding subfrequencies. Araki's solos, enlivened not only by bebop-informed rhythmic flares but also by subtle improvisatory motifs and recurring gestures across instruments that by the late 1950s would become his calling cards, offered lessons in execution, opportunities to fulfill the promises of his musical arrangements. The mambo section, as much a feature moment for Kawaguchi as an example of experimental sound engineering and inventive composition, offered a lesson in externalization, multiplication, and reconstitution. It allowed Araki and his bandmates to differentiate and compartmentalize capacities while keeping the resultant fragments connected to a larger whole.[74] The tune, like the album itself, was a way for a group to hear multiple selves and interiorities, reflected via playback, alive in layered time.

This collaborative exploration, coupled with Araki's facilities and the affordances of new recording techniques, again offered a different take on virtuosity, one that quite literally relied on spliced and layered takes and, effectively, a kind of smoothing and democratizing of traditionally masculinist virtuosic displays, productive, to my ear, more of shared delight in sonic possibility than hero worship. In this sense, despite its swing patina and bebop glimmer, the work really was a product of the late 1950s, its experiments resonant with those of other artists similarly exploring new group structures and musicking procedures. As was increasingly the case throughout the latter 1950s, the recording techniques being used by artists like Araki were part of a major shift in the conditions of sonic and social possibility bearing deep implications for creative musical praxes. Overdubbing drew attention to the studio itself as an instrument, to in-studio sound manipulation as an important domain of intellectual practice, a shift in musical thinking that only intensified in the decades that followed, particularly among Black musician-technologists. These techniques also, again, focused attention on the idea of an instrumentalist's signature sound: that alchemical blend of timbre, tone, touch, and kinesthetics that, by containing the traces of a lifetime of prior musical experiences, in effect functions as a portal into understandings of gender, race, technology, and location. A sound, however seemingly individual or signature, is always already relational and unfixed, a trace and a means of interaction.

Midnight Jazz Session's late 1950s studio experimentalism was also arriving at a complex historical moment: the decade had become marked by normalized anxiety; by ideological tussles between capitalist and communist world futures strung through everything from Levittown niceties to bleeding blacklists; by an arms race regularly reminding all of a paralyzing nuclear sublime; by rapidly changing social formations and self-awarenesses spurred by the rise of televisual mass communication. Modernity's polarizing engines and effects were being rendered visible in new ways: mounting efforts to actualize hopes of decolonization, for instance, were palpable throughout the Global South. Listening back for this historical context, we might ask, alongside Zakiyyah Iman Jackson, "If an essential feature of your existence is that the norm is not able to take hold, what mode of being becomes available, and what mode might you invent?"[75] Listening to *Midnight Jazz Session* through a question like this, we might say that one of the norms that was unable to take hold for Japanese and Japanese Americans alike under the internment, occupation, and nuclear shadow of American racial democracy in the mid-twentieth century, one of the essential features of existence denied, was the simple yet profound fact of human interiority—fears, feelings, complexities, dreams. The layered time to which overdubbing gave new form, focalized by Araki's musical vision but evocative of a strong group bond and a transnational entanglement with Black musical experimentalism, was a dense and imaginative response to that denial.

* * *

It's unsurprising, reading historical news clippings from back in the late 1940s, that many Japanese jazz fans back in the postwar Tokyo scene expected Araki to pursue a career as a professional musician when he returned to the United States. When Araki spoke with journalist Mas Manbo for a 1948 profile in the *Nippon Times*, he expressed those aspirations himself: to make it big in the United States, to land a seat with a big group, to lead a stellar band of his own. Excited to continue his education via the GI Bill and ingratiate himself in major Los Angeles jazz circles, Araki, then twenty-four, returned to the United States in late autumn of 1949.[76] "[But] before I finished my second year," Araki recalled, "I was called up to serve in the Korean War.... I lost three semesters [as a music student at UCLA]. I left regretfully."[77]

After completing this second brief window of compulsory military service, Araki returned to Los Angeles, pursuing undergraduate and later graduate studies while performing regularly in Little Tokyo, Downtown Los Angeles, and the Bay Area with his own combo and as a sideman. In Northern California, he played often at Treasure Island for the navy; in Southern California, he performed regularly at the Cosmopolitan Ballroom of the Nikabob Restaurant on South Western for JACL (Japanese American Citizens League) events as well as at the Zenda Ballroom on Figueroa with singer Frances "Chickie" White and bandleader Tetsu Bessho and the Nisei Serenaders.[78] He also played frequently with jazz bandleader Lionel Hampton. As Araki tells it:

> Lionel used to sit in and jam with us. . . . He was, I believe, the first black musician that made a big-time band. Then came Teddy Wilson, the pianist. Well, Lionel used to come in, and he was by then a successful bandleader—he was known for his world-famous compositions like "Flying Home" and "Midnight Sun." He had a big band in Los Angeles. . . . He would relax in the evenings by coming down, and so we used to play with two pianos at once. He would play the piano using two fingers as he would play the xylophone, and then I would play chords on the bottom. I'd never played with him before. . . . One night he brought in some key members of his band and I happened to have my alto saxophone there. His pianist played the piano and I played the alto sax. He liked what he heard and asked me to join his band, and he said the first thing would be a recording session a few days hence. So that recording session was the first time I played with Lionel's band. I was sight reading the music. It was at Norman Granz's studio in Hollywood. We recorded twelve tunes. . . . On two of his swinging numbers, he had to have a better drummer, so he signed up Buddy Rich, who of course was then known as one of the two best drummers in the world. . . . Those were two very enjoyable numbers to record.[79]

After that August 1955 recording session in Hollywood—Hampton at the helm, Araki sight-reading in the saxophone section, Buddy Rich keeping the energy high on classics like "Midnight Sun" and "Airmail Special"— Araki faced a choice.[80] Granz's by-then huge Jazz at the Philharmonic began touring Europe and Japan as part of the United States' Cold War–era efforts to spread American-brand democracy via jazz ambassadorship, and Hampton had just invited the young Araki to participate in a European tour.[81] "Lionel subsequently was going to Paris," Araki recalls. "He said, 'Jimmy, you are coming to Paris with us.'"[82]

Araki declined. For reasons pragmatic and personal, familial and vocational, Araki turned down the invitation to become a formalized jazz ambassador, instead diving deeper into a research interest he had cultivated in the futures of Japan's cultural pasts, in the preservation of historical Japanese literary forms and artistic practices. "I decided to make Japanese language and literature the subjects of my course of study," Araki remembers.[83] He joined others in doing so in the wake and under the threat of unfathomable loss. To extend what Teju Cole has written of mid-2010s precarities: the shifting intellectual and academic currents of the early 1950s were set against a backdrop of "mourning and premonition."[84] Mourning: the loss of a shared conscience in pursuit of Pyrrhic victory, the evaporation of humility in pursuit of nuclear belligerence. Premonition: the hard-won knowledge of rubble's possibility, the foresight alchemized from wounds and ash. Despite the surety sewed into burgeoning suburbia, despite the manyfold euphorias of the baby boom, the atrocities of the war—including, as Junot Díaz puts it, those "two atomic eyes [that] opened over civilian centers in Japan"—flooded a thoroughly Enlightened world with newly "triumphant calamity."[85] The psyches of leaders and laypeople were irradiated with an enveloping anxiety, a hum measurable in everything from soil samples to pedal points. What existed in a new, terrifying guise was victory's sublimity: futures for some, destruction for all.[86] In such a world, for a Nisei experimentalist with transoceanic entanglements, I imagine studying an ancestral past and improvising a layered future must have felt grounding, meaningful. A calling.[87]

* * *

Listening to Araki's only full-length record today, in a present marked by intensified anti-Asian violence in the United States, linked as that violence is to long histories of racism, xenophobia, and viral nationalism, to white fears of changing demographics intensifying amid the recent world-transforming global pandemic, I think, again, about the enduring significances of relation and collaboration among nonwhite youth of color, differently positioned yet similarly inspired. I think about the importance of Black musicking in recent histories of such relation and wonder what new articulations are being animated by today's youth in this ailing world they've inherited. I wonder what it is still possible to learn from those who have preceded us, listening near and across, attending to difference and distance, stacking sounds and stories and, if lucky, making time a friend.

As my copy of *Midnight Jazz Session* spins on repeat and the sun begins to rise outside my apartment building, the gray-black of the sky warming to a predawn navy, the birds beginning to rustle and chirp, the group's flourishes animating the still air, I sit quietly with the fact that Araki, like others, experienced the humiliations and traumas of Japanese internment, experienced the tensions of traveling across the Pacific in the aftermath of World War II to occupy Japan via the US Army, experienced the possibilities afforded by studying Japanese cultural history and literature, experienced what it felt like to find form in a recording studio. It's true he was exceptional in many ways, musically and literarily, but his life was also like so many others in the ways it was shaped by larger structures and forces intimate in their expression and global in their effects. What music like his helps us hear today, I believe, is how, in this case, technology and the "labyrinthine language of bop" created new conditions of possibility to articulate truths of Nisei emplotment in and beyond flawed empires in an irradiated world.[88] The multitrack dream space and overlaid histories his music mobilizes clarify, at least for me, a trifold idea: that world-scale tensions and calamities express themselves at the level of individuals; that individuals, messy and exceeding categorization, express world-scale tensions; and that overinvestments in the primacy of individuals and intense policing of who counts as them propels conflict across scales, across times. These things keep me listening, marveling at sonic inexhaustibility.

As my copy of *Midnight Jazz Session* winds its way back to Araki's "Day Dream," his piano playing in so many times at once, I hear a dreaming that meant experimenting, testing the limits of expressive and experiential possibility, multiplying the ways one's self and one's surroundings can be rendered; I hear a dreaming in a recording studio; a layering, excavating, revealing; an allying of machines; a creation of a liberatory, transnational, racialized but not overdetermined imaginative "interior," filled and contoured by "musical daydreams": "reveries, hallucinations, each shrouded in the half-light of their own specific unreality."[89] As I close my bloodshot eyes, long overdue for rest, time folds on itself, and I remember, near sleep, Duke Ellington.

"This isn't a piano," he once explained. "This is dreaming. It's dreaming."[90]

three.
quartered notes

When I close my eyes, and my breathing slows, and the waking world recedes, I can still picture the archive that blazing afternoon, silent save for the rustling pages and squeaking chairs and droning air-conditioning units, the space ignited by beams of golden-hour sunlight thick with dust-mote dancing. I can still recall, there in that vault ostensibly removed from a world in flux, in that place of promised posterity, in that vestige of colonial logic, the smell of old wood, faint and sweet and hardly placeable. I can still recall the plastic boxes laid out before me, full of documents ordered into one of an infinite number of possible arrangements, full of the intimacies and aspirations of persons long deceased. I can still remember the feeling of handling a specific individual's paper trails, taking care not to fold the thin pages, knowing they were written on by someone who, by their late twenties, my age then, had been imprisoned for nearly a decade, subject to carceral ruthlessness. I can also still recall, after rifling through these fragile traces of another's time alive, after trying to find in them some instruction or call or dismissal, the feeling of accessing an old disk, putting on my headphones, and listening to an archived recording of a poem, written under duress, performed live near a microphone for the very first time, the speaker's voice melodious and cadential like my late grandfather's, the sentiments shaped by songs and scenes long since evaporated.

"Quizas que puede decir que fue la llave que abrió las puertas de la prisión para mi" (Maybe you can say this was the key that opened the prison doors for me). "I've never read it in public.... I would like to offer it to you now: A Trip through the Mind Jail."[1]

The poem, now a classic of Chicanx literary writing, is a masterwork by author Raúl Salinas. Delivered live for the first time on this 1973 recording, the piece—and particularly this performance of it: the syncopated rhythms and bleeding registers, the surfeit of languages and sustained pitches, the kinesthetic energy and idiolectic bebop prosody—conjures a world of superimposed time and variegated speed and shifting place, an altogether different archive of sound and sentiment than the one housing the recording today. Composed while Salinas was incarcerated, "A Trip" and its nuances evoke the relations, structures, and histories of a midcentury turn toward carceral ubiquity, doing so in ways that foreground the entanglements of text and context, embodied experience and experimental musical possibility.

Salinas, born in San Antonio in 1934, was like others in his generational and local cohort in that his youth was filled with bebop, Black radical sound. This sound—again, a consolidation of after-hours jam sessions in Harlem, an experiment traveling westward through circuits of touring performers and distributors—was a long tone sustained throughout Salinas's life: through an early interest in jazz and its live performance in East Austin nightclubs, through jazz poetic experimentation, and through late-life performances and studio recording sessions with jazz combos.[2] It was also sustained during his lengthy incarceration: from 1957 to 1972, he served time in Soledad State Prison, Huntsville State Prison, Leavenworth Federal Penitentiary, and Marion Federal Penitentiary on various charges, mostly related to drug possession and distribution. During those years and beyond them, Salinas, like others, turned to Black experimental musicking as an entry point into understanding relation and solidarity amid the storm of suspension and recollection that, following Nicole Fleetwood and others, we might understand as the double time of carceral experience. Like others, from behind bars, Salinas reached for his own suitable vocabulary, his own unfettered dream space, turning to poetry, fiction, essays, and music criticism, attempting to write like his favorite musicians sounded. (His poetry was so well received, in fact, that academics and writers sent impassioned letters to government officials on his behalf, vouching for his literary talent, helping him secure his release.)[3] Striving to bring the world he knew and heard into focus, Salinas eventually participated in a Chicano literary renaissance linked to transnational efforts for social justice, pushing for new modes of relating, for deep ways of listening.

In this chapter I want to listen with this fellow Tejano and trace how he and others near him processed Black experimental musicking as the world smoldered and the walls closed in. I want to read and listen to Salinas's prison and postprison work to follow further some of the ways Black experimental musicking traveled, how it resonated with differently positioned nonwhite listeners in and beyond midcentury calamity, how it created conditions of possibility for new relational understandings and commitments. As with the preceding chapters, I want to do so through a "loose and dreamlike" form that attends at once to scenes of reading and writing, sounding and listening, in order to make specific and significant the manifold times and spaces that texture our dreams of better worlds. Considering together the histories I've researched, the personal influence of my grandfather's storytelling, as well as my own gendered, racialized body, I want to ask: How did the rebellions of young Black musical experimentalists in Harlem resonate among Mexican American youth in the postwar years? How did those sounds help illuminate the naked injustices of the American criminal justice system and the larger racial capitalist infrastructure of which it is part? What did it mean to try and write like musicians sounded, particularly in the context of a prison in which live musicking was more memory than daily possibility? In what ways can such writings enrich contemporary understandings of the functions of music criticism, the possibilities of poetic language, the formations of racialized masculinities in the United States, and routes to solidarity and shared fate under racial capitalism?

In asking these questions, I'm interested, too, in pursuing what Shana Redmond has described as the duality of "*doing* and being *inside of* time," particularly as it relates to incarceration and resistance.[4] Consider, on the one hand, the myth "of the prison as a location where time stands still," as a place for "failed citizen-subjects" without futures, living idle in a protracted Now somehow outside history, and, on the other, a reality "inside the prison" where incarcerated citizen-subjects refuse those characterizations through resistant performances, gestures, and artworks."[5] "Within prisons," Redmond writes, "identity performance is compressed and tightly regulated, as time and place become inextricably paired over the course of one's sentence. Time is the only structural excess available to inmates, and even it is not discretionary; prisons are intended to wait people out, to allow slow human expiration in order to prove the vengeance and power of the state. The prison is therefore built of and on the time of its inhabitants—those incarcerated workers and forced idle."[6] This surplus of times—of foreclosed possibilities, of enforced presents, of spent days, of missed sunrises, of forced dealings with the dreams of others' designs, of grappling with the fact that "the carceral state's dream of the prisoner's future is one of incapacitation, slow death, and nothingness"—this temporal geography creates urgent occasion to listen and read for carceral dreams, memories, and relations.[7] The carceral timescapes and penal chronologies that began to intensify after the war and that have only worsened exponentially in recent decades prompt us, I believe, to listen for what layered times have existed for incarcerated subjects and, importantly, for how things like temporal arts, "adornments of time," have offered creators and collaborators different ways of hearing their most formative relations to others, to institutions, to histories, to possibilities, to selves that are ever permeable, to communities that are always evolving, forever unbound.

* * *

Cristina Rivera Garza, drawing on French writer Antoine Volodine, notes that prison writings "are always talking about something else": "an incarcerated community whose members will ultimately die." "Their memory, in the narrator's hands," she continues, "is the only thing that will survive." Prison writers, then, often work on this aspect of memory, writing to become part of a historical record beyond the terms enforced by the state, to imagine and pursue a different system of being, "first [in] memory, then dreams"—to enact, as Rivera Garza puts it, an "afterlife in dreams."[8]

The printed version of "A Trip through the Mind Jail," written at Leavenworth Penitentiary in 1969, is a tapestry of such dreams and memories. Its collage of impressions, affects, and desires draw attention not only to a scene of writing (*la pinta*) and a subject of remembrance, a specific historical referent (La Loma, East Austin), but also to the entwinement of literal and metaphorical trips, personal recollections, and communal protentions. Composed of fourteen stanzas—sinewed, detailed, semiautobiographical scenes written in free verse—the sections advance by refrain, with "neighborhood" opening each vignette like a call or a conjuring.[9]

The poem's opening sets up its central tension, its core losses and urgencies:

> LA LOMA
> Neighborhood of my youth
>   demolished, erased forever from
>   the universe.
>   You live on, captive, in the lonely
>   cellblocks of my mind.[10]

As the recollections unfold, the speaker moves through the neighborhood, past its "endless hills" and "muddied streets," its "dilapidated community hall," its "Fiestas for any occasion" at "Guadalupe Church," its "Buena Vista," "Santa Rita Courts," and "Los Projects," its "Spanish Town Café." With each re-membered space comes a cluster of people, impressions, associations, and retrospective judgments. The "Rhythm n' Blues" and "Chalie's 7th St. Club" from Salinas's youth, Chitlin' Circuit venues where he began chasing his interest in Black musicking alongside other "Chicano jazz enthusiasts" who would "quiz each other," make a meaningful appearance, the sites of "loud funky music" and "purple clouds of Yesca smoke" that "one day descended & embraced us all."[11]

The poem, filled, too, with lamentations of neighborhood fratricide, detached representations of sexual becoming, and deeply personal critiques of the American carceral system, reaches a climax when the chain of local specificities is broken, the sights and sounds of La Loma gone, and the speaker returns the narration to its starting point within the cell, the scene of writing:

> Neighborhood of my childhood
>   neighborhood that no longer exists
>   some died young—fortunate—some rot in prisons
>   the rest drifted away to be conjured up
>   in minds of others like them.
>   For me: only the NOW of THIS journey is REAL!

As Salinas dealt with the immense existential difficulties of having lived behind bars for nearly a decade by then, La Loma and all it contained—its buildings, its people, its events, and, importantly, its sounds, its musics—became essential:

> I needed you then . . . identity . . . a sense of belonging
> I need you now.
> So essential to adult days of imprisonment,
>   you keep me away from INSANITY's hungry jaws;
>   Smiling/ Laughing/ Crying.

La Loma, "Neighborhood of my adolescence/ neighborhood that is no more," became, for Salinas, a long tone sustained through hardship, transformed by time and context, renewed with each new breath:

>   YOU ARE TORN PIECES OF MY FLESH!!!!!
>   Therefore, you ARE.
>   LA LOMA—AUSTIN—MI BARRIO.

The power of this poem resides in its reverent yet sobering portrayal of barrio sociality, in its close attention to the specificities of structure and circumstance that beget senses of place and home.[12] Through each of the poem's lines, La Loma, Salinas's multicultural East Austin barrio, becomes, in some ways like Harlem, a local symbol of dispossession and communal striving, a sign of song and difficulty, hope and heartbreak.[13]

The printed text is also a weave of different sign systems: not only the English, Spanish, and caló (a Pachuco argot), arranged and punctuated to emphasize multilingual rhymes and homophones, nor only the creative use of page space as in concrete poetry, but also pictography: the tenth stanza features, as Ben Olguín points out, "stylized Chicana/o graffiti and hand-drawn symbols of Salinas's barrio placas" that become "the nexus around which La Loma will be transformed into both a nostalgic representation of the free world—any place outside the penitentiary—and also a manifestation of the effects of the U.S. carceral system—that is, colonization and the related local effects of underdevelopment."[14]

Interesting, too, is that among the pictographs in the poem is a reproduction of one of Salinas's tattoos (see figure 3.1), an image inked onto his right hand that features symbols that "proclaim his nickname, his barrio, his spirituality, his love of music and the number 13, signifying the letter 'M,' which he noted to [Louis Mendoza] symbolized marihuana, his drug of choice."[15] The image has long entranced me, over the years becoming tattooed in my own memory, its details consistently reminding me of another's symbolic commitment to a self, to a nuanced identity in a carceral state premised on anonymization. Predictably, among the details that hold me is the eighth note at the image's center, positioned at the heart of the poem, tattooed on the fleshy part of Salinas's right hand, just where his pen would rest as he wrote—a notational ambiguity that for many practicing and professional musicians still marks a gateway into interpreting rhythms as even or uneven, straight or swung.[16]

After listening to that archived 1973 recording of Salinas performing "A Trip" live for the first time, it's hard not to hear his body of work as a whole as swung, stylistically and referentially indebted to a Black experimental musicking tradition in both sound and relational social awareness. As he performs the poem's fourteen stanzas, he uses syncopated rhythmic gestures

FIGURE 3.1 One of Raúl Salinas's tattoos, which appears in the text of his poem. Source: Salinas, "A Trip through the Mind Jail," in *Un Trip through the Mind Jail*, 58.

and melodic shapes, a jazz-informed vocal prosody, to bring to new life the energy and memory indexed on the page—a set of gestures that aligned him aesthetically (if not politically) with many other Chicano and Black radical poets, as well as distinguished his performances across decades of artivism, including during jazz poetry recording sessions in the early 2000s with musicians including Tejano jazz artist Tomás Ramírez and the late Asian American radical composer Fred Ho. As the audio recording of Salinas's 1973 reading plays out, the grain of Salinas's voice imparting new layers of information on the landmark printed work, the elements comprising the *musicalities of his language*—the sound of his voice, the music that so shaped his youth, the hairpin multilingual modulations and registral shifts—become inseparable, evocative of the limit points between media. As a printed work, "A Trip through the Mind Jail" is as much a linguistic and visual odyssey as it is a musical score, a transcription of a Xicanindio's soloing, a lead sheet for new improvisations across bars and bar lines. As a recorded audio performance, it is a reminder of a person, a life, a direct link between word and body.

* * *

The musical bones of "A Trip" are those of an East Austin that once was, a place in which place was made improvisationally, where the soundtracks of youth were thickly and specifically multicultural. Within limits, we can time-travel there. Picture it: a party in 1949, a throng of teenagers experimenting with booze, pot, and sexual fumbling, and Salinas, hearing the new Harlem sound for the first time, being introduced to it by a knowing older friend. "It seemed rather strange to me that I had never heard any of these records before," he recalled of his first exposure. "'Crazeology' by Chas Parker and his Pebon Boys," "'Dance of the Infidels,' by Fats Navarro."[17] As the joints, roaches, and beers pile up and the chemical waves begin to crest, "Dizzy [goes] into his trumpet solo on 'Groovin' [and] everything seem[s] to cave in on me all at once. . . . I could hear the music as if coming from some deep chasm, and it sounded like the record was going at a faster speed than usual."[18] A faster speed, a layered moment, a drug-swirled time.

By then, Salinas was already a musicophile. As he recalls, when he was a small child, he used to spend hours in front of the neighborhood juke-box listening to rhythm and blues. ("Sitting there listening to the music, I often felt like I was in a trance"; "The important thing to me was that [the music] swung . . . that meant everything.")[19] But like others in his scene, after hearing musicians like Dizzy Gillespie, Charlie Parker, Fats Navarro, and Kenny Kersey, his musical interests intensified, paired as they were with the kinds of drug consumption that not only clouded bebop's articulation in the popular press but also conflated narcotics with Black and Latinx communities, further yoking the logics of racialization to that of criminalization. (Mainstream American media in the late 1940s and 1950s, as George Lipsitz reminds us, perpetuated a neo-Victorian culture of repression, linking "opposition to dominant ideology" with vice, and Blackness with "greed, gluttony, laziness, and licentiousness.")[20] And as these matters always do, they found local expression and, crucially, pushback. Through the mid-twentieth century, Austin city planners and officials harnessed and hardened local segregationist energies, creating the conditions for East Austin to become an area distinguished by differently marginalized communities in close proximity.[21] The proximity of these ethnic communities in an Austin beset by Jim Crow laws, while at times producing conflict, also often resulted in alliances, convergences, and solidarities—a truth highlighted by the importance of East Austin's music and venues as contact zones, points of entry into relational understandings of class and gender, race and space.

As members of East Austin's youth cultures knew well, music and its performance sites were affording promise and pride to marginalized community members of differing ethnicities, as well as to veterans returning from war.[22] Music venues, in all their variety, were flourishing as "spaces of autonomy in a society otherwise dominated by whites," helping to "foster a sense of pride in the talents of the community" by nurturing "self-value and dignity in an atmosphere of white supremacy."[23] Music venues, too, were also providing opportunities for differently racialized boys to intuit (if not name), through sound, difference, and cross-identification, the ways "nonwhite men" who combat "structural subjugations by white supremacist patriarchal systems of power in the U.S. body politic" have historically become overly "loud in their heteromasculine pose and swagger," as Frederick Aldama and Arturo Aldama write.[24] Through music, hegemonic and alternative masculinities, as "phenomen[a] of place," were becoming newly heard and discussed.[25] Slowly, glacially, masculinities were beginning to be understood by young, differently racialized boys entering into new social terrains as localized, intimate habits and patterns—and, eventually, as expressions of intimate violences necessarily unmarked within the "prison house of racialized neocolonial heteropatriarchies," violences that perpetuate themselves via a stultifying normalcy, a numbing everywhereness.[26] As Salinas and his young friends eventually came to understand—in different ways as boys and, later, as older, racialized nonwhite men—music and its venues could provide new social visions beyond the social systems propping up the hegemonic mainstream, beyond the American racial democracy into which they'd been born.[27]

"'We were just kids, fuckin' kids, takin' on the world,'" Salinas once put it. "'But it was also making alliances with the Black community out of social and political necessity. We used to quiz each other, listen to records and ask 'Who's that?' I'm speaking for about 30 die-hard Chicano jazz enthusiasts who followed *Downbeat* and *Metronome* magazines religiously.'"[28]

During the early 1950s, Salinas, told by an Austin juvenile court "to join the military or leave town," decided to move to California, as he recalled, "to work in the fields [picking cherries] first with relatives and later with friends."[29] "By then," he once reflected, "because of my friendship with Chuy and my reading, I already knew what to look for [on the jazz front]. So wherever I went, I'd check the papers to see who was playing."[30] Thoroughly steeped in the music of Pancho Haygood, Babs Gonzales, Joe Albany, Jimmy

Raney, Joe Farlow, Red Rodney, Herschel Evans, Bud Powell, Fats Navarro, Sonny Stitt, Gene Ammon, Max Roach, Thelonious Monk, George Shearing, Stan Getz, Shorty Rogers, Chet Baker, Chris Hamilton, and many others, here on the West Coast, Salinas began exposing himself to the same thriving Bay Area and Los Angeles scenes that were nurturing figures as diverse as then proto-Chicano writer Oscar Acosta, tenor saxophonist Dexter Gordon, trumpeter Art Farmer, and multi-instrumentalist James Araki.[31] These California scenes, particularly those in Greater Los Angeles, were thriving in ways particular to West Coast postwar conditions. "During a period when many Mexican American Angelenos were frustrated with their socioeconomic position yet hopeful about the benefits of assimilation," Anthony Macías writes, "African American music and style proved to be an ideal model of both participation in and resistance to Anglo American society"; too, the "detached attitude, or 'studied indifference' of the pachucos, and later, the cholos, resonated with disaffected blacks, as it eventually would with many white youth."[32] In this environment, as in East Austin, musicians like Mexican American bassist Ralph Peña were creating a "community of exchange amongst Chicano jazzmen, Black jazzmen, and their white allies" by transforming home garages into "jam room[s]" for "interchange."[33] So were Japanese Americans, still grappling with the devastating economic, social, and personal repercussions of wartime internment, actively contributing to the scene's polyracial, multicultural character. Fresh from a similar yet distinct social situation in his multiracial community of East Austin, surrounded by different jazzmen "[drawing] from their upbringings in U.S. barrios and borderlands" and thus asserting them as "crucial sites of jazz production," Salinas, like other Mexican Americans circulating throughout the United States and finding freedoms in bebop, was primed to extend his sense of music's social, political, and imaginative horizons further, to find a voice, some footing.[34]

But a dark cloud hung over these scenes and their contributors, Salinas included. Like Charlie Parker, Art Blakey, and many others systematically targeted, exploited, and abandoned by the American project, in his youth Salinas became hooked on heroin, shooting up as a young adult "throughout '54 and '55."[35] Bouncing between California and Texas, stumbling through a marriage and fatherhood, Salinas was awash in problems created by solutions that seemed to solve them. Hoping to kick his habit, he traveled from Austin to Los Angeles in 1956, all the while sinking deeper into the drug trade, moving increasingly larger volumes of marijuana out of the Lighthouse Club in Hermosa Beach, where he worked with the owner and "kept their stash in the jukebox."[36] The precarity of this situation came to a head when, in

1957, "a major set of drug raids" in the city landed "over 100 people behind bars."[37] Detained at Los Angeles County Jail and eventually transferred to Soledad State Prison, Salinas received a sentence of five years to life. He was twenty-three years old.

* * *

As a Chicanx person with American citizenship, as well as someone who grew up proximate to the geopolitical border between the United States and Mexico, statistically, I've so far been deeply lucky that I've not been detained or incarcerated myself, nor has anyone in my immediate kinship circle. Still, like others, I have seen enough to know that carceral technologies of social control—prison walls, border fences, police cars—are inextricably linked to histories and proposed futures of racial inequity, nation-state fortification, and corporate profiteering designed to keep people, many of whom look like me, in prescribed social positions. Thinking about Salinas's case as I have been here, writing in a contemporary in which the American penal state is also an arm of the border climate industrial complex, in which the myths of white nationalism are also the everyday necropolitics of resource hoarding, in which fears of changing demographics signal sprints away from functional democracy, I join others in anger over the emergence of mass criminalization, over how many lives have been affected by racist greed.

It's no secret, that is, that unchecked incarceration, surveillance capitalism, and pandemic-era necropolitics have all become tightly entwined in (and increasingly beyond) the contemporary United States, enmeshed in what Jackie Wang describes as "carceral capitalism": a modality of racial capitalism in which "predatory lending," "parasitic governance," and contemporary carcerality create a toxic feedback loop of precarity, plunder, and profit, advancing violent "imperatives of global capitalism," shattering lives and families in the name of a rarified safety.[38] As of 2021, "there are currently over two million people behind bars in the United States"—a nation-state that, while making up only "about five percent of the global population," "holds nearly a quarter of the world's prisoners."[39] "Black Americans are incarcerated in state prisons at nearly 5 times the rate of white Americans," and "Latinx individuals are incarcerated in state prisons at a rate that is 1.3 times the incarceration rate of whites."[40] (To say nothing of how techniques of nightmarish confinement, honed over decades of war, are also being used against refugees and migrants in black sites and detention facilities along the US-Mexico divide, in makeshift prisons like the ones I grew up near.) In aggregate, the numbers outline the effects of a carefully curated system of racial criminalization that "brands people, often at very young ages," per Michelle Alexander, "as 'criminals' and then ushers them into a parallel social universe in which they may be denied the right to vote and be subject to legal discrimination in employment, housing, and basic public benefits for the rest of their lives."[41] The pattern is inseparable from the histories that created it; as Fleetwood conceptualizes it, "For the millions of blacks, Latinos, indigenous people, and other dispossessed groups imprisoned or under some form of penal surveillance, penal time exists within centuries-long practices of dispossession and captivity."[42] And while poems and songs can't on their own topple prison walls, they might well shake them; as many others have written before me, listening for the ways incarcerated individuals connect, experiment, collaborate, and dream otherwise, in spite of the circumstances they have inherited, can help us understand in granular terms the stakes and opportunities of abolitionist praxis, the necessity of dissolving the "mind jails" of contemporary life.

While incarcerated, Salinas, like other inmates near him and elsewhere, was working to fuse the strivings he heard in the work of his favorite Black radical musicians with his own emerging Chicano cultural specificity, his own memories of far-off people and places and times, his own dreams of possible futures, all amid a punitive present tense of carceral punishment, amid an extractive, vampiric, and incapacitating Now. Like others, he was responding to a penal logic that "fundamentally reconstitute[d] *being* in time," that rendered life a slow death, doing so by creating new temporalities out of the sedimented times of music, memory, verse, and dream. After having been steeped in Southwest jazz circles for years, awash in the criticism of Ralph Gleason, the uneven poetry of the Beats, the drugs of youth circles, and the sounds of Austin, Bay Area, and Southern Californian undergrounds, Salinas, in a sense still a teenager, began experimenting with the capacities of literary language, searching for prosodies that might create effects congruent with those of radical musicking. From within carceral fortresses, monuments of blood and brick, writing became, for him, a sanctuary, music his muse.[43]

* * *

In the 1950s many other authors, most living outside prisons, were also working to blend emergent improvisatory musics with literary aesthetics and cultures, resulting in things like the compositional richness of Ralph Ellison's *Invisible Man* and the experiential (if sheltered) excesses of most Beat poetry. The Beats, in particular, became important touchstones in the East Austin, San Jose, and Los Angeles scenes Salinas knew before being incarcerated. But their approach was experientially irrelevant for many nonwhite bebop listeners, to say nothing of incarcerated poets; the most famous Beats of the late 1940s and early 1950s, self-professed countercultural figures including Ross Russell, Jack Kerouac, Allen Ginsberg, and Neal Cassady, sought language to capture the immediacy of improvisatory musical experience and, by extension, a broader, emergent rebelliousness in the postwar moment in ways that, philosophically and politically, at once fetishized and downplayed race, effectively eliding cultural specificity, rendering Blackness ontologically plastic, and taking time itself for granted.

Here's what I mean. Part of the Beats' efforts involved what scholar Phil Ford, after Fredric Jameson, has described as a "nostalgia for the present," expressed as an inherent deficiency of writing as a technology; as Ford explains, many of the Beats in the late 1940s and early 1950s drew attention to an (overstated) gap between writing and experience, dramatizing the writer's craft as less an imaginative practice than an art of perpetual catch-up, subordinating writing to a continually unfolding present.[44] Within this framework, the most engaged writing seemed to be that which merged the act of writing itself with the present-tense unfolding of experience, transforming it into a "live" (as opposed to a "studio") art, though still implicitly preserving a separation between the "Now" of experience and the "then" of written trace. (As Ford cogently explains it, "Experience takes place in a specific and concrete time and space that writing, by its nature, does not occupy. Beat writing makes immediacy in time and space its great theme and performs the impossibilistic gesture of moving beyond its own inherent abstraction from that immediacy. It attempts an alchemical transmutation of pure experience into words and words back into experience.")[45]

But what if one's present moment, one's Now, wasn't all that great? What if the present tense was defined and enforced by fortified concrete walls and iron prison bars, by a carceral imaginary that rendered time a weapon to be used against the criminalized, the dispossessed, and the vanished? What if liveness, what if musical, improvisational radicality, was a memory, an echo in the mind's ear? What if dreaming up a more adequate present didn't mean tripping and dissociating in the grungy corners of alternative white masculinities but rather remembering and projecting joy, listening out of now, in both directions at once?

The Beats' fetishization of an ideal Now, evacuated of any consistent politics, seems, to me, quaint; it makes sense only for those who have the luxury of a present tense that feels good. By contrast, a writer like Salinas, incarcerated as a young Mexican American man who first came to know the world via Jim Crow Texas, wasn't fetishizing the present in his writings, on music or other topics. He also wasn't thinking of language as secondary to experience, of written words as afterthoughts subordinate to the "real" experiences they ostensibly trailed. Rather, writing became for him and others a technology of excavation, a route to new socialites, a means of listening for a different beat from some other place and time.

With that in mind: formally speaking, many of the poems Salinas wrote in prison aspire to the quality of improvisatory musicking while embracing the formal and medial constraints of the written word.[46] Stretching ourselves to read his poems allegorically, as actual improvised solos (as opposed to ekphrastic imitations or performance documentations), gives us a different quality of insight into their construction: just as informed improvising musicians invoke and evoke their tutors and rivals through "intermusical citation," so, too, does Salinas turn to bebop musicians to generate musical statements that are at once homages and departures.[47]

As I've gathered from my time in and outside the archive: one of the earliest poems Salinas wrote at Soledad State Prison was a tribute to Charlie Parker: "Did Charlie Have a Horn?" (see figure 3.2).[48] In the poem, written in 1958, Salinas turns to a variety of poetic techniques and aesthetic stances to capture something of Parker's lasting importance: rhythmic modulation, thematic development by permutation, hypothesis over certainty. With it, Salinas didn't attempt to capture the "moment" of one of Parker's solos, as writers like Kerouac had before him; instead, he worked to translate his knowledge of musical structure and jazz aesthetics into a poem that, of its own accord, might itself produce effects analogous to those of the music he admired. Through its intentionality—its rhythmic engine, its interrogative and speculative content—the poem addressed freedom through discipline, not ecstasy. Based in a slow kneading of question and answer, call and response—"Did Charlie Have a Horn?" "I bet he had a horn . . ."—the piece's bluesy design and context of construction highlight an early exploration of writing's liberatory potential, of music's capacity to help one live.

A few months later, Salinas produced another Parker poem, a memorial entitled "Lamento."[49] Where "Did Charlie Have a Horn?" evokes musical structure while working within a single medium, "Lamento" is a multimedia composition, an experiment with combinations of live music and poetry. The piece, finished on January 17, 1959, was an "experimentation in sound" dedicated to "the memory of 'BIRD,'" a "musical genius & soother of early societal wounds."[50] Designed to entwine the music and lyrics of Cole Porter's "Night and Day" with Salinas's own original verse, his own "soloing," the poem translates a compositional operation Parker himself had used with

DID CHARLIE HAVE A HORN?

"I have always been suspicious
  Of a thought that's quite delicious,
And it keeps me humming this refrain.........."

Did Charlie have a horn?

I mean the day that he was born.

He must have had a horn, to upset the world like this.

Combo or strings,

If it could swing,

Charlie had a way of finding its groove.

Technique superb, cool as the Bird's-----

Word. Based upon a soul full of blues.

And if he had a horn,

I maen the day that he was born;

He surely raised a storm , the way he still does today.

The listening field,

Finally dug something real

Instead of CORN!!!

And all because of Charlie's horn.....

"With this bit of retrospection,
  I will bet my BIRD collection,
That wherever Charlie P. may be:
  I bet he's got a horn.........."

LYRICS: Roy Salinas
MUSIC: Edward Mitchell

Composed at Soledad, Calif.

1958

FIGURE 3.2 Raúl Salinas's earliest version of "Did Charlie Have a Horn?" (1958). Source: Raúl R. Salinas Papers, M774, box 2, folder 2, Stanford University Special Collections.

Porter's tune years earlier alongside big band arranger and conductor Joe Lippman, building something new out of something existing.[51]

Night and Day

"... you are the one,
only you beneath the stars
and under the sun ..."

ON AN ENDLESS FLIGHT
    FROM A MUSICAL JOURNEY INTO PERFECTION

A WEARY BIRD, TORMENTED
    FROM WITHIN
SOUGHT REFUGE IN AN ALIEN WORLD.

No human ear was there to heed
  his sad/ plaintive/ WAIL ...

  a
      Golden
          Voice
             was
                laid
                   to rest.[52]

As with the Lippman arrangement and Parker's performance, Salinas notes that "Lamento" should "be read contrapuntally with lyrics of Cole Porter's 'Night and Day' interwoven," effectively taking Parker's lead by transforming Porter's 1932 smash hit for *Gay Divorce* into a new work celebrating informed innovation.[53] The poem also extends Salinas's prosodic experiments with quotation, capitalization, and punctuation, though it adds to them the possibilities of manipulated page space to imply (though not literally represent) musical performance. In its form and content, the poem is rooted in a diligent and relational praxis of improvisatory musical study that many Beat poets elided (with the notable exception of figures like Bob Kaufman, whom Salinas admired). Rather than fetishize the fiction of pure, spontaneous invention, "Lamento," like Salinas's other projects, foregrounds practice, discipline, and historical awareness as vital to creative activity.

* * *

Eventually, Salinas was released from Soledad State Prison. Not long after, in 1963, he attended a concert by Ray Charles and His Orchestra at Austin's then-gleaming Palmer Auditorium.[54] Charles was still touring his monumentally popular *Modern Sounds in Country and Western Music*, an album of country standards filtered through jazz and rhythm and blues styles, and Salinas was trying to find his footing in the world, about to turn thirty. As Salinas once wrote of that night, of the concert's haze, sweat, and volume, "Cuando tocaban 'You Don't Know Me,'" a wistful ballad of unrequited love, a couple of officers, either suspicious or with a tip, pursued and cuffed him for possession of marijuana.[55] "Se me caia el canton en coma. They wouldn't let me up."[56] Not long after, Salinas, having just violated his parole, was on his way to Huntsville Prison, Texas's execution capital, to serve the early days of an overkill fifteen-year sentence.

Once at Huntsville Prison, not at all far from what was once Camp Huntsville, a facility for Japanese and German prisoners of war, Salinas again faced the harsh realities of prison life: alienation and isolation, depression and disillusionment.[57] To bide his time, he sought out other inmates, finding solace in "sit[ting] around reminiscing about the good old (1950's) days of San Anto / Austin street life, the players, the hustle, the lounges."[58] To stave off creeping dread, he "joined the choir" and fell in, as Louis Mendoza writes, with others keeping abreast of "current affairs" via "books, magazines, and newspapers."[59]

He also kept writing poems that developed his interest in the relationship among bebop, poetry, history, and politics. In 1964, from his cell at Huntsville Prison, he synthesized his thoughts into "Jazz: A Nascence"—at once a capsule history, a bildungsroman, and a musical sketch. "Jazz: A Nascence" provides a poetic, contrapuntal narrative of jazz development, itself taking the form of a tune: "(Part I)," "(Chorus I)," "(solo)," and "(out)."

(Part I)

> Spawn of coital bed
> enjoyed by slave-ships & the sea
>   weaned in scarlet-red bordellos
> suckling milk from Lulu White.
>
> A raggi-tag-a-longin' kid
>   behind So'thern funeral caravans;
> stowaway up river
>   with Satchel-Mouth & Joe the King.

>   Smothered with caresses
> in crazy Town of Winds;
>   reward for shyness lost:
> Big Apple ... Pie for Youuuuuu!!!
>   (Chorus I)
> (solo)
>   Late night SHRIEKING Sounds!
>   commence
> sweeping out the mental cobwebs
> awakening brains from their torpor
> tonal (poem) cascades
>   Gently
> washaway
> musty/ dust settled within
> thin lines of genius/ madness
>
> O' JazzBird fluttering in the darkened sky,
> the willows have shed their tears too long
> does no one hear their mournful cry?
>   (out)
>
>   La Tejana / Huntsville
>   1964[60]

The poem begins with an invocation of the Middle Passage, linking the rise of "jazz" to a broader colonial history and to the emergence of a Black countermodernity. The poem then jumps from "slave-ships & the sea" to "scarlet-red bordellos," which are revealed to be in New Orleans, jazz's first home, by the mention of "Lulu White," a Black woman entrepreneur and brothel madam. The following lines moves us through the famed jazz "funeral caravans" and riverboats—through figures like "Satchel-Mouth" (Louis Armstrong) and "Joe the King" (Joe Oliver) and big cities like Chicago and New York—to arrive, ultimately, in the time and place of a solo, an unfolding present tense perhaps best captured in the repeated gerunds: "SHRIEKING," "sweeping," "awakening."

And while this historical recounting is interesting, it's only part of the whole. What entrances me most about "Jazz: A Nascence" is actually that its form is quite literally contrapuntal. Take a look; as the opening stanza unfolds, so, too, does a dual narrative: a single human life—the "spawn of coital bed," nursed by "Lulu White," who travels upriver as a stowaway and discovers a new voice in the big city—and, through that single, "smaller" story, a larger history of musical migration and experimentation. In this allegorical reading, the twin narratives converge as the solo begins, making the improvisation historically and historiographically significant. The sound of that solo—the literal sounds of the spoken words and the sounds of the music they reference, conjure—names a moment on multiple levels:

> tonal (poem) cascades
> Gently
> washaway
> musty/ dust settled within
> thin lines of genius/ madness.

So, too, does the poem's closing apostrophe to Charlie Parker, that theorist of midcentury experience that Salinas once said was as important an intellectual as Amílcar Cabral and Malcolm X:

> O' JazzBird fluttering in the darkened sky,
> the willows have shed their tears too long
> does no one hear their mournful cry?

The very moment of improvisation, as Salinas describes it here, becomes a meditation on individual actors, broader historical forces, and the ways one narrates their interrelation.

In this way, Salinas's approach differs from that of more renowned Beat poets, who, again, often tended toward a "nostalgia for the present" in their work—a nostalgia that led to treating the act of writing as less a process of imaginative consideration than a method of trying to capture, in real time, a sense of "pure spontaneity." These ideas were, as Ford has argued, partially shaped by the postwar popularization of sound-recording technologies like the tape recorder, but they also drew on notions that improvisation was, *somehow*, unconstrained and ahistorical—notions divorced from the Black, countermodern forces indexed by each solo.[61]

By contrast, Salinas's prison writing, as I read it, was more grounded. In it, Salinas was concerned with how something like a solo emerges from and contributes to a broader historical weave—as something that, again, is a true counterpoint of individual experience, broader cultural historical developments, and the ways we narrate them. In a postwar period in which histories of race and struggle were becoming increasingly important to index, this mattered. Salinas, an incarcerated Mexican American intellectual deeply moved by bebop's illuminating architextures, was working to study his world and relate to other thinkers and histories through music, to write like his favorite soloists sounded, to conjure old haunts and envision new arrangements beyond carceral horror.

* * *

One day at Huntsville Prison, Bart Edwards, then editor of the *Huntsville Echo*, a largely prison-circulated and -produced newspaper (although also distributed throughout the small surrounding town), learned of Salinas's "in-depth, first-hand knowledge" of jazz music and culture, and he asked him to write a monthly column: Quartered Notes.[62] That column, which became a fixture of the local prison-town press, even after Salinas's eventual release from Huntsville in 1965 (other incarcerated people, including musician Carmen Scoleri, Mickey Barker, Louie Spears, Herbert Alexander, and Lloyd Palmer, continued the column when Salinas left Huntsville), became an opportunity to survey, critique, and celebrate a multitude of jazz styles and artists—from Hank Jones's piano solos and John Lewis's Bach-inspired jazz fugues to the corrosive stuff of fake hipsterism and the closing of New York's Birdland jazz club. The pieces engage hard bop, a fusion of bebop's harmonic provocations with more audience-friendly blues riffs; modal, an abandonment of chord changes and championing of quartal movement; third stream, a controversial hybrid of jazz and Western high classical; and still so many others. They also span nearly the total range of readily accessible forms of music writing—profiles, introductions, album reviews, think pieces, even a concert review. Their concerns, to me, evince close study: What counts as music? What makes a solo good, a performance great? What can listeners, professional critics, and performers teach each other?

In relation to the broader music and jazz critical ecosystems of the United States, this kind of prison-written and -circulated criticism was radical and, in Salinas's case at least, generative of new approaches to the activity. For context: throughout the 1950s and 1960s, a number of different approaches to what John Gennari has called the new jazz criticism emerged, including the clinical encyclopedism of Martin Williams, the literary pyrotechnics of Whitney Balliet, the grounding diligence of Nat Hentoff, the radical visions of Ralph Gleason.[63] Each writer conceived of the critical enterprise differently, in some cases eschewing the sociological forces shaping musicians and their communities to instead focus on the qualities of "the works themselves," in other cases acknowledging outright the centrality of struggle and striving in Black musical praxis and history. As Gennari puts it, "Williams and Balliet endeavored to make jazz criticism a branch of literary criticism—Williams through an academic approach modeled on the literary New Criticism he studied as an English graduate student at Columbia in the early 1950s, Balliet through a poetic style that itself aspired to the category of literature."[64] Hentoff and Gleason, by contrast, approached their critical activity differently, understanding jazz to be "part of a larger set of social issues and concerns, civil rights and civil liberties preeminent among them."[65] The contrasts of these four major critics, themselves emblematic of a broader jazz critical field, underscore the stakes of jazz critical activity in a period of broader political turmoil, shifting popular tastes, and jazz's elite institutional codification in the United States—namely, whether or not the trajectory of jazz practice and the futures of the United States were isomorphic.

These were the stakes, too, of Salinas's jazz criticism, produced and distributed on a much smaller scale though wholly invested in the deeper meanings listeners ascribe to music and its makers. At the heart of this issue of deeper meanings was indeed the critic's race, gender, and social position. As many writers and musicians have pointed out—from Louis Armstrong and Ralph Ellison to James Baldwin and Amiri Baraka—the vast majority of jazz critics even beyond the 1960s were white men.[66] (As Baraka put it in *Black Music* in 1967, three years after Salinas started his prison column, "Most jazz critics have been white Americans, but most important jazz musicians have not been.")[67] This fact, combined with a legacy of cultural pilfering, with a compulsion to attend to Black music and not to Black people, created a palpable, lasting animosity between many musicians and critics. This animosity, as well as the enormous power differential and information gulf between him and writers like Gleason, Hentoff, Balliet, and Williams, wasn't lost on Salinas as he wrote for a primary audience of incarcerated men from his constraining prison cell. As he once put it in a 1994 interview at Stanford University, "'Here I was a Mexican Indian in one of the most racist prisons in the country writing about African-American music.' To me that certainly was a form of defiance and a form of resistance."[68] When we read Salinas's words in the context of what was a predominantly white, male-dominated jazz critical establishment, in relation to a largely Black musical sphere, they highlight a lesser-celebrated kind of relation: a nuanced sense of unity and difference, an appreciation for specific communities and their musics, even a solidarity born of proximity and related struggle.

And while Salinas's articles in the *Echo* left a paper trail worth following, they didn't nest into the jazz superstructure in a traditional sense. There was no integration or communication between the *Echo* and the mainstream record industry, a kind of communication that had become something of an open secret among critics; there were no magnates to please, no major labels to court, no big commissions to vie for. It's highly unlikely, too, that any of the high-profile musicians Salinas covered—John Coltrane, Thelonious Monk, John Lewis, Nancy Wilson, and others—ever even knew Salinas existed, let alone that he wrote well of them. This meant that the role of the critic, for Salinas, was one that was decidedly *local*, limited to a readership that Salinas knew or knew of in Huntsville Prison. To write jazz criticism from behind prison walls, as a Mexican American, a proto-Xicanindio artist-activist, was to dream radically, differently—to hear in Monk and Dizzy and Charlie "Bird" Parker, in their "*Black speculative musicalities*," routes into new, antiracist worlds of social-aesthetic possibility right where one was standing, willingly or otherwise.[69]

For readers accustomed to engaging with jazz criticism produced mostly in New York, in magazines like *Downbeat*, *Metronome*, or the *New Yorker*, I imagine it must have meant something to have a music critic in their own ranks, as well as to have the power to influence the direction of that critic's articles. Salinas, receptive to his readers' requests and rejoinders, occasionally commented on this: "Such loyal interest expressed by the handful of faithful readers of this column led to the writing of this portrait," or, "I must respond to several complaints hurled at this column."[70] The dialogue between writer and reader preserved by these comments fills in a picture of his conception of the critic's role in a community; the production process's permeability and the transparency of Salinas's practice highlight the importance of the audience in Salinas's work. The articles' local and historical specificities—Salinas's acknowledgments, for instance, of where he was writing from and whom he was speaking to—make clear that while they are deeply informed by an existing jazz critical tradition, the columns aren't simple reproductions of others' tastes and styles but instead Salinas's own local attempts to model the engagements he espouses.

Among the most interesting of the columns, for me, is a response to a February 1964 *Time* magazine cover story on Thelonious Monk that praised the artist for his musical complexity, "inimitable piano style," and deft, signature dancing.[71] In March of that year, Salinas reflected on Monk's aesthetics and considered his increasingly broad reception (read: serious consideration among the elite critics of New York) alongside his distinctive, kinesthetic style. While an analogy to painting forms the surface of the column—"When Monk plays his music, he is like a painter who stands away from his easel and slings paint at his canvas. But you can't object because of the beautiful colors he chooses"—what Salinas heard wasn't only an array of beautiful musical colors and brilliant corners but also some sense of justice, some meditation on who *is* and *has* an inside, an outside—musical, social, and otherwise.[72]

To get there, let's take a trip. Literary theorist Brent Hayes Edwards once wrote that Monk's "entire aesthetic revolved around the inside: the elaboration of a closely guarded interior beneath layers of masks and shells that often seemed impassable, forbidding, eccentric."[73] For Salinas, in prison, Monk's work was a meditation on *being* inside, on being boxed in by categories and expectations, knowing it, and actively working against those strictures. As Salinas writes, "Thelonious Monk has always been considered somewhat of a weird and offbeat character, and his music has been described as the meanderings of a madman. Still, he remains an individualist, a prime requisite in the performing arts. Monk has yet to be swayed by the numerous schools and fads which have arisen since the advent of jazz. He lives in a wealthy land of dissonant chords, harmonic interplays, and rhythmic interpolations. From these he has never deviated."[74] In a carceral world and especially an American prison system designed to actively repress and pathologize the inner lives of the incarcerated, the vanished, finding ways to live the "weird and offbeat," to thrive by "meandering" in a lush dream space of "dissonant chords, harmonic interplays, and rhythmic interpolations," could be an urgent and restorative practice—it could mean striving for self-consonance in a racial capitalist world in which color and justice had a deeply difficult relation, could mean hearing a future beyond the temporality imposed by the state, could mean renewing, as critic Richard Boyer put it in a prescient take on Monk in a 1948 issue of the *New Yorker*, a fierce "intere[st] in basic principles of life."[75] As I read him, Salinas heard a fundamental link between that which was "weird and offbeat"; that which was staunchly individual, genuine, pursued in good faith; and that which was just.[76] Monk's music, known for its kinesthetics, its melodic asymmetries, and its percussive interplays, often prompted Salinas to test the possibilities of the blank page before him. With each writing effort, whether by focusing on phrases, sentences, stanzas, or whole pieces; whether by accepting the conventions of grammar, page space, and monolingualism or rejecting them with style; or whether by simply focusing on the "inside" or the "outside" of his experiences, Salinas, like others, was working to articulate what he knew of justice. Or, better, what just is. Or, better still, what might be.[77]

"Justice is somewhere there, somewhere inside what holds us together, but only in fragmentary evidence, in the sound of clues that rise at an angle, step by step, and break back down to hint again," writes Edwards.⁷⁸ I think it's only fitting, then, that still there in that university archive, among the pieces of "fragmentary evidence" that help us tell stories of pasts that aren't even past—among those "clues" "ris[ing] at an angle" and "break[ing] back down to hint again"—there rests a small scrap of yellowing notebook paper bearing a quote Salinas attributed to Monk, that "weird and offbeat character": "Beyond justice, everything gets complicated" (see figure 3.3).⁷⁹

Again, as much as he wrote for himself, Salinas also wrote for and with others—a fact especially pronounced when considering his jazz criticism for Quartered Notes. By writing his column for a limited, *listening* prison public, Salinas was able to name and animate values, to put worldviews on display for open debate, to help cultivate modes and habits of relation that could form the basis for new social connections. In the company of others, who commented regularly enough on his writing to warrant Salinas's own published responses, he was able to grapple with the interplay of musician, performance, listener, writer, location, and historical context; to explore thoughts about experimentation and respect, freedom and justice. And contrary to other critics whose primary prerogative was the "elevation" of jazz to the status of high modernist art at the expense of context and history, it allowed him to explore a mode of language about music that attended to not only the intricacies of musical structure and the personalities of practicing artists but also the truths of one's life revealed by the act of notating a listening experience.⁸⁰ To write with and for others was to map the curvatures of a community's ears, to reveal fundamental assumptions and create new openings.

* * *

In 1965 Salinas was released from Huntsville Prison.⁸¹ By 1967 he was back behind bars, arrested for trafficking heroin (felony racketeering) with a number of others in Austin.⁸² In contrast to his previous prison sentences, however, once he arrived at Leavenworth, Salinas began a political maturation, the contour of which has provided the basis for virtually all extant scholarship on his work. "It was at Leavenworth," writes Ray Reece, "that Salinas himself began to think radically, to perceive his life in systematic political terms, and so at least to burst through the grates of his mind jail."⁸³ At Leavenworth, Salinas met a number of infamous prisoners—Pun Plamondon, Lolita Lebrón, Rafael Cancel Miranda, Andres Figueroa Cordero, Irvin Flores Rodríguez, and others—and, through them, was introduced to the writing of Frantz Fanon, Karl Marx, Mao Zedong, and Malcolm X. At Leavenworth, his sense of the world became increasingly transnational

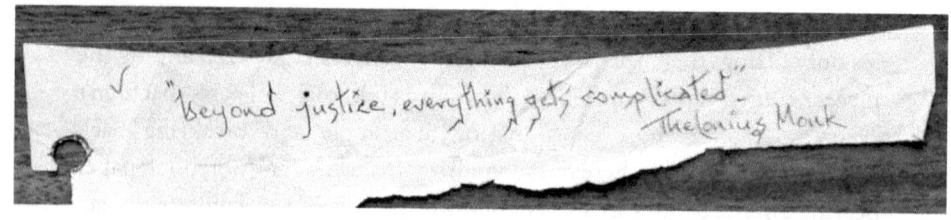

FIGURE 3.3 A quote Raúl Salinas attributes to musician Thelonious Monk. Source: Raúl R. Salinas Papers, M774, box 1, folder 9, Stanford University Special Collections.

through attention to civil rights struggles, antiwar initiatives, workers' revolts, and decolonization efforts. "Through his interaction with these men and others," Mendoza reflects, "Salinas began to question the wisdom of his involvement in the drug trade and organized crime" and "to see how race and class functioned in prison and the outside world to keep people from discovering constructive solutions to individual and group empowerment."[84]

As Salinas came to political consciousness, so, too, did his writing evolve: atop the themes of remembrance and invention bolstered by the Black improvisatory musical tradition he knew well were layered new vocabularies for "societal justice and people's liberation, mutual aid and economic democracy, self-determination and human dignity."[85] And by the time Salinas published "A Trip through the Mind Jail" in the 1970 inaugural issue of *Aztlán*, a Leavenworth newsletter, he had already established himself as a poetic witness to some of the hemisphere's greatest ills. As opposed to the "often ideologically inconsistent counter-cultural stance of many of the Beat poets," Mendoza notes, "the context and conditions of Salinas's confinement shaped him into becoming a 'rebel *with* a cause' in an era rife with revolutionary potential."[86] In his cell, isolated yet conscious of constitutive relationalities, Salinas found purpose among others.

Newly emboldened in the early 1970s, Salinas filed a lawsuit against the prison; when it failed, officials punished him by transferring him to Marion Penitentiary. As Salinas once recalled in a personal journal, he and his cohort had thus reached "the last stop on the prison shuttle express," "the big granddaddy zoo," the "hole" of maximum security. "Like most people who live in the hole (isolation cell) for any length of time, we were becoming accustomed to living the existence of solitary confinement."[87] Yet, by then, his activist and literary efforts, in concert with the struggles for social justice happening beyond the prison walls, had also earned him enough of a reputation to have prominent academics write letters to prison officials on his behalf, winning him favor.[88] With their assistance, after roughly fifteen years in and out of prison, Salinas was released for the last time in late 1972; newly cognizant of his position in a broader world-system, he began writing, speaking, and teaching in the Pacific Northwest. In 1973 he participated in the first Festival de Flor y Canto at the University of Southern California, and by 1977 he had published his first major collection of poems through Pocho Che Press: *Un Trip through the Mind Jail y Otras Excursiones*. Newly endowed with a sense of political purpose, Salinas completed a key change, a slow modulation into a new realm of aesthetic and activist imagining.

* * *

I've been reflecting here on the arc of this carceral odyssey imbued with musical memory just as I have been for months now; whenever I rehearse these stories, for myself and others, I'm invariably moved by the importance of Black experimental musicking for this Xicanindio poet, born in 1934, the same year as my late grandfather, and raised not all that far from where I grew up at the border of South Texas and northern Mexico. I'm also impressed by the various ways this poet's musical and relational commitments persisted and found aural and literary form once he settled into his new life beyond prison walls. Nearly fifty years after writing his first poems in prison, that is, Salinas took to recording studios throughout the Southwest, collaborating with Latinx, Black, and Asian American musicians on three jazz poetry records variously informed by his and his friends' bebop-inflected youths: *Los Many Mundos of raúlrsalinas: Un Poetic Jazz Viaje con Friends* (2000), *Beyond the BEATen Path* (2002), and *Red Arc: A Call for Liberación con Salsa y Cool* (2005). The albums, recorded and mixed in different parts of the country—San Antonio, San Diego, Austin, New York—allowed him, after a lifetime of thinking sonically, of improvising literarily, to present, as poets like Langston Hughes and others had before him, "his voiced words as instrumental offerings," to fuse "the rhythms of his voice" with the articulations of his bandmates in the context of an unfolding "jazz performance," to position "his words in dialogue with the notes of the musicians, with shared acts of listening operating as communicative bridges between the performing poet and the performing musician."[89] As I hear them, these records allowed Salinas to synthesize his political activism, prison experience, youthful memories and aspirations, and "jazz and beat influences" into formal experiments that could "showcase the musical dimensions of his work, particularly jazz," that had been there for over half a century.[90] As

I see and hear them, the records are a kind of culmination, a set of fully realized, multimedia and multicultural improvisatory enunciations, records of a lifetime's dreaming. They're worth sitting with; let's take a trip together.

The first of these jazz poetry records, *Los Many Mundos of raúlrsalinas*, was recorded in the greater San Diego area, at Earthling Studios in El Cajon, California, in late September 2000. Built around poems Salinas wrote throughout his life, the record features musical accompaniment by musicians Mikey Figgins and Kevin P. Green, as well as a guest appearance by Tomás Ramírez, one of Austin's premier jazz saxophonists. The fourteen poems-as-songs—each rendered musically in ways that, like Salinas's raw voice, seem to resist predictable tonalities—float in negative space: between decades-old poem drafts, between newly reconstituted memories, between in-person, in-studio collaborations. Together, they amount to a radical experiment, an exploration of a many-worlded Xicanindio jazz interior, an extension of a "life's work," as Abel Salas describes it in the liner notes, "across a more ample spectrum," into a "limitless terrain of multi-media convergence."[91]

Among the songs Salinas and his collaborators recorded for that project was "Tejazz." Salinas had originally composed the text for it five years earlier, for the dust jacket of an entirely separate album that his studio collaborator, Ramírez, Austin's "Jazzmanian Devil," released in 1995: *Tējazz*. As a print piece, the text is layered: on one level, it's a response to Ramírez's record, a tour of its musical contents: verse as liner notes. On another, it's an impression, the trace of a *way* of listening: Salinas's response to Ramírez's music produces a poetic portrait that reveals both player and listener, place and memory. On still another, the written text, which initially framed a record as front matter, became a prompt for new music, an occasion for new collaboration.

Textually speaking, the poem responds to the musical content of Ramírez's record. Salinas describes the album's opening track, a post-Coltrane saxophone cadenza called "Nomás Tomás," as

> coloreando
> in not-too-subtle
> Shades
> blending hues
> rendering ballads 'n' blues
> Dues dearly paid for.[92]

He describes Ramírez's "Nothing Yet"—a sixteen-minute psychedelic opus that ebbs and flows with extensive percussion, distorted guitar solos, pensive electric piano moments, hejira-esque bass interjections, and Ramírez's occasional multiphonic saxophone wailing—as a fusion of "urban / rural / Jazz Manias." The other tunes get their nods—"Sentimental Journey" as "Sentimental Viajes," "Quintana" as "Quintana / Grownup / uptown / uptempo," "Ochoas Rios" as "8 ríos to cross," "Elephant Flashpoint" as "subterranean elefantes in flames."[93] As one reads the text on the page, one sees and feels the echoes of a lifetime's musical engagement; as one listens to the audio version produced for *Los Many Mundos*—Salinas intoning his verse, transforming his tight voice into a horn; Ramírez soloing in response, at once hearing Salinas and responding to his being heard and written about; the track's unspecified bassist and drummer, creating a loping feel and providing interjections where necessary—one hears those echoes coming to bear on a new project. The track emerges from the space between typewriter and saxophone, poet and musician—emerges from Ramírez's and Salinas's shared memories of and in Austin, separated as they were by a generation. For Salinas and Ramírez, exploring these ideas through distinct yet complementary forms and media was the point; as the latter put it in an interview, "Music is poetry for the ears."[94]

Another memorable jazz poem Salinas recorded in 2000, with Figgins, Green, and others, for *Los Many Mundos of raúlrsalinas* was "Riffs I," a piece he originally drafted back in December 1981 while visiting Managua, Nicaragua, that was later published with slight modifications in his 1995 collection, *East of the Freeway*. As I hear it, the audio recording that emerged from that session at Earthling Studios highlights the retrospective qualities of Salinas's text—the ways it evokes a musical boyhood in East Austin, defining jazz as "1950s hipster days of dingy, yellow chords" and "cashmeres of fresh green"—while also imbuing words with new intermusical layers. As Salinas performs it on the recording:

Whenever I hear Lester blow his tenor saxophone . . .

Jazz was 1950s hipster days of dingy, yellow chords, cashmeres of forest green. Clean and keen, we called each other "Miles" and "Diz" and "Serge." We sat in East Austin town cafes and grills, thrilled with talks of Herschel Evans, Chu Berry, and the Prez. Enigmas of Joe Albany, Tristano, educated tunes. No "Moonlight in Vermont." Those stigmatized sounds so close to Bird and Bud, to Jug and Stitt, blues up and down, blues up and down.

Whenever I hear Lester blow his tenor saxophone . . .[95]

Accompanied by Figgins on bass and Green on drums, Salinas opens by setting his line—"Whenever I hear Lester blow his tenor saxophone"—to the melody of bassist and composer Charles Mingus's "Goodbye Pork Pie Hat," originally written as an elegy for Lester Young, all the while interacting with Figgins's bass playing. At 0:29, Green begins a quick swing pattern on his ride cymbal, and shortly thereafter, Figgins walks up and down the neck of his bass, blurring the key center. Salinas then interjects forcefully, half-singing his poem, stretching the lines into half melody. He sings boldly, motivating the piece toward tension; the group then crests at 1:25. Two consecutive instrumental solos then follow: a wandering bass excursion until 1:48 and a more purposeful drum solo until 2:30. Figgins then reenters, and Salinas picks up where he left off, with "No 'Moonlight in Vermont.'" Salinas then continues moving through the text, propelling the group until a wash of cymbals overtakes his voice; at 2:47, the tune bleeds into a final reprise of Mingus's melody, Salinas's words. Musically, the work isn't a hit, by any means, but that wasn't at all the point.

Like with his earlier print piece "Jazz: A Nascence," when Salinas recorded "Riffs I," he was tracing a counterpoint among improvisatory musicking, cultural history, and live art. With "Riffs I," the counterpoint unfolds throughout the poem's entirety, and on different scales, with different elements: the pairing of the opening line with Mingus's melody, both of which commemorate tenor saxophonist Lester Young, who anticipated the bebop generation and was a great inspiration to players including Charlie Parker; the rounded form of the musical piece itself—beginning and ending with Mingus's melody, turning it into a chorus or "head" figure, adding new creative constraints to the original, free-floating recollections of the initial text; and the strategies used in the body of the text itself. As with most all of Salinas's poems (and many improvised solos, which often, as noted in the preceding chapters, involve subtle, audible citations of other musicians and tunes), the text is densely referential. The musicians name-checked: Miles Davis ("Miles"), Dizzy Gillespie ("Diz"), Leon Brown Berry ("Chu"), Herschel Evans ("Tex"), Eugene Ammons ("Jug"), Charlie Parker ("Bird"), "Joe Albany," Lennie "Tristano," "Serge" Chaloff, Sonny "Stitt," "Bud" Powell, and, of course, the "Prez": Lester Young. These musicians were, for Salinas and his boyhood friends, personal lodestars. Identifying with "Miles ... and Diz ... and Serge" meant rejecting the mainstream; there was, for him and his Black and Mexican American compatriots in East Austin, no "Moonlight in Vermont"—none of the smooth, crowd-pleasing lilting of John Blackburn's 1944 hit of that title—but instead the challenging work of bebop musicians at the cutting edge. On the *Los Many Mundos* recording, all of this becomes clear, sonically, as the tune drifts in and out of key centers and rhythmic feels. The text—a piece improvised from the interstices of poem and song, solo and accompaniment, personal memory and live recording—enjoins readers to track the multiple histories evoked by a single utterance: bebop, East Austin, Chicano letters, San Diego, Latin America, the new millennium. It points listeners to the limits and immense capacities of language, to the complementary poetics of memory and liveness; it points to a way of dreaming in and through sound, of writing worlds at the edge of the everyday.

* * *

Let's continue our trip together. *Los Many Mundos* was followed up by a second project that Salinas completed with nearly twenty musicians at Pablito's Studio on the south side of Austin. Recorded in 2002, this project, *Beyond the BEATen Path*, builds on *Los Many Mundos*' experiments and engages a wide range of genres and styles, including bebop and hard bop, rhythm and blues, and folk (see figure 3.4). From an instrumental standpoint, its scale is impressive: strings, trumpet, saxophone, drums, guitar, percussion, bass, keyboards, backup vocalists, accordion. Its stylized title, too, marks a notable, decades-long distance from the Beats and the paths they walked. Stephen Bruton, the album's producer, noted that the album's production process actually took three years to complete from beginning to end. "It had to," he writes in the liner notes. "The poetry in this album took a lifetime to write."[96] Among those poems—"Letter to Lefty," "Unity Vision," "Amorindio," and others—was, notably, "Did Charlie Have a Horn?," a poem first typed up by Salinas nearly fifty years earlier while behind bars in his midtwenties as a way of finding strength in musical memory, as a means of seeking freedom through a distant musician's sounds.

That said, the real culminating album project actually came a few years later, out of a collaboration with revolutionary Chinese (Asian) American baritone saxophonist, composer-improviser, writer-activist, and self-proclaimed "popular avant-gardist" and "revolutionary matriarchal socialist and aspiring Luddite" Fred Ho.[97] In September 2004 the two met at Edit Point Studios in San Antonio, Texas, and recorded an album, Salinas's third, entitled *Red Arc: A Call for Liberación con Salsa y Cool* (2005). The project, as the *Texas Observer* described it, "is a poetic fusion that defies categorization. It is Zen, but it is angry; it is Chicano, but its rhythms are those of Charlie Parker and Thelonious Monk; it is regional in its setting and imagery, hemispheric in its vision. In short, it is raúlrsalinas—one long enjoyed bop calling for liberación con salsa y cool."[98] Engineered by Donney Meals and later mixed, edited, and mastered by Jon Rosenberg in Brooklyn, New

FIGURE 3.4 Raúl Salinas bathed in black and blue on the cover of his second jazz poetry record, *Beyond the BEATen Path* (2002). Source: Raúl R. Salinas, *Beyond the BEATen Path*, Red Salmon, 2002, CD.

York, the album unites Salinas's resonant, swung verse with Ho's weighty, insistent baritone sax lines; across each of the twelve tracks they collaborated on (many of which Salinas later collected and released as printed poems in a volume entitled *Indio Trails: A Xicano Odyssey through Indian Country* [2007]), Ho and Salinas converge to overwhelm American binary oppositions, to break the categories enforced by global capitalism and racial democracy by turning to the sounds, memories, and dreams of the exploited, the oppressed—Black, Indigenous, Chinese, Japanese, Vietnamese, Chicanx, Latinx, and more—while finding a common revolutionary language in Black radical music, in the echoes of Bird, Monk, and Rahsaan Roland Kirk.[99]

During their sessions for *Red Arc*, Salinas and Ho recorded a number of new pieces, a few of which I'd like to focus on here. One piece, which Salinas eventually published as a printed work called "Loud and Proud," foregrounded political relationality in both word and sound. In musical dialogue with Ho, echoes of Gillespie and Cuban percussionist Chano Pozo's Latin jazz cu-bop collaborations floated through the air; as Ho put it in the album's liner notes, "I quote from the legendary Afro-Latin song 'Manteca,'" in the context of an "11/8 ostinato." ("Manteca," a 1947 collaboration among Gillespie, Chano Pozo, and Gil Fuller, became a watershed Afro-Cuban jazz release. As Gillespie writes in his autobiography, "'Manteca' was probably the largest selling record I ever had.")[100] Jason Borge explains that Pozo "lent virtuoso chops and compositional energy to Gillespie's big-band ensemble" of the mid- to late 1940s, "chang[ing] the landscape of jazz forever by injecting the music with a rhythmic complexity it had rarely known before."[101] Ho also draws on previously composed original pieces: "a 6/8 blues" "entitled 'Free New Africa! Boogaloo' and 'Big Red! (For Malcolm X and Mao Zedong).'"[102] (The latter, a twelve-minute opus recorded with Ho's Afro Asian Music Ensemble and released in 2011, is a radical exploration of timbres and an indictment of American imperialism.) These three musical samples alone—an upbeat, movement-compelling Latin jazz piece by Gillespie and Pozo, an original blues composed as a soundtrack for the undoing of American imperialism, and a driving, impressionistic, Kirk-inspired, syncopated musical diatribe against jingoistic atrocities and racial capitalism—already create a radical, postnational musical vision for life beyond the physical and onto-epistemic violences of the American system.[103] When Salinas's poem and voice were added into the mix, the vision became even richer, more relational.

Salinas's poem is an anti-imperialist, post-9/11 call to sing, to produce sound, to connect the human right and moral imperative to speak out against injustice with the communal act of music making:

> In loud voices we must sing.
> Cantaremos porque . . .
> Silence means consent.
> Cantaremos porque . . .
> Silence equals death.[104]

Importantly, the "one collective / and united / voz" that "must not be stilled"—the communal song—is based in difference, based on a multitude of distinct "voices," rather than an anonymizing uniformity:

> No need for nationalistic,
> Jingoistic, patriotic pap. Remember world war II?
> "We're gonna' have to slap
> the dirty little jap,
> and uncle sam's the guy who can do it."[105]

In the poem Salinas aligns himself in solidarity with oppressed peoples from around the world: Japanese, American Indigenous ("let me exercise my rights—aboriginal and otherwise—"), Mexican, Chicano, Irish, Lebanese, Palestinian, Afghan, Iraqi, Puerto Rican ("wrap me not in waving rags / that gag the wailing / of the masses en Acteal. Irlandeses both protestants and catholics / their paths plowed under/ Lebanon plundered / and as the colony crumbles / Palestine rumbles, / Intifada!"). "Cantaremos / of the niños mutilados / en Irak, / Atenco, / and Kabul," "Vieques," he continues. "Loud and proud / i sing."[106] As Salinas writes, incisively:

> my ritmos and rimes
> in these times
> of patriotismo gone astray
> disgusting display
> bustin' out all over town;
> including the brown.
> Flying of the flags
> used to disguise body bags
> that carried medal of honor winners
> back to hick towns of
> coffee-serving refusals
> & cemetery of heroes burial denials.

The goal: to "[bring] to our / gente decente / that other realidad."[107]

The recording, like the others on the album, reiterates that syncopated rhythms and superimposed meters and performance temporalities are at the heart of Ho and Salinas's collaboration. At the outset Ho begins his 11/8 ostinato, which modifies Gillespie and Pozo's "Manteca" metrically as well as harmonically, moving the piece from that song's original's Bb minor pentatonic to a more modal-feeling E minor without the second or third scale degrees. Salinas's delivery of his lines is, like Ho's line, rhythmically articulate. At 0:15, when Ho switches gears and plays a bluesier, repeating riff, the rhythms of Salinas's vocal delivery change as well—Salinas hears in Ho's change the space for more sustains, and so he supplies them, stretching vowels across bar lines. Ho then returns to his modified "Manteca" riff at 0:26, and Salinas, slowly, drifts back toward a more percussive delivery. At 0:41, Ho stops playing, and Salinas, in a singsong voice, mockingly and seethingly performs the racist song he heard as a child, critiquing its "Jingoistic, patriotic pap":

> "We're gonna' have to slap
> the dirty little jap,
> and uncle sam's the guy who can do it."

At 0:46, Ho then breaks into his third riff—freer, with longer phrases—and Salinas erupts. At 1:09, Ho begins using percussive pops, modifying his line for interest. At 1:30, Ho changes gears again, shifting into a syncopated, 6/8 blues before eventually, at 1:45, moving back to the 11/8 "Manteca." At 2:00, Ho shifts again, eliding pitch altogether and performing percussive pops that outline a 7/8 groove (two-bar phrases). As Salinas continues moving through his piece, Ho's phrases become increasingly percussive. At 2:58, as Salinas intones a call to "lift our voice," Ho then begins a repeating groove based on an ascending scalar figure, and as the two move toward the piece's end, the intensity mounts, concluding in a united call for a better future, for "that other realidad" for "our / gente decente."[108] Anti-imperial, antiracist, and multihyphenate, I hear "Loud and Proud" as a braid of revolutionary energies and histories, a relational critique of racial democracy at the level of words and music.

Ho often used extended techniques in his playing—percussive pops with his mouth and saxophone keys, multiphonics, extremely high-pitched wails that revealed his six-octave range. Salinas's sonic signatures were his rhythms—his sustains and syncopations, his irregular patterns disrupting standard musical expectations. Paired together, their efforts created a new articulation of relational, ethnic American poetics—a new language of memory, critique, and layered temporalities. This emerges on one of the heaviest works on their 2005 album, *Red Arc*: "Solidarité," a poem linking (in)justice, jazz, race, imperialism, poetry, and wartime trauma. Originally written in Austin, Texas, on Survival Day, August 5, 1984, "Solidarité" pays tribute to "Shigeko Samsaori and the other Hiroshima/Nagasaki hibakusha," to those who survived the United States' atomic bombings of Japanese cities, civilians.[109]

The piece begins with Salinas reciting the title and dedication of the poem while Ho erupts with a sustained saxophone scream, high in the instrument's register, that then descends into a short blues lick. Salinas then devotes the first four stanzas of his poem to a narration of the US bombing of Hiroshima on August 6, 1945. He represents mass suffering directly:

> Moaning people wander
> Rag-like flapping skin
> Searching carnage stacks

> For friends not pulverized in blast
> Reuniting parents
> Burnt beyond recognition
> Flesh fused with flesh
> Human shadows etched in concrete
> On streets of once communal land.[110]

Meanwhile, Ho provides his main riff for the piece: a four-bar groove in 7/8 (4 + 3) based on a diminished fifth (tritone). Ho's note lengths are on the shorter side, giving the riff a biting, abrasive quality. Salinas's delivery, like Ho's performance, is also rhythmically precise.

After a short window during which Ho plays by himself (1:44–2:08), Salinas reenters, shifting his narration from mere moments to long years after the bomb's detonation:

> Consciousness regained
> Realization
> No babies forevermore.

He then ends by drawing historical parallels between the atrocity of the atomic bombings of Hiroshima and Nagasaki and US-backed conflicts in Vietnam and Latin America:

> Lying to the South
> New vietnams
> Nu cold? War
> Waged against the natives
> México
> Guatemala
> Nicaragua
> El Salvador
> América central
> Lying to the south
> New Hiroshimas
> Glow![111]

In Ho's saxophone cycles and Salinas's poetic treatment of these horrific events is anger, fear—anger at the injustice of it all, fear for those who have suffered and who continue to be affected by American imperial violence. In their music making is a call for justice, a call to move beyond what just is.

Ho and Salinas's relational investments in Black life and art were aligned and expressed sonically in the studio in important ways. (The artists, along with Nuyorican-Gitana poet Magdalena Gomez, even toured for a spell together in the two years that followed, with Salinas and Ho performing material from *Red Arc*.) "After becoming a professional musician," Ho once wrote, "I came across a statement by V. I. Lenin . . . 'Ethics will be the aesthetics of the future.' Twentieth-century African American music is part of an extramusical ethical/spiritual/sociopolitical revolution. . . . It is the triumph of the human spirit, of spirituality and ethicality in the midst of cannibalistic and corrupting capitalism."[112] Salinas, too, held such beliefs to be true, as is evident across his musical collaborations, prison and post-prison writings, and radical artivism. For Salinas, an aesthetics implied an ethics, a way of being, moving, and communing with others; as a lifelong sound shaper and practicing jazz improviser, he was invested in listening with big ears, in relating to those around him, in hearing and being heard.

*   *   *

What does this all add up to? These details and fragments, relayed "loose and dreamlike," these archival "clues" "ris[ing] at an angle" and "break[ing] back down to hint again"?[113]

I've been tracing the contours of this Xicanindio poet's (audio)biography in part because I believe such stories offer us tools, models, and guidance for living and dreaming in a broken world. For to dream in sound is to test limits, to push the boundaries of form and medium. To dream on the page as a Xicanindio prisoner in the post–World War II decades—and, in the post-9/11 years, onstage and in recording studios as a poet-improviser among performing musicians—was to imagine alternative possibilities for individuals and communities, to trouble the limits of the written and the spoken, to disrupt the colonialist musical dichotomy of improvisation and composition, to refuse the partitioning of languages, geographies, traditions, and communities. It was to bend poetic language in the direction of liberatory music, to quite literally "name" newly imaginative "interiors," those "unfettered dream spaces" of American life beyond mainstream prescription and policing.[114] It was, as Josh Kun has written of Langston Hughes, a way of pursuing and contributing to a tradition of radically experimental poetics that "merge[s] the scriptural with the aural and test[s] the structural and discursive possibilities" of form itself, that disrupts the "opposition between oral and literate, page and performance."[115] There, at the limits of the sayable, in the combination of vamps and verses, intoned lines, accompanimental interjections, and solo improvisations, resides the promise of a new map for being.

These days, as I read them, Salinas's poems encourage us to consider the challenge of attempting to write like musicians sound, and in effect to become acutely aware of our capabilities with language, of the possibilities of different written forms, and of the affordances of different media. For to write like musicians sound is to trace the curvatures of one's ears—to note, for poetic use, the ways an individual's listening experiences bounce off the expectations created by genres, contexts, and musical discourses.[116] At its most intense, it's to strive for what Della Pollock once called "performative writing": language that "does not describe in a narrowly repertorial sense an objectively verifiable event or process but uses language like paint to create what is self-evidently a version of what was, what is, and/or what might be."[117] Or, differently, it's to approach what Daniel Albright once called *pseudomorphosis*, the result of "ask[ing]" "a work in a single artistic medium" "to ape" or "do the work of some alien medium," which "typically involves a certain wrenching or scraping against the grain of the original."[118] Salinas's attempts at this, regardless of what name seems to fit his process today, guide my sense of how significant literary art was for him and others like him—what it did for them then, and what it does now to highlight how aesthetic affinities interface with racial capitalism, carceral time, and social possibility. As Nicole Fleetwood puts it, "Incarcerated artists deliberately take the status of being labeled a social problem or failure as the very grounds for their artistic experimentation. Failure amplifies their aesthetic improvisations and the risks they will take to produce works and worlds that exceed the prison."[119]

When I read Salinas's writing today, in a moment beset by a racial capitalism with an insatiable thirst for souls, I remind myself of this context, his time of composition, and remember that in the troubled decades following World War II, his work offered incarcerated readers and musicians a music-shaped poetics built beyond a white gaze—beyond, too, any tacit assumptions of "freedom" as a given of American citizenship. He was *raza*, a *pinto* poet writing in relation to his histories and his fellow inmates, drawing on his experiences in the Southwest, tapping into the insurgent, revolutionary spirit at the core of Black musicking in ways that illuminated relational suffering under American racial democracy, as well as the philosophical and political openings of experimental work. Writing and publishing while in prison, cut off from the outside world, relegated to a space of confinement and loneliness, strikes me today as a way of affirming the grain of one's life in the context of a nation-state committed to denying nonwhite communities nuances, interiorities, dreams that might otherwise unsettle a brutal, protracted normalcy.[120]

As Salinas reminisced in a 1994 interview at Stanford, "Music became another form of resistance. I said it somewhere, 'Here I was a Mexican Indian at one of the most racist prisons in the country writing about African-American music.' To me that certainly was a form of defiance and a form of resistance. So I began to write jazz articles. Then as I developed my writing, my poetry, I began to write jazz poetry. I then took the next logical step of development and transformation and then I actually picked up a horn."[121] As he was penning the material that would form part of the bedrock of the Chicano Movement's literary axis, so, too, was he pursuing the intricate relationship between literary practice and improvisatory musicking, entwining musical knowledge with poetic and political truths to effect lasting, large-scale "transformation." Like his efforts in Soledad and Huntsville Prisons, these attempts were always connected to real people, locales, and situations. As he recalled later in that 1994 interview, "My brother's in the next cell with me, and he happens to be black, and I am brown, and next to us our brother is white, and you can't afford anymore to make those distinctions."[122] The prison, as experienced and remembered, became for Salinas a microcosm of the world beyond the walls, a world he knew to be vibrant, diverse, and swung. And the world, as Salinas knew from his readings and experiences, was in many ways imprisoned, chained to fear, habit, and hierarchy. Through art, he theorized how one might break free alongside others, producing work that could accommodate the transcultural, transracial, and thoroughly musical bonds he had formed in prison and in East Austin. And in the process he crafted a self-conception that was idiosyncratic yet familiar, drawing as much from the lessons of an African American musical tradition as the legacies of conquest shaping the category of Chicano. As he put it:

> As a player and a lover still today of music, the lights, the sounds of people on the streets certainly gave me that affinity with other people marginalized such as we consider ourselves to be and we lived in a community that was both Chicano and African-American. We were in a black community and a brown community that was mixed and so the music of that particular community certainly became a part of us. To this very day . . . I am

a lover of jazz. Jazz is a music that I love and respect. I knew individuals and I followed it and became a student of jazz history.[123]

* * *

My time in university archives, in quiet rooms precisely lit and maintained, clean save for the ambient dust of time's insistence, eventually taught me that Salinas planned a follow-up to his 1977 *Un Trip through the Mind Jail y Otras Excursiones*, but the book was never published nor realized in full. In outline, though, it stretched across decades of practice. Called "Jazz Jaunts" and preserved in the archive as a set of fragments, it remains, beyond his late-career albums, Salinas's only self-assembled collection of music writing (see figure 3.5). It was planned to be thorough: "poems/prose/essays/letters/songs/bop prosody/ & musical trips."[124] While unfinished, it bears instructions for its completion: "Blue Notes," or "(vignettes/biographical sketches/anecdotes/tragedies of people in the music world)"; "Wailing Walls," or "(letter/poems from the HOLE)"; "Quartered Notes," or "(16 monthly jazz columns from The ECHO—prison newspaper Huntsville, Texas—Jan. '64 / April '65)"; "Drum Trouble: A Short, Short Story."[125]

I find myself reflecting on this abandoned project often, especially here in my apartment in Los Angeles, not far from the Los Angeles County Jail, where Salinas was first locked up some sixty-plus years ago, just a drive away from a few local archives still preserving his works for posterity; I find myself thinking about what sustained him through the many troubling years he endured. I find myself meditating on sustains in general: on holding out and across; on nourishing, protracting, and protecting; on making "'a way' out of 'no way,'" as Daniel Fischlin, Ajay Heble, and George Lipsitz write; on stoking the "the capacity to discern hidden elements of possibility, hope, and promise in even the most discouraging circumstances."[126] Aswirl in sound and sentiment near a tower of notes and a stack of Salinas's late-career records, now, at this unnamed hour, I find myself reflecting on how Black musicking and local memory sustained many in his generation, including my own grandfather, helping them navigate modernity's many "mountain[s] of brick."[127] I find myself reflecting on how, for Salinas and others, the numbing sameness of prison pain was offset by close listening and creative writing, both of which unlocked the significances of old episodes and provided difference, texture, and direction amid the thousands of missed sunrises.

I think of this, too, whenever I replay the final line of that first live performance of "A Trip through the Mind Jail," still captured on that archived

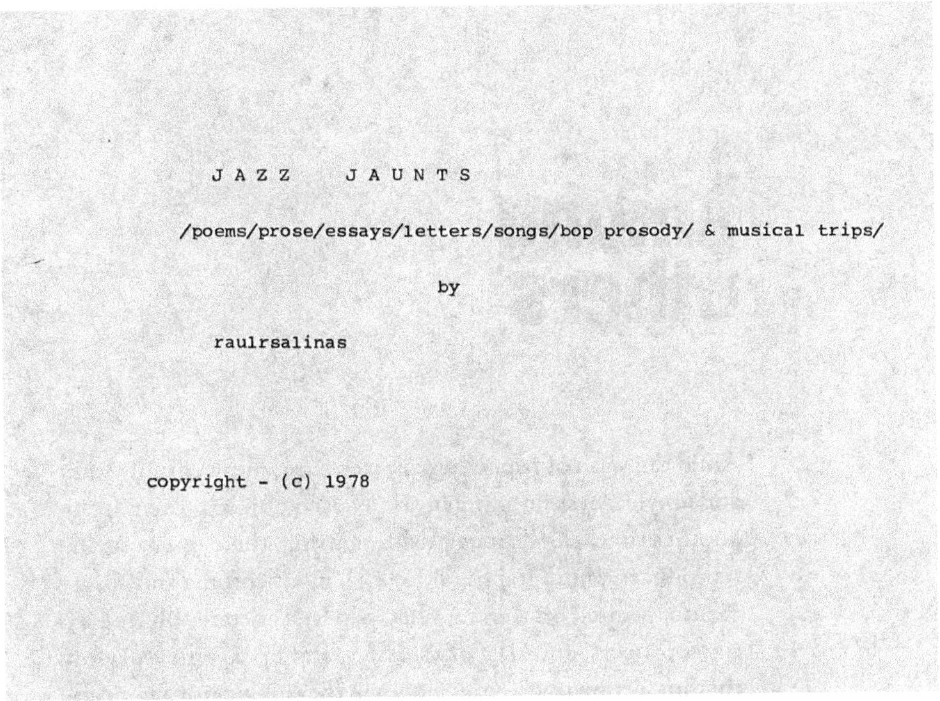

```
J A Z Z     J A U N T S

/poems/prose/essays/letters/songs/bop prosody/ & musical trips/

                              by

raulrsalinas



copyright - (c) 1978
```

FIGURE 3.5 Front matter from Salinas's unfinished jazz writing manuscript, "Jazz Jaunts." Source: Raúl R. Salinas Papers, M774, box 27, folder 8, Stanford University Special Collections.

recording. "Somewhere, someone remembers." This time, as the recording ends, I turn back to the photos I took of "Jazz Jaunts," that fragmented record of relational musical experience, and I mash up the two projects in my mind's ear, repeating the closing line of "A Trip" while scanning the dedications of a book that never was. To "the Chicano jazz crowd of the 1950's Austin Eastside." "Somewhere, someone remembers." To "Chuy z.," one of Salinas's first music mentors, one of his first shepherds through "yesca smoke" and syncopation. "Somewhere, someone remembers." To an Afro-Asian American multi-instrumentalist and arranger—"Chink" Wing, "(in whatever universe!)." "Somewhere, someone remembers." I reflect on these antiphonies, these layered times of making and living, and I note how someone remembering might still be the most radical dreaming a colonized world can produce. I rise from my desk, taking stock of my freedoms, of this life unquartered. I crack open a shut window, letting the outside in.

four.
among others

Amid the wash of papers, jewel cases, sheet music, drumsticks, and vinyl sleeves flooding my desk, each object a totem from another time, an effort against forgetting, there rests a small, reproduced photograph (figure 4.1), monochrome and chiaroscuro, printed on thin recycled paper; its details, blurred by time, process, and DIY physicality, add up to a five-person rhythm section tracking an album in the closeness of a midcentury studio, the musicians' sounds frozen, the vibrations paused, inviting a look, a listen.

Whenever I scan the photo, my eye notes its angularities, its sharp geometries—the rectangular lines created by the sound panels and fire escape ladder and music stands and microphone boom arms, the shadows cast, the depth of field flattened, the lines and shadows Mondrian-like in their squareness. I note the high contrast, the dodging, the drama of the shadow play, the saucers by each music stand forming a jagged line near the ensemble, each filled with the ashy evidence of ritual, the bones of good smoke. Handling my homemade reproduction, I note the physical proximity of the musicians, how close they appear to one another and yet how distant, each detail of the temporal slice evocative of individuals' specific routes through a collective moment, the heterogeneity of shared time. I note, too, the musicians themselves: at the back right, seated at the piano, Sir Charles Thompson, reading sheet music arranged by Quincy Jones as if an afternoon puzzle. In front of him, bassist Paul Chambers, a wide interval held between his left index and pinky fingers, his upright bass tipped at a shallow angle

FIGURE 4.1 Harold Wing (*left*, on drums) records in the studio with the Paul Quinichette Group. Photo by *Metronome*/Getty Images.

toward his torso. In front of him, guitarist Barry Galbraith, the sole white artist pictured, his left hand over rather than under the neck of his electric guitar, perhaps for an extended technique. To his immediate right sits guitarist Jerome Darr, eyeing up his guitarist neighbor, the fingers of his left hand outstretched at the bottom of his fretboard, perhaps to mute his strings, his wrists emerging from a smart suit sleeve sewn of thick winter fabric. And furthest from everyone pictured, yet closest to the camera, is drummer Harold "Chink" Wing, his eyes shut tightly, his brow furrowed, the bead of his left drumstick held at a shallow angle to the snare drum to facilitate the airy sound of ghost notes, a music stand by his side propping up a map of the piece in progress, unutilized in Wing's moment of sensory bracketing. As I see it, the photo captures a group in motion; it renders each participant's contributions to the musical occasion visible, differentiable, proximate, linked at the level of aesthetic form, physical presence, and vibrating air.

The group in the photo is assembled for a recording session in the mid-1950s, roughly around the same time my grandfather would have been woodshedding with instrumentalists in North Texas; roughly when James Araki would have been performing in the variously multicultural creative music scenes of California; roughly when Raúl Salinas would have been attending avant-garde performances throughout the Southwest, listening for guidance and escape; roughly when a generation would have been exploring contradictory, relational dreams spurred by category-challenging Black soundwork.[1] When I look at this image, I try to keep this in perspective.

I'm most interested here in the last figure mentioned, the least famous musician pictured.[2] "Chink Williams," legally Harold Wing, was a mixed-race (Chinese and African American) drummer, pianist, and arranger (1927–1993). Based largely in Newark, New Jersey, Wing played drums for a number of top-tier jazz musicians in the 1940s and 1950s, including Dizzy Gillespie, Charlie Parker, Miles Davis, Bud Powell, Joseph August, Erroll Garner, James Moody, Babs Gonzales, and Sarah Vaughan; he was also an avid songwriter, composing songs that were performed by a number of artists, including material cowritten with Ella Fitzgerald and the Sy Oliver Orchestra.[3] In the 1970s, in the wake of the 1967 Newark upheaval, he continued his work as a drummer while becoming more prolific as an arranger-composer, writing songs recorded by Etta Jones, Shirley Horn, Junior Mance, and others; he also rose to local prominence as a community leader by serving as the music coordinator for the Division of Parks, Recreation, and Community Affairs for the city of Newark for a period of nineteen years.[4]

In what follows, I'd like to track some of Wing's work in and beyond Newark to get a sense of how his immersion in bebop today evokes a sense of invention, community, and accompaniment—of a virtuosity beyond heroic individuation, of "decorating time" and building community. I'd like to think through what it has meant to be, live, and dream "among others," to sit with the tensions implied by that very phrase: on the one hand, to be minoritized and anonymized by the market logics of the music industry (e.g., the unnamed, undetailed mass connoted by the throwaway "among others," typically appearing at the end of a list) and, on the other hand, to be *part of a community of relation*, to be and become *among others*. Drawing on audio recordings, literary writings, newspapers, liner notes, reviews, and interviews—including conversations with Newark musicians and music historians, as well as an extended personal interview with Eugene "Goldie" Goldston, a vocalist and elder statesman of the Newark jazz scene who was one of Wing's former musical mentees—here I extend my interest in how Black radical musicking shaped a generation of nonwhite youth by listening closely to an Afro-Chinese American's drumming and songwriting, situating it within a distinct local scene and the cultural shifts of the postwar years. I work to engage Wing's racialization and musical training in Newark, his professional output in the 1950s, and his contributions as a songwriter and civil servant. Throughout, I offer close readings and listenings that emerge from a sense that every note and scrap bears traces of a larger story—or, as Emily Lordi puts it, in an interpretive mode "grounded in a moment-to-moment description of what is happening in the music" to draw a song and a performing group's details "close," making "personal" the efforts of artists who "throw themselves into the moment of performance as if there might not be another."[5] As a drummer myself, I listen with a sense of physicality in mind; I offer transcriptions of historical materials that I've played myself in attempts to crawl inside the music differently and in effect, as Michiko Theurer writes and models, to pursue a research practice that can "[open] up (even [necessitate]) investigation from different and sometimes contradicting angles and methodologies," "to map relationships between sounds" from within one's own musicking body, to blend things like "pitch-class analysis" and "poetic interpretation" with performance practice to create the conditions for a different closeness, an intimate, tactile engagement with previously organized sounds.[6] Working across modalities and methodologies, here I seek to highlight imaginative, musical, and social horizons of playing more often felt than heard.

As I do so, I also draw inspiration from another Newark-rooted drummer, composer-improviser, and theorist: Tyshawn Sorey. In a recent interview, Sorey, responding to questions about how his drumming has changed over the years, notes:

> Everybody talks about virtuosity as being about how fast you can play or how loud you can play or how much technique you have available. There's nothing wrong with having great technique at your disposal, but how you use that technique is what's going to make the difference.... The real virtuosity ... is not in how fast you can play or how many notes you can play or how technically advanced everything is. It's really about how we breathe together, how we move together, how we listen, how we experience each other, what it feels like to play as a trio but not sound like three people. The way I've always viewed the notion of *trio* is that *trio* means one.[7]

This model of linking creative musical approaches with collective constitution inspires me both as an artist and as a scholar; virtuosity, so long linked to celebrity and mastery, to masculinist so-called triumphs over others and their musical offerings, becomes a route into the expression of different virtues. The development of a *communal virtuosity*, in which "breath[ing]" and "mov[ing]" and "listen[ing]" together, "experienc[ing] each other," in an ideal situation, can also mean the development of a politics of solidarity out of musical closeness and aesthetic affinity. Throughout this chapter I listen for the echoes of that kind of communally virtuosic making that can only occur among others; I listen against the grain of the more traditional, masculinist, heroic virtuosities, masteries, and historiographies typically ascribed in retrospect to creative musicians who (co)developed new vocabularies. I listen, through an individual's musicking among others, for a coming to a new consciousness, for an arrival at a conception of oneself as a community practitioner.

To get there, this chapter poses a few primary questions. What did it mean to practice bebop as an Afro-Chinese American in midcentury Newark? How did the efforts of Harlem's Black musical innovators intersect with those of musicians across the Hudson? How did direct participation in music ensembles, particularly as a so-called sideman, an accompanist, illumine life in the postwar United States' racial democracy? What can the nuts and bolts of music production history reveal about agency, collaboration, and solidarity? In Wing's case, that of an Afro-Chinese American man from Newark, what did years of direct, professional collaboration with celebrated bebop virtuosi reveal about racial democracy? How do his efforts fit into a broader tradition of Afro-Asian jazz practice, and what kind of world did he and others dream together?

* * *

As I've gathered from archives and interviews, Wing came of age surrounded by Black genius. In nearly every Newark club on almost every night of the week, he witnessed Black musicians pursuing a new idiom through improvisations that gave form to contradiction, autonomy, divergence, and collective activity. Born in 1927 in a city marked by ethnic and racial divisions, a city cleaved into ethnic enclaves that often begot difficult crossings, Wing was also doubly racialized yet singly acculturated—something that "Chink," his pejorative nickname, came to highlight.[8] In both African American and largely Chinese and Chinese American immigrant populations, Wing was like others in that he was othered owing to his phenotypic features; to my knowledge, he also didn't develop pronounced connections to the cultural repertoires of his older Chinese family members and was geographically distanced from Newark's Chinatown, as he and his immediate family lived in the city's Third Ward. Rather than efface his Chinese ancestry, however, he embraced it creatively, loosening the white-knuckle grip of the pejorative label by drawing it close, linking it to his art and livelihood.

That decision was substantial. Wing's claiming of "Chink" as a nom de musique effectively kept the scars of Newark's Chinese immigration histories in view for years, creating productive challenges for his collaborators to develop ways of talking about it all. As Eugene Goldston told me, reflecting on the stories he had heard of Wing's family, "His father was Chinese.... We knew about that in the neighborhood, but very few guys my age knew his father personally. His father had a Chinese laundry; his mother was African American. Everybody knew [Wing's] father here in the Black community."[9] Too, as James Moody recalled, "We called him Chink. That was his name."[10]

Virtually every nickname, and perhaps especially so in music scenes, is a "capsule history"; what that capsule historicizes is, as Ralph Ellison once put it, the "change from a given to an achieved identity, whether by rise or fall," effectively mapping "the nicknamed individual's interaction with his fellows."[11] The names (to say nothing of the languages) we accept, traffic in, refuse, and denigrate at once reflect and instantiate social and political arrangements, bringing the link between the institutional and the interpersonal into plain view. A name, as Laila Lalami puts it, "carries inside it a language, a history, a set of traditions, a particular way of looking at the world," and what one does with the names one is given is always a world-making action: an exercise in self-crafting and community articulation.[12] And as Farah Godrej writes, "We reclaim words and phrases so that we refashion their meanings to correspond to our particular goals. We rescue or salvage them from their earlier—often derogatory—meanings so that they have the authority of our ownership behind them."[13] In that sense, to reclaim pejorative names can be to work toward an ameliorative discourse, to dull verbal blades by displaying the scars they leave. To do so within musical circles largely composed of differently marginalized citizens is to constantly remind collaborators, audiences, and superiors of the need to remain invested in each other's well-being, to accompany one another on the path to healthier social arrangements.[14]

And though Wing was Afro–Chinese American, his music, as T. Carlis Roberts's theoretical framework in *Resounding Afro Asia* helps us understand, was not "interracial," meaning that it didn't bring together sounds that, in the United States, had come to signify both Blackness and Chinese Americanness. Rather, he performed a Black music—a radical Black music that, again, offered a set of "barbed challenge[s]" to anti-Black mentalities, and "exhilarating invitations" to those, as James Baldwin captures in "Sonny's Blues," who were listening deeply.[15] Wing's dreams, his visions of change, informed as they were by his compound racialization, were thus mediated by a sonic Blackness, by his biracialized body, by his relationships with others, and by the various names he went by.

Among the musicians Wing idealized in his youth were local champions—Gus Young, Dan Gibson, Charles "Brother" Kelly. "When I was a little boy," Wing once said, "I used to peek through the window at the Golden Inn on Charlton Street to see Gus [Young]," a local drummer.[16] Young, a musician about ten years Wing's senior, became a creative model; he was himself a precocious performer and often played sets at the Colony and Kinney Clubs in the late 1930s and eventually recorded on the Decca and Coleman labels.[17] Wing admired him and his playing style. As Goldston told me, "Wing gave a lot of credit to . . . Gus Young. Gus was older, a well-regarded drummer in the area. He played in a bar for many, many years on Washington Street called [the Conlan Bar]. He was older than him [Wing]. He told me that Gus was one of his mentors. Whenever he had a chance, he would go listen to Gus."[18]

Wing also paid close attention to Herman Bradley, remembering him fondly even into his later years.[19] Bradley, yet another well-respected musician in Newark's creative music cosmos, had established himself in the area during the 1930s, playing with groups including the Rhythm Dons and contributing actively to Newark's communal sound.[20] As a teacher, he was effective: "Herman taught me how to read music," Wing recalled, "and by the time I was 14 I was playing six nights a week in local clubs."[21]

Wing's most formative early relationship, though, was with Charles "Brother" Kelly, a musician who "adopted" Wing, introducing him to many key members of the Newark jazz scene, taking him to concerts, teaching him how to perform onstage, and ultimately giving him his first opportunity to sit in with a band when he was thirteen.[22] A surrogate brother, Kelly guided Wing through the confusions of adolescence and the uncertainties of wartime, teaching him music-industry norms while providing motivational support.

These mentors helped shepherd Wing through the technical and social dimensions of creative musicking in Newark, helping cultivate his talent and directing his ambition to write original material. Like other mentors for many other scene participants, they did so in ways that proved lasting, that were generative of "a congenial atmosphere for learning by conveying the view that student and teacher alike are involved in an ongoing process of artistic development and that the exchange of knowledge is a mutual affair."[23] At a crucial point in Wing's artistic development and, frankly, his upbringing generally, his interactions with his mentors, steeped as they all were in bebop's codes and challenges, helped introduce him to the horizontality of an accompanimental sensibility, a communal imagination, a sense of shared time in a city he was only beginning to meet. As Wing once put it, those "were the guys who really inspired me."[24]

Eventually, as a teenager, Wing left the local arts high school to attend the Newark Conservatory and, across the Hudson, the Henry Street Conservatory of Music. Like many others even today, over half a century later, as a music student in these institutional spaces, he received a very different type of instruction than he was getting as a young member of Newark's creative music scene. At Henry Street, he studied so-called classical music and theory, arranging, orchestration, and composition; as a drummer, he was exposed to a variety of percussion instruments from Western classical traditions; and as a piano minor, he anchored his studies of functional harmony and composition in an embodied musical practice.[25] Yet, predictably, Wing was barred from studying at school what he was practicing at home, as his "music teachers limited themselves to a narrow range of music that they considered acceptable."[26] This isn't really a revelation.[27] But it highlights that, as a student, Wing joined a tradition of Black creative musicians who, when they could study music in formalized settings, found no representation in the curriculum and thus studied in two separate, power-differentiated musical spheres, oscillating between the prosodies of each educational space.[28]

At fifteen, Wing was performing downtown regularly with a group led by trumpeter Leon Eason.[29] Already having adopted his complicated (and lifelong) nickname, Wing began seriously pursuing a multi-instrumental practice that, as with James Araki (and in a looser sense Raúl Salinas), would ultimately inform his musical imagination in the following years. Audiences noticed: on April 20, 1946, for instance, Billie Smith of the *New Jersey Herald News* reviewed a concert she attended, praising the night's "great jammers" like "Dug Clifford Phifer, Pancho Diggs, Tod Smith," and "Harold Wing," "who can drum with any band."[30] Just a few weeks later, Smith followed up with another concert review: "Things that happened at last Monday's Jam. My boy Chink Wing took the ivory. I didn't know you played a little box too Chink. Bush was on the bass, little Dannie was on the sax and I failed to catch the name of the drummer. The boys got together and knocked everyone out."[31]

By studying and performing on both piano and drums, Wing developed skills that would eventually inform his work as a studio musician and songwriter. Like others who have followed similar paths, he learned to cross-pollinate concepts and repertoires across both piano and drum set, developing musical ideas out of each instrument's material affordances. This, combined with the experiences he was having in jazz clubs and at the conservatory, contributed to an accompanist's sense of how multiple voices, instruments, and people can converge to produce layered musical ideas and temporalities—overlays and relationships that could be at once contrasting and synchronous, greater than the sum of their parts.[32]

Too, by the late 1940s, his songwriting efforts led him to cowrite and register songs with Florence Wright, a Newark-based jazz singer, arranger, and bandleader; William "Billy" Ford, a trumpeter and singer who would eventually lead one of the US State Department's jazz ambassador tours; and Albert Armstrong, a trombonist and arranger known in many of Newark's best clubs. The attractions of songwriting, beyond notoriety, were the formal opportunities it presented for combining skill sets and techniques yoked under the concept of musicianship.[33]

Writing for pleasure and performing for a living, by the end of the 1940s, Wing was establishing himself among Newark's best musicians, playing with a number of the biggest acts in the city. It was even his fortune, as he told historian and longtime reporter Barbara Kukla, to play "with [Charlie] Parker at the Sterling Bar on Clinton Avenue."[34] (A concert flyer for that gig, kept by Parker's wife, Chan, for a project commemorating her husband's life, bears Wing's and Parker's names; see figure 4.2.) As a result, Wing's opportunities in studios and with touring bands began to multiply: a record with blues singer Joseph August, a tour with singer Ynomia Harris, and even a television show, *Stairway to the Stars*, for which he served as bandleader.[35] Like others in his scene and certainly many in his generational cohort, Wing was cutting across boundaries and categories while developing a craft, rendering the "chaos" of midcentury living into varying ephemeral forms.[36]

Wing's understanding of what it meant to create art was deeply connected to the idea that bebop was a racialized, countermodernist art music—to the facts of the "discourses of art and blackness meeting head-on and tussling it out in both musical and critical terms," as Guthrie P. Ramsey Jr. puts it. Drawing as much from his music school experiences as from the immersive musical education he was receiving in jam sessions, Wing was, like others, pursuing a "blackened modernist aesthetics," an "Afro-modernism" that was "at once more populist than its European counterpart, yet committed to articulating its elite position relative to the more commercial genres."[37] To pursue this as a biracialized young man coming of age in a

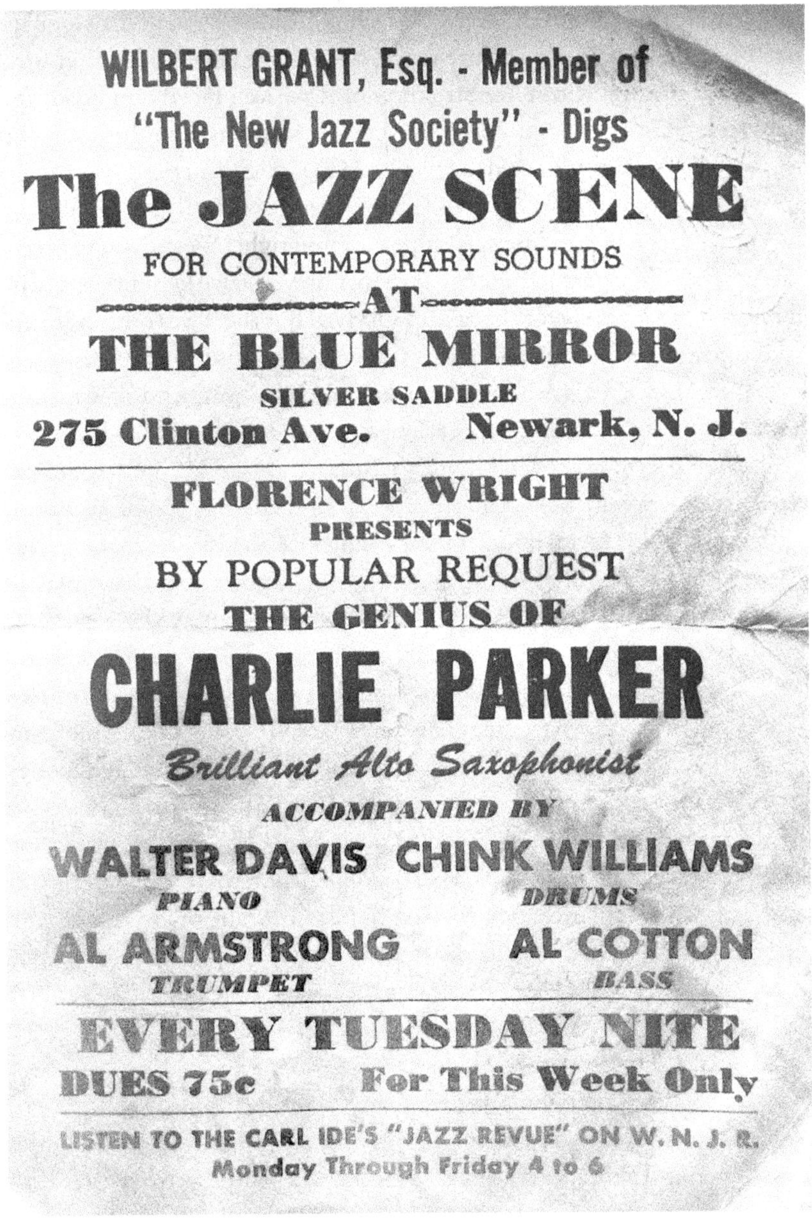

FIGURE 4.2 Flyer for a Monday-night session organized by Florence Wright.
Source: Parker and Paudras, *To Bird with Love*, 289.

difficult city and a tumultuous historical moment was to find a language in which to demand dignity and respect, to pursue new modes of musical and social relation within the strictures of American racial capitalism and democracy. Dizzy Gillespie, reflecting on his memories of those days, put it this way: "We never wished to be restricted to just an American context, for we were creators in an art form which grew from universal roots and which had proved it possessed universal appeal. Damn right! We refused to accept racism, poverty, or economic exploitation, nor would we live out uncreative humdrum lives merely for the sake of survival. But there was nothing unpatriotic about it. If America wouldn't honor its Constitution and respect us as men, we couldn't give a shit about the American way. And they made it damn near un-American to appreciate our music."[38] Yet while some musicians were able to make their living performing this new, countermodernist style, others were not, including Wing. In the late 1940s, after touring with Eugene Phipps Sr., Buddy Johnson, and Nat Toads; after making "club dates with Dizzy [Gillespie] and Charley [sic] Parker"; and after playing "one nighters with Miles Davis and Bud Powell's groups," Wing, inspired by his favorite drummer, Danny Gibson, "formed his own combo, which was forced to disband later due to the public's slow acceptance of the new sound and modern progressive concept."[39] Despite Wing's passion for and commitment to the form, his combo just couldn't bring in enough money.

But Wing was pragmatic; like others, he knew he needed to make a profit to justify continuing his career as a musician, and he knew that, in his case, that would mean playing what bigger-name collaborators needed from him, as well as what audiences were paying to hear. In short order, "he became one of Newark's most popular drummers," writes a reporter in *New Jersey After Hours*; behind the kit, he became the local "ace man."[40]

* * *

Beyond the harmonic, melodic, and formal innovations of bebop were, again, its intricate rhythms. "For many contemporary observers," Ramsey notes, "bebop rhythm was the music's most radical and controversial feature when it first appeared."[41] The style's rhythmic identity, difficult to execute and instantly recognizable, can be said to have emerged from three general musical tendencies: instrumentalists playing melodies on the backside of the beat, lagging slightly behind the pulse established by the rhythm section; musicians playing syncopated phrases that shifted the overall pulse from downbeats to upbeats; and soloists ripping through arabesque figures in double time, producing dense, rapid flurries of notes atop often-familiar chord progressions.⁴² Fluency with this rhythmic approach identified a musician as being part of a new musical order. Rhythm united performers and became a means of articulating "their social affiliation with an avant-garde cultural movement."⁴³ To demonstrate this rhythmic intensity, particularly in ways that some listeners found "disorienting," was to challenge a public's musical expectations and to stage dramatic departures from the relative rhythmic consonance of earlier jazz styles.⁴⁴ And, as Ramsey puts it, "Much of the musical enchantment of bebop emanated from its new conception of accompaniment in the rhythm sections, which created brilliant sonic tapestries supporting the dramatic solos. Pianists, drummers, guitarists, and bassists supported bebop's themes and solos with a rich and sometimes cacophonous mix of timbres, harmonic substitutions, and polyrhythmic accents that complemented and at the same time challenged the soloists."⁴⁵ Wing had ample opportunities to practice these new, rhythmically intricate accompanimental approaches, as well as to transfer their lessons to other styles, to abstract this "new conception of accompaniment" from bebop's musical architecture and to apply it to other genres.

For, again, working musicians, and especially drummers, needed to be fluent across a variety of styles. This was as much an economic imperative as an ethical one—to play well with others, to nest into any number of styles, at any tempo and in any key, was to ensure that more work and music would come. But the experience of actually performing this labor, of musicking itself, also created opportunities to explore ways of relating to others beyond the market forces helping to create the conditions for collaboration in the first place. For many drummers, the goal was to enact a musicality rooted in *complementarity*, a musical approach crafted from a sense of relation rather than heroic individuality. It was to be attuned to difference, to the specifics and quirks of others—to personalities.

"The way I look at it," said bebop drummer Kenny Washington, "all these different people that I play with, they're all personalities. They all have different personalities and you have to play differently with each one of them. Like every piano player I play with, they play differently, and the thing about it is that you have to know their styles and know what to do and what not to do."⁴⁶ Tyshawn Sorey, speaking on this matter decades after Washington, reiterates and elaborates the point: "Yes, our job as drummers is to make a lot of things happen in the music, to move things along . . . but at the same time, we have to make everybody in the band around us sound better. We have to deal with the instrument in a way that is about *giving*."⁴⁷ As a multi-instrumental accompanist, Wing worked in this "giving" spirit while occupying different roles in ensembles and in relation to soloists and bandleaders; he worked in these different roles to elaborate the musical aims and "personalities" of the main acts with whom he collaborated. In the process, his ideas found form among others in quite an on-the-nose way. His story, like those of others in similar positions, reminds us that to accompany others in and beyond music making is to build worlds with them, alongside them, among them.

* * *

As our story continues: on a crisp night in 1949, Erroll Garner, one of creative music's most distinctive and influential piano voices, visited Teddy Powell's Holiday Inn on Meeker Avenue in Newark, "where many top entertainers including Billy Holiday, Red Foxx and Billy Eckstine performed."[48] There, a few years after first playing with Charlie Parker, Dizzy Gillespie, and James Moody, Garner performed with the club's house band, reimagining time-tested classics and workshopping new numbers. At the end of the night, after the crowd had dispersed, he decided that Wing, "the young house drummer," "was just the man he needed to liven up his trio."[49]

Wing accepted Garner's offer. In early 1950, shortly after completing recording sessions with Joseph "Mr. Google Eyes" August and "opening at the Apollo Theatre" and "Birdland in New York City" with Garner, Wing went on tour with him and John Simmons, playing shows in the Northeast and the Midwest: Kansas City, Detroit, Pittsburg, Cleveland, and Chicago.[50] Performing with these older musicians, as he put it, introduced him as a young man to what musical collaboration could be on an "'A class level.'"[51] Wing's experiences with Garner and Simmons almost immediately elevated his musical output, granting him recognition (and, importantly, work) as both a songwriter and a drummer with top-tier artists: James Moody, Babs Gonzales, Ella Fitzgerald, Paul Quinichette, Quincy Jones, and others, all within the span of a few short years.

After returning from performance dates in the American Midwest and completing a studio session during which a couple of Wing originals were recorded ("Cologne" and "The Quaker"),[52] Garner, Simmons, and Wing returned to New York for a second session.[53] It was a marathon: the group recorded at least *fifteen* songs (well over an hour of music) after weeks of solid bookings. To my ear, standing apart from many of the tunes this lineup recorded—including slower ballads like "I'll Be Seeing You" and "Poinciana," midtempo numbers like "Confessin'" and "Trees," and even zippier one-offs like "Futuramic," named after the 1950 Oldsmobile Futuramic 88—is a brisk, sprawling, and quixotic tune: Garner's bop-inspired "Perpetual Emotion."[54] Clocking in at just shy of ten minutes, the tune's sprawl, energy, and tonal recursivity bring to mind unbridled, searching jam sessions while also mimicking the impossible perpetual motion machines the title evokes. Tonally speaking, the song is based on a near-endlessly recurring descent: the changes consist of major chords built on a descending chromatic scale (Bb, A, Ab, G, Gb, F, and then back to Bb to repeat the cycle), and the melody, infectious and madcap, ascends and descends the first three scale degrees of each major chord. As the cycle repeats—and as it becomes apparent that it could do so forever, the verses encircling themselves like a strung-out Ouroboros—the piece, clocking in at 220+ beats per minute, becomes a tour de force for each of the players: for Simmons, the challenge is keeping the changes interesting; for Wing, it is keeping the pulse racing; and for Garner, it is creating a musical arc out of an infinite staircase.

As I hear it, the endlessly repeatable harmonic cycle at the core of "Perpetual Emotion," hypnotic and funhouse as it sounds, creates what Timothy Hughes describes as "an alternating sequence of expectation and fulfillment" that "extends forward through time."[55] As he explains it, some musical patterns are "designed to lead the listener to expect [their] beginning to follow [their] ending. The recursive mechanism that leads our ears in this way can be rhythmic, harmonic, melodic, timbral, or any other sort of mechanism—as long as it leads us to anticipate the beginning."[56] In the case of Garner's tune, starting and ending each verse with material in Bb major—and effectively sandwiching a descending chromatic scale between the same major chord, creating a distinct key center—is enough to create a cycle of harmony-based expectation and fulfillment atop which new lines and patterns can be layered.

As the ten-minute track proceeds, we can follow this layering, as well as track how improvised musical ideas float from one part of the room to another, evocative of what we might describe as a collaborative imagination. An example: looking to explore thick polychords after having blazed through lean melodic lines, at 2:45 Garner creates sonic breathing room by shifting to longer rhythmic values (see example 4.1). He lands on this idea: displaced whole notes that anticipate the start of each new measure (and eventually, when shortened into displaced half notes, each half measure).

As I hear it, one effect of this open, syncopated idea, given its contrasts from the material that precedes it, is the creation of a new, shorter-lived cycle of "expectation and fulfillment" layered atop the one governing the tune as a whole. Wing, latching on to this rhythmic shift, responds (see example 4.2).

EXAMPLE 4.1 Erroll Garner introduces a new rhythmic idea in "Perpetual Emotion." Transcription by author.

EXAMPLE 4.2 Harold Wing echoes and supports Erroll Garner's idea in "Perpetual Emotion." Transcription by author.

As Garner begins exploring different chords and voicings, Wing doubles Garner's rhythmic idea on his bass drum while keeping time on his ride cymbal and hi-hat, dramatizing in miniature how musical patterns build in-the-moment expectations not only for audience members but also for active sound-making participants in ensembles.[57] While far from revolutionary, the moment is an example of improvisatory exchange, an instance of a drummer listening to a soloist, supporting an emergent idea by repeating it, communicating recognition.

Moments like these, while by no means linearly indicative of good character, politics, or ethical judgment, prompt us to consider, again, musical dialogue, ethical encounter, and improvisational activity within Black creative musicking circles and traditions. For many drummers working as professional accompanists, the prevailing wisdom has historically been to be felt and not heard—to listen intensely and communicate efficiently; to offer timbre, texture, and pulse; to "facilitate control over *the flow of motional energy*."[58]

The rest of the song proceeds similarly: Garner, rhapsodic; Simmons, steady; Wing, complementary. Its length, roughness, and repetition place it in that nebulous, generative space between so-called pure spontaneity and notated composition. When the song ends, it does so arbitrarily, abruptly, with a stop that feels like a random imposition on a pendulum that could swing forever. It ends with friction: an unresolved seventh, a rumbly sustain, a final kick.

For me, the group's performance highlights, again, bebop's rhythmic intensities: "shimmering wall[s] of syncopation on all levels of the music, in both the solos and the accompaniment."[59] "But the heady sense of propulsion," Ramsey writes of the style—"the playful and sometimes bewildering give and take that listeners experience in bebop"—"emanated *primarily* from bebop drummers. The dramatic crashes they provided seemed to shake heaven and earth."[60] How better to relate to others than through syncopation, comment, and surprise? How better to move toward unnamed worlds than through the fluid space of shared time?

Whenever I play along to the recording myself, taking on Wing's drum set parts, mapping the sounds across my limbs, I find myself wondering, amid the track's whirling gyres, what "emotion" needed to be so "perpetual" in the first place (or whether Garner even had a nameable emotion in mind). I also find myself wondering what became of that feeling when, after recording the tune with Wing and Simmons on May 12, 1950, Garner rerecorded it in later years with different personnel and under new titles: "Erroll at the

Philharmonic," "Margin for Erroll," "Garnerology."[61] Working through the tune, following the group's slight dip in tempo near the recording's end, I find myself wondering, What happens, generally, when emotion and entropy collide? When boundless feeling and frictionless fantasy meet the imperfections of the waking world?

While Wing, like Simmons, was becoming an expert accompanist, friction was still part of his equation; the growing disagreements he had with Garner throughout the early 1950s were both interpersonal and institutional, "evidence of problems yet to be solved, discussions yet to be conducted, understandings yet to be developed."[62] The most pressing of the problems afflicting the two was a common one: How can one foster horizontal musical and social exchange in a market environment that promotes and prioritizes heroic individual achievement? That breezes past accompanists to make profit an endless rhythm? If a key part of any reparative and sustainable creative collaboration is *trust*—and if part of the challenge, then, is the development of structures and opportunities in which people can foster trust in the face of systems that atomize individuals and pit them against one another—how can one do that in the moment, especially when tempers run hot?

"The story goes," Eugene Goldston told me, "[and] I don't know if it's totally true or not, but I've heard it from several different sources, that Chink played five years with Erroll Garner. And while Chink was on the drums, he was listening, taking notes.... One day, when Erroll Garner was late for a gig, and the whole band was set up, Chink got on the piano and started playing the tunes.... Now, he wasn't as good as Erroll Garner, mind you, but he was a piano player. So Erroll fired him."[63]

* * *

Bebop's musical and social infrastructures—the cutting contests, those competitive exchanges one might hear between dueling soloists after-hours— have long figured in lore and scholarship as the occasion for the negotiation of midcentury masculinities. Dominance was asserted, vied for; players, often young men, came of age understanding both musical and social participation as premised on "notions of power and legitimacy and privilege," notions that "extend[ed] outward into patriarchy and inward into the family," that symbolized "the power of inheritance, the consequences of the traffic in women, and the promise of social privilege."[64] It's not surprising, then, that the competitive patterns of the cutting contest, born of a racialized, heteropatriarchal social logic, often easily spilled out into other sectors of the music and entertainment industries, effectively perpetuating hierarchical social arrangements by promoting individuals over collectives. Musicians duked it out with one another for recognition and the promise of economic security. Some triumphed; others got fired.

Considering this competitive logic in racial terms in and beyond musicking yields a thicker understanding of American racial capitalism and democracy. As stated in the preceding chapters: once their new music left the Harlem underground, "beboppers quickly became seen by black and nonblack observers alike as symbols of a serious, politicized, and sometimes pathological black male creativity," eventually marking "the emergence of the figure of the modern black jazzman as a defiant, alternative, and often exotic symbol of masculinity, an image that is common in postwar American arts and letters."[65] Key to that exoticism, again, was a racist fear that young, Black, predominantly male jazz musicians who were dreaming dissonantly under American racial democracy posed "sexual threats to white superiority."[66] For bebop was "a style that challenged many assumptions about black male creativity and the power of pop and mass culture in the making of 'art.'"[67] To refuse a stereotype was to negate a worldview.

Considering these points in ways that trouble the United States' prevailing Black-white racial binary thickens the analysis even more. As Matthew Salesses writes in a powerful autobiographical piece, historically speaking, white male insecurities over their own emasculation, particularly in the late nineteenth century "during and after the construction of the transcontinental railroad," created "hypermasculine" *and* "emasculated" Chinese male stereotypes to justify racist immigration, anti-miscegenation, and labor laws.[68] By at least the early twentieth century, Salesses writes, "Asian Americans were forced to take any work they could get, namely the work white men didn't want, often service jobs like cooking and laundering. (This is where the stereotype of the Chinese American laundromat comes from.) This work was seen as 'women's work,' and further associated Asian American men with sexual and gender deviance. The effect helped both to address white male anxiety and to establish white heterosexual masculinity (and patriarchy) as the norm."[69]

Such characterizations affected not only how some Asian American musicians have engaged with Black radical music but also how Asian American jazz musicians have been considered in scholarship: "Part of the 'alienization' of Asian Americans has been the feminization or emasculation of Asian American males, who, stereotyped as either asexual eunuchs or passive males, are hardly the robust masculine figures jazz discourse produces in its

AMONG OTHERS · 131

valorization of the 'kings' of jazz. Jazz tropes such as the 'cutting contest,' 'blowing hard,' and the 'battle of the bands' betray a masculinist slant that forecloses Asian American male participation."[70] To be an Asian American jazz musician across the gender spectrum today, then, is to deal regularly with these racialized masculinist stereotypes, to work to overcome them and be heard on one's own terms.

For a young Afro-Chinese American man like Wing in the middle of the century, then, a musician whose mother was Black and whose father was Chinese American and ran his own laundry in Newark, to be an Afro-Chinese American bebop musician was to deal with these entwined racial and gender stereotypes in public, to navigate and improvise around the heightened indeterminacies and ontological plasticities of daily life in conversation with audiences and musical interlocutors. To learn to accompany well in and beyond music, to begin dreaming among others, was to start challenging those stereotypes and the systems creating them. It was to begin thinking beyond the discourses of heroic individualism and toward relational praxes, to begin pursuing an accompanimental ethos, a virtuosity of communally sustaining virtues.

* * *

In September and October 1951, Wing returned to New York yet again for more studio sessions, this time with fellow Newarker and early bebop innovator James Moody. A septet—John Grims on trumpet, Bob Range on trombone, James Moody on alto and tenor sax, Cecil Payne on baritone sax, John Acea on piano, Larry Goins on bass, and Wing on drums (credited here as "Chink Williams")—the group gathered to mark the occasion of Moody's return to the United States with a new record.[71]

James Moody was returning from Paris, driven from the United States for many of the same reasons other African Americans were, including James Baldwin. (As Baldwin wrote in "The Discovery of What It Means to Be an American," "I left America because I doubted my ability to survive the fury of the color problem here.")[72] Career savvy, and with his most famous single, "Moody's Mood for Love," already out, when Moody returned to Newark in 1951, he sought to return *musically*, to return to the domestic scene with a drove of new material. For this reason, he formed his seven-piece outfit and hit the studio to record a four-song EP.

The first of those tunes was "Margie," a standard played unhurriedly, with a variety of densities, volumes, and textures from one musical section to the next. The second was "Serenade in Blue," another standard, performed ruminatively, as if in the wake of something drastic. The third was "Wiggle Wag," an upbeat Moody original featuring backbeats and boogie-woogie elements. And the fourth, to me the most musically and occasionally interesting, given that its title marks the reason for the group's formation, was a fervent cut called "Moody's Home."

"Moody's Home," a fast, bright bop tune, is as much an announcement of Moody's return as a display of his growth as a soloist. Drawing on years with Dizzy Gillespie and Charlie Parker and his exposure to Paris's and Stockholm's postwar scenes, Moody weaves as much as possible into his jubilant return, his statement of sonic prodigality: arabesque lines, glinting ornaments, an evocation of literal wailing.[73] At all points, the song's core "subject," from form and performance standpoints, seems to be the idea of melody itself: what can constitute one, who can provide one, to what degree they are necessary at all.

This idea comes through in a couple of ways. First, "Moody's Home" doesn't quite have a "head" or main melody; instead, it has a brief introduction that returns once in the final ten seconds of the tune. The rest of the material, sandwiched between this introductory motif, consists of fairly standard chord changes and Moody soloing effervescently, scarcely repeating figures. The result is a diagonal response to a conservative concern about bebop's velocities, a reactive argument that melody had been sacrificed at the altar of speed, that technique had become an end and not a means to one. Moody and his group, not losing much sleep over that stance—their expressivity on ballads like "Serenade in Blue" was proof enough of their more traditional melodic aptitudes—on "Moody's Home" decided to meditate on what melody could become, not what it had already been.

Listening to the recording and playing along with it today, I find that melody's horizons find expression not only in Moody's impressive verses but also in Wing's two fleeting drum solo windows. In his first, at 1:02, Wing introduces a simple one-bar melody:

To give this melody texture and direction, Wing turns to pitch, timbre, and rhythmic density, nesting his smaller elaborations within the basic melodic idea (see example 4.3). His execution, controlled but not labored, shows off his technical capabilities in a way that highlights a sense of musical

EXAMPLE 4.3 Harold Wing's first expression of his melody on the drums during "Moody's Home." Transcription by author.

direction over raw athleticism.[74] Of special note is Wing's use of his snare drum's timbral affordances, using different playing zones—dead center, near the rim—to bring more nuance into his playing window.

Later, at 2:05, Wing has another brief window, during which he repeats his main melody, though he expresses it with a different inflection. Where earlier Wing keeps the majority of his frequencies high, using his snare drum to provide most of the content, here he turns to his toms, expanding his ranges of pitch and physical motion; he also adds increased rhythmic interest by implying dotted eighth notes within a downbeat-based theme. The total effect is a more guttural, syncopated take on the idea introduced at 1:06, motivating the song into its final moments of jubilant homecoming, arrival (see example 4.4).

In both brief solos, Wing invents a melody to trace an arc: from rhythmic consonance, to unexpected syncopation, and finally to clarifying resolution; in the process, he ends with a strong setup for the band to reenter, demonstrating how much room there is for musical development in even the shortest time spans.[75]

James Moody, when asked about his septet in an oral history interview, identified Wing first. Wing was important to his desire to reconnect and his aspiration to build on his already exceptional musical successes. As Moody put it, "At the beginning, I had a drummer from my hometown—I call Newark my hometown—'Chink' Williams."[76] Wing and Moody had spent ample time together as young people playing in Newark's vibrant scenes, joining a host of others in stating exactly what the community's guiding principles were, further distinguishing them from the Harlem sounds across the Hudson while linking to them all the same. They had also each done so as part of the process of navigating race and class strife, discovering what inclusion looked and felt like through the debates and hypotheses of improvisation.

Still cognizant of the racial histories they had learned and the personal experiences they had accumulated, Moody went on to clarify in that interview that he wasn't denigrating Wing by using his nickname. "Like,

EXAMPLE 4.4 Harold Wing's second expression of his melody on the drums during "Moody's Home." Transcription by author.

'Chink' Williams, that was his *name*. I don't mean that in a derogatory way. 'Chink' Williams because he was part Negro and part Chinese. And that was his name." Wing's nickname, again, was always a provocation, always a litmus test—at once a music-industry calling card and a capsule history of midcentury migration, racialization, and social relation. It was, for Moody, too, a complicated signifier of long-term friendship, an index that needed explanation.

When friendship meets the curves and edges of aesthetic form, accompaniment, especially in creative, improvised music, starts to feel different: less like one enlisting another in servitude than like joining another in co-investment.[77] For Moody, this feeling in music was essential; friendship was crucial for achieving technical sublimity and musical fulfillment, essential for achieving the subtler telepathies of superlative performance. By collaborating with friends, Moody worked to tap into relationships built off the bandstand, expanding them with musical experiences, and vice versa. At least one by-product was more "give" in the form and content of musical and social hierarchies. A verse here, a drum solo there—time shared among others.

* * *

I'd like to return now to that reproduced monochrome photograph from earlier, that visual slice of a 1954 recording session at Fine Sound Studios in New York, still sitting here on my cluttered writing desk, resting atop creased sheet music and a metal drum key. The more I look at the musicians pictured, the more significant their shared time feels; each musician, famous by then in his own right, brought a wealth of experience to the challenge-opportunity of building an artful moment together. Guitarist Jerome Darr had played with Charlie Parker earlier that year; just a few months before this photograph was taken, in fact, he'd joined Parker in the studio for what would ultimately be one of Parker's last recording dates. Guitarist Barry Galbraith was by then already being hailed as one of the premier jazz guitarists and pedagogues of his time; by the end of his career, he had produced a deep and wide discography as a session musician as well as a series of instructional books and arrangements, many of which are still widely in use today. Pianist Sir Charles Thompson had recorded with seemingly everyone, including Parker, and bassist Paul Chambers was in the process of changing the way people approached the instrument; Chambers would eventually contribute to some of the most well-known jazz records ever produced, including Miles Davis's *Kind of Blue* and John Coltrane's *Giant Steps*. And, of course, nearest the camera: Wing, the youngest player in the room, gaining experience by interacting musically with his esteemed collaborators. Not pictured were a few of the soloists—tenor saxophonist and bandleader Paul Quinichette, the "Vice Prez," who had assembled the ensemble; bebop trumpeter, arranger, conductor, and eventual world-famous producer Quincy Jones, who put the charts together; flutist Sam Most, who had a few featured moments on the project; as well as others who contributed to the album's A side.

In the studio that day, the ensemble explored some new directions in mid-1950s creative music, recording four songs that would end up forming part of a new LP entitled *Moods*, which would be released under the group name the Paul Quinichette All Stars (1956).[78] The goal of the project, it seems, was to link the then-current state of postbop with a booming (American) interest in Latin jazz projects; that is, where the album's A side features "Latin-ized" compositions and arrangements by Jones and the stylings of a different lineup—Quinichette on tenor sax, Herbie Mann on flute, Jimmy Jones on piano, Al Hall on bass, Willie Rodriguez on timbales, Manny Oquendo on bongos, and Tommy Lopez on congas—the album's B side features more straight-ahead tunes. While not a musical revelation by any means, today the project adds to our stories of midcentury musical relation, intercultural encounter, and genre capitalism, shaped as the LP was by both the "jazz" and "Latin American" cadences of twentieth-century American cultures.[79] The photograph strikes me a reminder of these trajectories, a scene of convergence.

Given *Moods*'s formal, instrumental, and stylistic bifurcations, a track of special interest to me is the last one on the record: "Pablo's Roonie," on which Wing plays drums (see figure 4.3).[80] At a time when mambo (first developed in Cuba) was reaching a high point of popularity in New York with long-established acts like Machito and his Afro-Cubans, Jones, Quinichette, and their ensemble put together a piece that today offers one of a few snapshots of how mambo and midcentury American jazz commingled. (Another is Chico O'Farrill's *Afro-Cuban Jazz Suite* [1949], featuring Machito, Charlie Parker, and Buddy Rich.) With "Pablo's Roonie,"

Time	Section	Style
0:00	Introduction: Vamp	Mambo
0:06	Introduction: Most Enters (Flute)	
0:11	Theme A: Quinichette Enters (Tenor)	
0:21	Theme B	
0:42	Feel Shifts	Postbop
0:53	Theme B	Mambo
1:03	Feel Shifts: Quinichette Solos (Tenor)	Postbop
2:27	Thompson Solos (Piano)	
3:08	Most Solos (Flute)	
3:51	Theme C: Quinichette Returns (Tenor)	
4:12	Transition	
4:22	Theme C	
4:33	Recap: Introductory Vamp Returns	Mambo
4:38	Recap: Most Enters (Flute)	
4:43	Recap: Quinichette Enters (Tenor)	
4:52	End	

FIGURE 4.3. Stylistic shifts in "Pablo's Roonie," from Harold Wing's *Moods*. Image by author.

that snapshot, formally, didn't involve blending the two styles but rather maintaining their differences—preserving the identifying characteristics of what many understood to be discrete musical systems, then bringing those differences into close proximity through formal oscillation (and ultimately uniting them through the connective tissue of Quinichette's breathy tone).

Much of this oscillation is accomplished by the rhythm section pictured in the photograph, especially via the interplay among Wing, Chambers, and Thompson.[81] At the tune's beginning, for instance, Wing performs his take on a mambo groove—eighth notes on his toms to approximate congas and a pattern on his cymbal bell to evoke the cascara—while Chambers and Thompson imply a 3–2 clave with a riff played in unison (see example 4.5). (Note: After the first four bars, Thompson continues the riff while Chambers switches to half notes.) At 0:42, however, these musicians change tacks: where Thompson mostly lays out, Wing shifts to a standard swing pattern while Chambers plays a walking bass line (example 4.6). These two patterns constitute the two main "feels" or "zones" of "Pablo's Roonie": on the one hand, a mambo filtered through standard jazz combo instrumentation; on the other, a postbop clubscape brought to life in a familiar way.

Through moments like these, we can appreciate the importance of accompanists on the level of *genre*, specifically. For while it's true, as Anthony Brown notes, that the "rhythm section" "provid[es] a highly diversified, textural mosaic, which not only support[s] but also interact[s] with the 'frontline' (horn) soloists," it's sometimes forgotten that the players constructing this mosaic are usually responsible for supplying key sonic identifiers of popular musical genres.[82] Or, put differently: accompanists in (and of) the background don't just prop up the foreground; they also build specific environments, create detailed ecosystems, and at times *evoke tangible places* in which foreground musical enunciations make specific kinds of sense.[83] So in the case of improvising creative music ensembles, accompanists, and especially drummers, not only support but also transport the lead figures they play with, zipping them across terrains, creating bridges between imaginations, making new kinds of relationality possible.

The rest of the song largely plays out along these lines. Quinichette's, Most's, and Thompson's solos are carefree; Wing, Darr, Galbraith, and Chambers's foundation is sturdy but not brittle, allowing for slight fluctuations in tempo. By the song's end, when the introductory mambo material returns in full, the whole has come into focus: a feeling of genre mixing as normalcy, of polymusicality as standard.

EXAMPLE 4.5 The Paul Quinichette Group's rhythm section creates musical environments through rhythm. Transcription by author.

With "Pablo's Roonie," the septet, conducted by Jones, sought to evoke Latin jazz energy and postbop cool through a fast-yet-effective approach: not deep fusion but methodical oscillation. Their result was a purposeful antiphony that, if nothing else, is a record of encounters and implications. *Moods* as a whole strives for much of the same, splitting onto two sides a personal and communal survey of musical expansion and transnational exchange.[84] In form and content, the project and its players volley not only between scenes of encounter and cities in flux, between indices of genre and markets in bloom, but also, by definition, between geographies of style.

The project was also fun, if short lived. As bassist Paul Chambers put it, reflecting on his time with the group, "Everybody has dreams of going to New York one day or other, because that's where you can probably make a reputation. So, I just waited for Paul Quinichette to come along. . . . I played with him for about eight months, which was a good experience. We had Sir Charles [Thompson] on piano, Chink Williams on drums and a guitar. . . . The jobs weren't too plentiful, though, so [Paul Quinichette] had to break up his band—that was in 1954."[85]

AMONG OTHERS · 139

EXAMPLE 4.6 The Paul Quinichette Group's rhythm section shifts to a standard jazz swing groove, which contrasts with the preceding mambo section. Transcription by author.

* * *

The mid-1950s United States, as Newark's Amiri Baraka (LeRoi Jones) put it in *Blues People*, "was a changed place from what it had been only a decade and a half before" when the first after-hours jam sessions were happening at Minton's in Harlem. "Heroic wars 'to make the world safe for democracy,'" he continues, "had dwindled grimly into 'police actions,' the nature of which many American soldiers did not find out until they were captured. Even the term *democracy* was blackened by some ambitious, but hideously limited, men who thought that it meant simply 'anticommunism.'"[86] Vaughn Rasberry, in *Race and the Totalitarian Century*, develops his concept of "racial democracy" by picking up on many of the same tensions Baraka identified; after World War II, racial democracies like the United States—in which "the rights, privileges, and affective dimensions of citizenship are distributed to or withheld from citizens on the basis of race" via a "network of disciplinary, punitive and terroristic measures meted out to racial subjects by state and non-state actors"—needed to signal internal confrontations with these "strategies of exclusion and persecution" in order to avoid "the perception of a preponderant affinity with . . . totalitarian adversaries" on the world stage.[87] Executive Order 9981, which initiated military desegregation in 1948, was one step; turning Dizzy Gillespie and other Black performers into jazz ambassadors, as scholar Penny Von Eschen has written about compellingly, was another.[88]

Newark, too, was changing rapidly. In the 1950s the city's Black population increased dramatically via the "second wave" of the Great Migration; meanwhile, nearly a hundred thousand white residents fled the city for new suburbs.[89] A number of Chinese and Chinese Americans left, too, following decades of traumatic discrimination and persecution; as Newark Chinatown historian Yoland Skeete-Laessig notes, "The desire to destroy Chinatown [in Newark] was an old idea that finally succeeded in the 1960s when all but the last Chinese families left."[90] The old city, rather than confront its histories of racial violence and lack of supportive infrastructures, courted wealth and repressed dissent in the glow of postwar victory.

By the early 1970s, Newark had become a much different city still. Shuttered or rebranded were many of the clubs community members like Wing had frequented in the 1940s; dispersed and tired were many of the young audiences who had grown up with bebop. The city, like others in the United States, had buckled over time, caved in where history, neglect, and poverty had proved too great a strain. And years before, without ceremony but with ample warning, the brick city had burned.

From July 12 to 17, 1967, the events that came to be known as the Newark Rebellion had left the community reeling. Like most calamities, the rebellion was a kind of revelation, an apocalypse confined to twenty-six square miles. What it revealed was a northern city hit hard by many of the mid-twentieth century's most racially and economically skewed phenomena, set in motion by policies that a virtually all-white power structure had engineered and enacted: the invention of suburbia and its accompanying white exodus from downtown; the persistence of corruption at the level of local government, including missteps made by mayor Hugh Addonizio; and city and state neglect of Newark's growing impoverished populations. Demographic change throughout the 1960s had transformed Newark into a majority-Black city for the first time ever, yet white citizens still held political control of the vast majority of the city's governing boards; unforgiving policies and the absence of consistent, livable-wage work had funneled the city's lower-class Black and Latinx populations into already stressed neighborhoods and housing arrangements, and those locations were receiving less and less support from city and state governments; and the rapidly changing city population had created unprecedented tensions between local white law enforcement aiming to retain control and underserved residents seeking representation. All of this, as has been well documented, culminated in an overwhelming (and deadly) clash of fear and need.[91]

That clash, as historian (and longtime activist) Robert Curvin puts it, played "a major role in validating the grievances of community activists," ultimately paving the way for "a black takeover of City Hall in 1970" with the election of Newark's first Black mayor, Ken Gibson. It also, in a distant sense, provided the occasion for Harold Wing's new involvement in the city's future. For shortly after being elected mayor, Gibson, a longtime musician himself, appointed Wing as music director for the Department of Parks, Recreation, and Cultural Affairs.[92]

Wing, out of the spotlight for the better part of this period, was returning in the early 1970s to a city still reconfiguring itself after that upheaval, a city working to claim the responsibility of its redefinition. After having called the city home since his earliest days—since growing up the son of a Chinese American and an African American, since throwing himself completely into the music cultures of the Hudson—he took to his new role with a special intensity, working until shortly before his death.

* * *

As music director, Wing and his team were able to help foster an ecosystem of music practice and enjoyment by addressing a lack of government-backed representation for the city's most aggrieved populations; the way he did so is evocative of a "cultural ecosystem" model of arts practice and production. This ecosystem, as Jeff Chang has explored in a variety of forms, can be sketched by asking, "Who has access to the means of production of culture? Who is represented in cultural production and the structure of cultural production? How does their representation, misrepresentation, or underrepresentation impact the notion of artistic *quality* and the reproduction of inequality? And, who has the power to shape culture and cultural production?"[93] Working for the city with access to city resources, including funds and infrastructures, Wing and his collaborators were able to provide opportunities for a number of musicians and audiences to think about where Newark might be heading.

As Eugene Goldston told me, "Chink, being the coordinator for the city's music, through the recreation department—he got us gigs all over the city. All these establishments—restaurants, jails, etc. From there, we got opportunities all up and down the eastern seaboard. We traveled a lot—on the weekends, you know, because we had to get back to work. Anyway—as soon as I got that job, as soon as we all started working, we had steady gigs for about ten years. Chink was playing both drums and piano."[94] Having dedicated himself to composition and community involvement, Wing joined others in doing what he could to make Newark a place of new musical opportunity.

Among the efforts was the creation of a seasonal jazz festival, which provided residents with good music and helped young professionals like Goldston find their footing. During the summers, as Goldston recalled, "We played in the parks.... In fact, that helped a lot of us become established. Because if you were playing in the parks during the day, well, you were playing for a lot of people coming through. And even when it was slow, we'd be there performing as if we had an audience of a thousand."[95] During the winter Wing would modify bands' setups, taking trios or quartets to nursing homes in the area to play for the elderly. "He would also put together programs that brought together the elderly and little children via jazz concerts," his daughter told me. "It was an all-around benefit: the musicians got exposure to one another, solid gigs, and good playing experiences; Newark's audience got good music, atmosphere, everything." Throughout his nineteen-year tenure as music director, Wing and his team put on "thousands of concerts for young people, senior citizens and other special audiences," all of which helped combat the negative media coverage of the city proliferating in the aftermath of the rebellion.[96]

Many of Wing's events were covered in local papers, including concerts he put on for local prisoners and students of different ages.[97] But among his deepest commitments was the expansion of access to formal music education in Newark. As director of music at the John F. Kennedy Recreation Center on Howard Street, a program modeled after Wing's experiences at the Henry Street Conservatory of Music, though by contrast accepting of many styles and traditions, Wing worked to provide young student musicians opportunities to study and perform. "When I see a young kid that's really interested in trying to learn something," Wing told C. Alan Simms of *Information*, an English- and Spanish-language newspaper, "I do all I can to try and help him." For "practically any jazz musician can read. He knows music, chords, scales, harmony, theory, and all, because he's studied." The opportunities for the bulk of Newark's youth to study formally, though, were slim, particularly in the decade after the rebellion. Wing worked to respond by pushing to "get the kids studying vocally and instrumentally" despite limited space and resources. "If I had the position," Wing said, "[I would] have music in all the centers with a staff and have all these kids I've been telling you about coming to these centers, studying free of charge on the city."[98] Working quite literally in a supporting role (albeit one with more institutional power than those of his music combo days), Wing channeled his efforts into the enrichment of local youth music education, connecting skill sets and knowledge bases into efforts that today read to me as accompanimental: present for individual needs, judicious with constructive criticism, and cognizant, ultimately, of layered, dynamic structures shaping social practice and inner life.

* * *

Wing maintained a serious songwriting practice throughout the 1970s, becoming noticeably more prolific after assuming his role as Newark's music director in 1973. Building on his years of experience in the music industry, he wrote and registered nearly forty new songs between 1970 and 1976 as a member of the American Society of Composers, Authors, and Publishers. As implied by their titles, the songs explored everything from romantic love to Black political power to religious feeling.[99] While the vast majority were unfortunately never recorded in studios, a select few were, including "Consequences of a Drug Addict Role."

Recorded by jazz pianist and vocalist Shirley Horn in 1972, "Consequences" is an experimental prose and sound poem that offers reflections on the temptations and destructions of drug use, on the relief and empowerment drugs promise and the strife and death they so frequently deliver. Lyrically, it proceeds through a series of long, percussive sentences linked by internal rhyme: "The drug addict role, so horribly cold, has a multi-toll: black, white, young, and old—enchanting, its dreams, inviting it seems, the carefree air, pockets bare, comforts rare, a daily dare; seeking help, periodic wealth, a neglect of self, a challenge a day, no work or play, nothing to say but, 'How's the stuff today?'"[100] Largely an impression of narcotic dependence, the prose poem's rhythms arrest. So, too, does its general approach: rather than fetishize users or use in the ways many sensationalist white jazz critics had grown accustomed to in the 1940s, 1950s, and 1960s, particularly in their responses to heroin use by Black creatives like Parker, it instead describes a "horribly cold" repetition, bearing witness to its weight. "always bent, money spent . . . go out to cop, a grueling hop, looking for the tops, trying not to get popped; it's an atmosphere." In the wake of a "virtual epidemic of heroin addiction" among the prominent voices of midcentury creative music—Elvin Jones, Art Blakey, Hampton Hawes, Jackie McLean, and others—bearing lyrical witness to personal desperation and narcotic ravaging was a route not only to a kind of narrative rehabilitation but also, in effect, to a rehumanization: to describe in lyric and sound was to become proximate, to draw the ailing close enough to begin to measure experiential distances.[101] For Wing, this work was personal: like others, he, too, had suffered from addiction, once even appearing before a judge for "use and possession of narcotics."[102] Unlike many in his situation, he was lucky; he survived.

Musically, "Consequences" is avant-garde and impressionistic—an event-driven piece that, through its hazy beginning, stabilized middle, and evaporative end, slowly traces an arc of feeling, a parabola of intensities—a trip. Some moments are carried entirely by suspended cymbal work; others feature a rapidly bowed cello. Harmonic grounding is largely withheld until roughly a third of the way through the piece, when out of the instrumental fog emerges a repeated sequence of contemplative block chords in the piano. The vocals, arriving in rapid bursts between long pauses, flicker in and out of focus via electronic processing that disperses Horn's typically pure, vibrato-less tone. Sitting at the border of song and spoken word, "Consequences" evokes the experience it condemns: a chemical ride that begins and ends in disunity.

Horn recorded "Consequences" during a period in the early 1970s when she wasn't touring much but rather performing primarily in Washington, DC, where she could commit to raising her then-teenage daughter. ("'That album was all about me,'" her daughter Rainy once expressed in an interview. "'Mom was trying to figure it out. I didn't admit to it for a long time, but I listened to it a lot.'")[103] With this framing, Horn's decision to record Wing's song—and, in her delivery, in her embodiment of and additions to its messages, her decision to make it her own—underscores both her solidarity with Wing, her lifelong, recovering friend, as well as an effort to communicate something of importance, of "consequence," to herself and her kin.

And through the song, Wing was able to explore a confessional mode that captured a terrible (and far too common) experience in a way that would potentially reach a large number of listeners—not only those suffering from addiction or withdrawal but also those who routinely put aggrieved people out of their minds. The argument of his piece—essentially, that addiction is never cause for the ontological reclassification of human beings as lesser, irreparable, illegible—points implicitly to the racist debates around bebop, drug use, and Black musicians and communities since the 1940s.[104] For people like Wing, such dismissals and punitive responses, deeply entwined with the processes of racialization contributing to the very conditions of possibility for substance abuse, were part of the monumental apparatuses he was attempting to overcome by turning to art as a maker and a public servant. That is: when "Consequences" was released in 1972, it named, literally, *effects*, experiences all too common among marginalized communities in a city still stunned and smoldering, rocked as it was by late 1960s upheaval: Newark, the "Brick City."

* * *

"Every city in the world has a legacy," Amiri Baraka once wrote. "If those legacies are known, kept before the peoples of the world, and that legacy is rich with history and culture, the city itself becomes an object of glamour, excitement, and curiosity." "But when the best legacy is hidden or forgotten," he continues—when "the city becomes identified with a set of negative or dangerous characteristics"—"then it will look like Newark looks after five p.m. on any evening."[105]

In the aftermath of a more-than-local calamity, at the mercy of shifting economic winds, Wing joined others in working to make Newark an "object of glamour, excitement, and curiosity." Like those around him, he was working to transform the city's emotional and social debris into songs that were at once danceable and poignant, into opportunities that were meaningful and numerous. And he was doing so in the face of mounting negative representations, in a landscape in which major news stories *about* Newark—typically not written *from* Newark—were about its decay, its failures, anything to justify its outright abandonment.

The bulk of the songs Wing wrote during these years remain largely unknown. In the absence of widely accessible recordings or sheet music, their titles and promises are all we have. The "micropoetics" of each title, absent any musical content, don't frame organized sounds but instead open out into speculative terrain; in aggregate, they suggest a thematic continuity, some sustained concerns: "All Cities and All Countries to Be Free!," "An African Girl Is Queen of the World," "Educate Your Mind," "It's Time for Us," "Martin Luther King, a Black American King," "Compensation."[106] Through such music, written from Wing's Newark apartment—through that larger cultural ecosystem that his music implicitly and explicitly indexes—we can understand that Newark itself was attempting a reimagining. Through Black representation for predominantly Black constituencies, through emergent solidarities and cohorts, Newark was attempting to reimagine itself as more than a city designed by white European settlers and controlled by nonlocal business interests; it was attempting to assist those people still ailing, those residents waiting for those in power to hear them. For Wing, like for others in his scene, the project was personal: after coming of age in an environment warped by racism, after hearing the relationality at the core of improvisatory invention, after discovering what was possible through accompaniment as social and musical practice, the community's Newark—a musical stronghold, a bastion of creativity—was so much more than a footnote to progress, so much more than a mere brick city.

* * *

In 1985, near the end of Wing's time as Newark's music director (and near the end of his life), residents from throughout the city sought to celebrate his contributions by collaborating on a concert held at Essex County College: "A Tribute to a Native Son." The program, built to honor Wing's work with the community, consisted entirely of his compositions, and it brought together nearly every facet of his activity in the music industry: student involvement, city support for Black art, and performances by his contemporaries, including some of the very musicians he grew up modeling—Eugene Phipps Sr., Jimmy "Chops" Jones, and others—as well as players he had helped get started, including Anne Bailey and Denise Hamilton. Among the cast, too, was Eugene Goldston: one of a number of people who had been inspired by Wing's energy. "We did a show entirely of his songs," Goldston told me in downtown Newark. "He wrote so many."[107]

One of the things the concert foregrounded was the sheer number of people affected by an individual's communal activity—by songwriting that shifted the emphasis from composing individual to enabling group and listening community; by drumming that supported and elaborated collaborators' visions and personalities in real time; and by government work that created opportunities for as many people as possible to benefit from music's social and aesthetic affordances. "All the musicians loved him," Newark jazz historian and reporter Barbara Kukla told me. "They loved *playing* with him. He was a great guy."[108] Wing's different activities, variations on the same theme, helped "set in motion a process," as Barbara Tomlinson and George Lipsitz have argued of similar efforts in academic spaces, that "produce[s] different kinds of people through the organizational learning that emerges from practices and processes that build our collective capacity for democratic deliberation and decision making."[109] We might see this as a takeaway of these improvisations across domains in the postwar years: that the intimate formal, historical, social, and compositional lessons of a Black musicking community provided a guide through personal trials, local struggles, and racial discriminations—a route to understanding the contradictions and potentials of a people's shared time.

As an Afro-Chinese American performer and songwriter who came of age in and through Black radical music, Wing pursued what Tomlinson and Lipsitz have conceptualized as accompaniment as strategy: at once "participating with and augmenting a community of travelers on a road" and "augmenting, accenting, or countering one musical voice with another" to create the conditions in which others—in which communities—can shine.[110] Such efforts, in the 1950s and still today, tend to go unremarked, particularly in a racial capitalist society that privileges profit-generating virtuosi over reparative collectivities, ensembles, and networks. As Tomlinson and Lipsitz point out, it's only through a *fusion* of discrete actors' efforts that music achieves its affective potential and, relatedly, that communities advance in their struggles for justice and equity.

To have learned this as an Afro-Chinese American drummer, pianist, and songwriter coming of age in late 1940s Newark—a vibrant scene virtually at the epicenter of bebop, a music largely (mis)understood today as the domain of heroic individuals, troubled geniuses, hopeless junkies, and wallflower hipsters—was to learn jazz's democratic valences through practice and support. As a drummer, it was to provide rhythmic interest if a soloist nodded off, timbral variety if the arrangement changed course, tacit phrases if the occasion demanded reduction.[111] It was to facilitate temporal agreement: not metronomically inflexible, invariable pulses but rather a sense of cohesion and shared direction that unlocked the affective potential of melodic and harmonic content. It was to create a habitable planet of sound and sentiment—a textured plane suited for life, liberty, and the pursuit of newness—and it was to do so, primarily, by being felt, not heard.

Too, as a songwriter, as an artist engaging with a music industry and broader culture that still prioritizes the genius of the individual talent over the daily labors of the collaborator, it was to have understood the discontinuities between institutional reward and on-the-ground effort (to say nothing of a pressing need for more songs that could speak to a local population). Amid the immediate need to earn a living and the infrastructural pressure to build a professional brand, to pursue songwriting as accompaniment was to write with and for others, to center the collaborative imagination. It was to pursue the locally poetic: to remain concerned with economy and consequence in the communication of specific feelings and stories that map larger collective sentiments. As Baldwin notes in "The Artist's Struggle for Integrity," this has been the point for many artists who accept communal responsibilities: to bear witness to calamity; to transform the gristle of place, time, and person into forms that bring a sense of the whole into view; and to accompany others along the paths they walk, "reduc[ing]," again, as Ellison put it, "the chaos of living to form."[112]

We can hear the fine details of this relationality in the recordings analyzed and mentioned in the preceding pages—in piano melodies that leave ample room for a musical interpreter to add their own flair; in active listening that expresses itself in subtle calls and responses at the drum set; in melodic drum solos that build theme and development in extremely short time spans; in polymusicality, expressed by using different styles of musical time to propel and encourage bandmates, as well as to generate and juxtapose musical genres; in creative collaborations with iconic Black women musicians. Through all of this, this story of Wing's work evokes those of a great many people who developed purpose *among others*, who came into an understanding of "the human" "refract[ed]" through the prisms of musical performance and structure.[113] As I've been working to show here, we can learn a lot by listening for and with such people and their activity, deep as their sounds and traces may be in the archival mix. For just as accompaniment can name a musical and ethical approach, so, too, can it name a scholarly one: a mode of historical work that listens expressly for the overlooked and minoritized in order to recover forgotten people and stories, on the one hand, and to map the very intellectual precepts and institutional structures that have enabled their forgetting in the first place, on the other.[114] The results, always ad hoc and unpredictable, inevitably bend toward an enriched understanding of our institutional designs—of the effects they produce, the acts they promote, and the lives they occlude.

* * *

In a piece for his abandoned "Jazz Jaunts" project, poet Raúl Salinas once wrote of Wing, reflecting on their connection:

> I still think of Chink Williams on occasion. Especially on chilly, misty Northwest Sunday mornings on the Port Madison Reservation. Jazz comes through our patched-up, radioshack portable (veteran of the TRAIL in '76) radio, out of Seattle, far from the warmsongs of that southwest life still out there. Anyway, that's when i think of Chimk [*sic*].
>
> We olny [*sic*] met three times, but he made a lasting impression on me and my studies of jazz. The first time was at the old Doris Miller, an auditorium in the Black community, named after a local young man who died aboard a u.s. naval ship during the war). Chink was drumming with the Benny Green Orchestra and we rapped and we got high. i guess by then

i was sort of a bag man for musicians passing through. The next meeting was at the same place some two or three years later when he was playing with the James Moody band. If memory serves me right, i think we last saw each other in San Jose, California, at the old Palomar Gardens. Was he playing with the Erroll G Garner Trio?[115]

Sitting here at my desk in Los Angeles, with Wing, Simmons, and Garner's "I'll Be Seeing You" spinning on my record player, the monochrome photograph of the Quinichette session nearby, I find myself thinking about remembrances like this, the bonds they elegize, what it all might mean when the world is on fire. What it might mean, that is, to improvise among others when nothing feels possible, to sing in order to bring a tomorrow into being, to create new groups bound by "a desire for things to work out," by a "shared sense of what things are important, which things will matter for the future, which elements of the past are important to note, which tendencies to nurture and promote."[116] What it might mean, that is, to conceptualize *community*, as Anthony Reed theorizes it, "as a way of deorchestrating Time to create not a home but a resting place from which to imagine home," as a way of fashioning new time together to instantiate new space entirely.[117]

I think of these things as some of the key listeners mentioned in the preceding chapters begin returning to mind—James Araki performing in the same Los Angeles venues that Wing would have played on tour, Charlie Parker's sounds still ringing in both of their ears; Raúl Salinas relishing postprison freedoms and writing about the "lasting impression [Wing made] on [him] and [his] studies of jazz," "still thinking of [him]" some twenty years after their last conversation; Eugene Goldston speaking with me in downtown Newark about the reach of local figures and the eddies and countercurrents of Black radical musics, our conversation tracing musical flows from Austin to Los Angeles, Harlem to Tokyo, New York to the Rio Grande Valley and beyond.[118] I think of Goldston now, especially—a respected musician not wanting to boast about his own successes but rather to highlight his friend's spirit. I take note of how grounding his remarks felt the night we met, how familial. "By the time I met Chink," he told me, his voice breaking, "he had already done all of that famous stuff. He'd been everywhere, played with everyone. It always brings back fond memories, thinking of him. It was my privilege to meet him at a time when he was willing to share his learning and experience with me. I'll never forget him."[119]

As an Afro-Chinese American musician coming of age in the mid-twentieth century, Wing dreamed in ways that today reveal communal refutations of univocal (read: white, hegemonic) national strivings, strivings frequently alchemized into commercial incantations for upward economic mobility under racial capitalism.[120] The recordings and photographs that remain today evoke, for me, group contestations with multifold, everyday racisms and racist market structures, including difficult concert and vinyl economies and racialized genre categories.[121] The stories left behind ultimately highlight, as I hear them, personal struggles with the names one might be called while trying to make a name for oneself.

With all of this in mind, then, I offer, here, a refrain.

To dream in sound is to reveal the intimacy and strangeness of social and musical form. It's to attune oneself to relation, to vibrations linking bodies, surfaces, technologies, locations, and histories; to hear in unexpected resonances the traces of larger worlds. To dream among others, to listen for what worlds others hear, to sketch together new spaces of conviviality and coevalness, is to invent new ways of relating and becoming, to challenge the subordination and anonymization that racial democracy and capitalism demand, to resist becoming reified as the tossed off, as the invisible, as the "among others" so often depersonalized and effaced. As Frantz Fanon writes, it's to strive to understand a group *as such*, to "go beyond [one's] immediate existential being" so as to "apprehend the being of the other as a natural reality," to develop new names for the trembling worlds we're born into.[122] It's to find truth in that making together. It's to share time.

epilogue
affinities

As time has warped and shattered amid the suffering of these long pandemic years, I've found myself thinking often of my late grandfather—of his saxophone, glinting and silent, breathlessly awaiting new life; of his handwritten sheet music, his note heads always curiously facing the wrong direction; of his building a life with my late grandmother, their twilight dancing suggestive of a benevolent universe. He died before I could tell him most of this, before I could follow up with more questions, before we could potentially unearth together some of the journeys of which he seldom spoke. Gazing today at his old vinyl records, albums by his favorite artists, I am filled with questions I cannot fully answer, only deepen. What did he dream of when he picked up those albums, when he reached for his instrument? What guidance, if any, did he receive from the collective spirit musicking indexes? What and who should I be listening for today, amid so much? What was he listening for all those years ago, encountering and admiring a Black radical musicking as a young Mexican American man from the Rio Grande Valley?

These questions and their spirit undergird and animate the preceding pages, focused as they are not on my grandfather but instead others in his generational cohort, others with whom I imagine he would have gotten along. Through this book's linked (audio)biographical pieces on listeners from across the United States, I've worked to convey how a mode of Black dreaming created a framework for young, nonwhite listeners to pursue their own improvisations, to contextualize their energies and struggles under American racial democracy. I've strived to express that a cadre of Black musicians, varied and contradictory, reached listeners in unexpected and profound ways, creating new conditions of possibility for young people to hear themselves among others. I've worked to suggest that by pursuing a newly specific musical idiom and challenging an anti-assimilationist ethos, the musicians of Harlem's midcentury underground set a striking precedent for a new generation, stirring in many a desire to disrupt the standard logics of racial subject formation, to subvert rote and systematic denials of internal complexity, and to reject forced submission to dreams of colonial design.

For Harold Wing, what emerged were instead dreams in and of a different time, a shared time; dreams rooted in a sense of accompaniment, in a communal ethos that, as for many others in his scene, shaped his musicianship, multi-instrumentality, and composition not around an ideal of "heroic virtuosity" but instead around shared experimentation and mutual development. As I argued in chapter 4, "Among Others," Wing's experiences as an Afro-Chinese American bebop drummer, pianist, and songwriter—navigating the new sound's structural challenges, collaborating with its principal creators, performing and recording in and beyond Newark—ultimately shaped his approach to the relationship between art practice and community building. For Raúl Salinas, what emerged were dreams beyond carceral time; as I argued in chapter 3, "Quartered Notes," the challenge of finding language for the social, musical, historical, and punitive forces he was experiencing behind bars pushed him into new poetic and critical terrain, infusing his multimedia Xicanindio poetry and relational politics with a sense of what worlds music can bring forth, what mind jails it can tear down. And for James Araki, what emerged from his listening and experiments was a sense of layered time and formal possibility, of the imbrication of complex personal interiors, large transnational circulations, state-sanctioned violences and racisms, and novel technological affordances. As I argued in chapter 2, "Layered Time," the lifelong challenges of responding to injustice, experimenting with expressive tools, and attempting to translate the sediments of experience and history into locally meaningful aesthetic forms ultimately highlighted, then and now, some of the best of creative music's lessons.[1] Each of these individuals, like others in their communities, found in radical, creative music an interpretive code for their youthful experiences, a way to improvise in their own cultural keys. In contexts they knew well—recording studios, prison cells, army bases, bandstands, vanishing neighborhoods—dreaming across formal, medial, and social boundaries meant building a world with others in mind, meant evading the constrictions of midcentury racisms by envisioning different rules that might apply.

* * *

As I finished writing this book during pandemic lockdown, in the looming specter of end-times capitalisms, under protest curfew and amid multifold grief, I also thought often of the phrase *American dream*. Seeking its origins, I learned that author James Truslow Adams coined it nearly a century ago in his 1931 book, *The Epic of America*, and that when he did, he wasn't at all attuned to the kinds of differences and potential solidarities that radical, relational dreaming can and does foster. In his triumphalist epilogue, in fact, it seems he felt the nation-state's dreamwork was already wrapped up: the "dream of being able to grow to the fullest development as man and woman, unhampered by the barriers which had slowly been erected in older civilizations, unrepressed by social orders which had developed for the benefit of classes rather than for the simple human being of any and every class.... It has been a great epic and a great dream. What, now, of the future?"[2]

Langston Hughes's "Montage of a Dream Deferred," finished some three decades after Adams's book, took a different approach. In fact, the "conflicting changes, sudden nuances, sharp and impudent interjections, broken rhythms," "riffs, runs, breaks, and disc-tortions" that Hughes's Harlem portrait indexes—the "music of a community in transition" that his poem evokes and approximates—shows just how far off the mark Adams was.[3]

Hughes writes famously in "Tell Me," one of the montage's episodes:

> Why should it be *my* loneliness,
> Why should it be *my* song,
> Why should it be *my* dream
> > deferred
> > overlong?[4]

The frustration, incredulity, and desperation, the insistence on the personal, on the fact of one's existence and interiority—"*my* loneliness," "*my* song," "*my* dream"—spoke then and speaks still now of the urgent need for a different kind of radical creativity: "a way of imagining the self unfettered, racialized but not delimited."[5] A way of imagining oneself and one's community beyond inherited national myths—and, by extension, beyond a Western cosmology that has long functioned, as Zakiyyah Iman Jackson has argued, by systematically denying Black depth and complexity, by rendering Blackness a convenient ontological plasticity in relation to an assumed white fixity.[6] Hughes's retrospective 1951 poem, responding to a country and a world transfigured by catastrophic war, captured such a spirit by focusing on "how young, black, urban males, who were often treated as enemies of the state, wrested bebop out of the social experience of 1940s black male 'cullud'-ness," creating in ways that refuted white supremacist ideals and ultimately coalesced into a moment-defining improvisatory style.[7] In bebop, in its "broken rhythms" and "conflicting changes," was a frustratingly familiar code, an old blues newly presented in thick chords and jagged rhythms—and, in effect, the seeds of a new communal articulation:

> What's written down
> for white folks
> ain't for us a-tall:
> "Liberty And Justice—
> Huh—For all."[8]

I share this because I believe, again, that to dream in sound can mean to defamiliarize, to experiment, to make strange, to subvert "the material world for the sake of another one that feels perhaps even more real and worthwhile, always open to those who are searching for something to believe in."[9] Where the literal dreams of our sleep highlight that there's more to each of us than what we are immediately conscious of, hidden depths and currents that open out into forever, the figurative dreams of our arts and aspirations, mediated as they are by time and circumstance, remind us that there are possibilities latent in even the direst situations, that a tomorrow may still be possible, that justice may yet arrive. Dreams, as figures of complexity and continuance, evoke a now and an elsewhen, a thick, malleable time; hearing music as a mode of dreaming, experiencing dreams as a kind of musicking, highlights the hyperreal textures and temporalities of our hopes and our bodies, our matters and our meanings.

* * *

Musicking can serve, has served, as a doorway into reparative socialities and relations, a way of facilitating connective responses to long and tangled histories in which the divide-and-conquer strategy of whiteness (and possessive investments in its perpetuation) has kept people apart, reified differences, hardened stereotypes into essences, and kept resource inequity a constitutive feature not only of the United States as a project but of modernity/

coloniality as a whole. So, following multi-instrumentalist Rahsaan Roland Kirk, I wrote this book with my ear, my musicking body, narrating it in an (audio)biographical mode invested in the granular ways sounds constitute selves and communities. The connection between this mode and the book's argument is direct: the sounds we create, the selves we imagine, are always deeply related to those of others, near or far, family or not. Acknowledging this intimacy in art and research can bring new material to the fore; doing so in life can make new worlds possible.

And while this book has focused on individuals, its core arguments, again, don't sit at the level of individual experience or biography. Rather, the individuals' stories function here as portals into larger social concerns; the (audio)biographical mode has here functioned as an intellectual and stylistic strategy for drawing connections across scales, highlighting structures in which individual lives and works are always enmeshed.[10] And while stories "of individual mobility and commitment cannot resolve the more fundamental inequalities shaping a minority community"—single individuals' successes do not change systems of oppression—it's possible that stories about individuals *in relation*, if rendered with a sense of proximity, of shared fate, might still illuminate how intimate the nation-state's violences are, as well as how transformative our dreams can still be.[11]

Thinking through individuals, communities, and histories in relation by centering musicking as a form of subversive, alter-American dreaming has, again, informed my understanding of race in and beyond the United States. As Natalia Molina writes, analyzing race relationally "recognizes it as a mutually constitutive and socially constructed process"; it combats "essentialist notions" by resisting category reifications and attending "to how, when, where, and to what extent groups intersect"—actions that "push against the tendency to examine racialized groups in isolation, which limits our understanding" of long-interconnected systems.[12] "A better understanding of the relational nature of race," Molina continues, "also provides groups a framework and common ground for recognizing the ways in which their histories, and their futures, are linked."[13] As mentioned in the introduction and threaded through the subsequent chapters, approaching race in this relational manner has thus involved decentering whiteness and asking instead, "How are polylateral relations among aggrieved communities of color formed?"[14] How are these polylateral relations always already gendered? From a practical standpoint, this meant placing inquiries and hypotheses "in a dialogue with events, people, and literatures that may not immediately seem to resonate with or influence the conventional [scholarly] frameworks."[15] The motivation, to draw again on Frantz Fanon, was to recover stories of individuals and communities finding strength in one another, and to present those stories in a way that participates in the fight for "the birth of a human world," "a world of reciprocal recognitions."[16]

It should go without saying that today, in the United States, many African American communities, beset by discriminatory policies, police brutality, and systematic economic disadvantage, still grapple with what it meant for their ancestors to be seized, tortured, and enslaved; to be deracinated and desubjected, *dehumanized*, rendered bare flesh, and transformed into *property*.[17] And, vitally, to have been those "objects," as Fred Moten memorably put it, who continually refused this ontological designation by repeatedly "[speaking] back."[18] It should go without saying that many Latinx and Chicanx communities, beset by structural xenophobia and economic precarity, still grapple with what it meant for many of their indigenous ancestors to see white sails on the eastern horizon and shortly thereafter succumb to attack, disease, enslavement, rape, and erasure; to be read as always already doomed in the ideology of an invading force, kept alive and instrumentalized only to the degree that they could assist colonists in the erection of their New World. And, vitally, to have been those who, despite these horrors, have preserved lifeways for future generations. And it should go without saying that today, in the United States, many Chinese American and Japanese American communities, the subjects of both "perpetual foreignness" and "model minority" discourses, still grapple with what it meant for their ancestors to live through, for Chinese Americans, the late nineteenth-century "yellow peril" and the Chinese Exclusion Act and, for Japanese Americans, the internment camps and the biological and psychological inheritances of the United States' nuclear bombings of Hiroshima and Nagasaki.[19] And, importantly, despite these traumas and the specific difficulties of transpacific diasporic experiences, to have still found ways to keep those diasporic connections alive, all the while forging new bonds and cultures in a country so seemingly allergic to anything not white.

With these histories in mind, here I have worked to highlight dreams, solidarities, and relations that link these varying trajectories, no matter how small the detail, how temporary the connection. I've strived to treat local stories of "unfamous" people as historically important; I've worked to amplify a few of the ways that musicking has helped people find strength in one another.

* * *

In this book I've also worked to make musical affinity, the "raw power" of which "is such that a chance encounter can spark a lifelong engagement with a musical tradition not otherwise part of an individual's purview," methodologically significant.[20] This, for me, has involved relying on close listening as a critical, creative, and historical methodology, including thinking across media forms to gain insight into materials typically studied in isolation; considering archives and memories in contrapuntal relation, attending to what productive trouble they make for one another; and pursuing a model of interdisciplinary study that links discourses and disciplines by focusing on the ways individuals and their activities frequently cut across the analytics, theories, and social categories so often used to render the world digestible.

One immediate utility of an affinity-mapping approach like this might be its potential to tweak how things like music history and historiography are pursued, shifting the emphasis, as Ben Ratliff once suggested, to those "unfamous" figures whose contributions to music cultures exist beyond the purview of familiar narratives.[21] Another might be the way it encourages critical and reparative understandings of race and gender in the context of the United States' stultifying racial democratic and capitalist infrastructures, the way it emphasizes the fact that, as Luiz Alvarez writes, understanding racialized youth cultures is "virtually impossible without [also] accounting for how one [group] relates to [an]other."[22] Still another might be its path, in this case, to abandoning the term *jazz* altogether, as Nate Sloan, Tyshawn Sorey, and many other practitioners have argued for—its route to neutralizing the acidity of an outmoded category and instead focusing on shared spirit; on radical, communally creative praxis; on aesthetic and social improvisation; on experiments made of the stuff of the popular yet always two steps ahead (or, better, a few steps at a diagonal).[23] Yet another might be its potential to redirect studies of American culture more broadly, orienting them around unsung engagements, unscripted connections, and life-prolonging aspirations for life and love beyond labels.

On this front, the book *Legends from Camp* comes to mind for me almost immediately. In that work, a landmark collection of poetic and prosaic reflections on jazz and internment (and particularly on the work of bebop pianist Thelonious Monk), Nisei poet Lawson Fusao Inada reflects on the affinities he and his friends shared in their youths: "The music we most loved and played and used was Negro music. It was something we could share in common, like a 'lingua franca' in our 'colored' community. And in our distorted reality of aliens and alienation, it even felt like citizenship. It seemed so very American—'un-foreign,' on 'un-foreign' instruments—and the words it used were English. Not 'across town' or 'Hit Parade,' English, perhaps, but nevertheless an English that, in its own way, did the job."[24] For Inada, this Black music brought clarity to a "distorted reality of aliens and alienation"; it helped create a sense of belonging-in-difference: a "feeling" of citizenship, of *trust* among differently marginalized people attempting to carve space for themselves in an increasingly walled-off America.[25] Inada's affinity for this music, and, crucially, for those Black musicians making it, helped him conceive of a home that exceeded the centrality of whiteness: a chromatic hyperplane, a world otherwise.

That young people like Araki, Salinas, Wing, and my own grandfather were similarly affected reiterates the incredible reach of Black radical music; it also highlights the larger forces always expressing themselves at the level of individual experience: the shifting sands of racial democracy and the changing nature of American foreign relations, the mobilizations of popular musics and the radical responses to their co-opting, the power of folk traditions and the politics of knowledge production. That each of these people heard paths forward through radical sounds, through the speed and sentiment of a midcentury moment, toward the development of new forms and poetics, toward blueprints for more ethical relations, reveals not only something of the unifying potential of underground experiments but also, as with that memorable final scene of Baldwin's "Sonny's Blues," the liberatory possibility of listening closely, deeply, and consciously, of finally hearing, there in the depths of another's "loose and dreamlike" sounds, a different way to be.[26]

* * *

Tonight, as I quiet my mind, rest my eyes, and grant my memory space, I can still recall among my grandfather's possessions, tucked away there at the edge of two nations and still the center of more histories, a worn-out copy of Charlie Parker's unfortunately titled *South of the Border* (1953), a collection of Parker's Afro-Cuban experiments released shortly after my grandfather started music school at North Texas State College—later, again, the University of North Texas, where I attended music school some fifty years later. I've long wondered what exactly my grandfather heard in Parker's playing when he first heard it—and, more specifically, what he heard while listening to that record in the Rio Grande Valley, in the Texas-Mexico borderlands our family calls home, listening to Parker soar over a 2–3 clave while dancing to the record's Afro-Cuban rhythms with my late grandmother, a delighter in movement and a former clarinetist herself. Now closer to and further from them than ever, I think about their dreams, their musical lives, their senses of possibility and continuance.

I think about them as I consider a contemporary marked by an unequal distribution of fear—about resurgences of authoritarianism and fascism; the rise of surveillance capitalism and its attendant psychopolitics; a stultifying uptick in racial, misogynistic, and xenophobic violences; the existential bleakness of global pandemic—and, crucially, the movement for Black lives.[27] I think of them as I remember, sleepless, Arthur Jafa's 2013 film essay, *Dreams Are Colder Than Death*, which reflects on the unfathomable costs of US fantasizing and the legacy of Martin Luther King Jr. and his "I Have a Dream" speech.[28] I think of them as I recall the ways Jafa's film addresses the insistent anti-Blackness of this breathless nation-state, the viral caging and breaking of bodies at a spirit-crushing pace. I think of my grandparents and their generation as I return to poet-theorist Elizabeth Alexander's writing, and to a relational consideration of her question "Where is our dream space?"[29] Our abstract worldmaking haven? Our ionic zone in which the ostensibly hidden is revealed and refashioned, where intimate contradictions and layered dissonances announce new relations, where the everyday's boundaries begin to dissolve? I think of them, again, as I think of what music means for so many—a kind of collectively organized sound, a form of communal speculation, a means of negotiating difference, proximity, and potential.

My grandparents loved feeling music in motion, through dance, and I would like to think that in their movements together—hands leading hands, feet shifting in time, twirls and dips perfectly synced with musical rises and falls—there was some trace of a better world, an imminent togetherness. Tonight, as I think of them, I hear an echo of their faith somewhere deep within myself, and I begin to listen a little harder: for sounds, for stories, for dreams that "can convince us—in [their] brutal complexity, in [their] myriad contradictions, and [their] nuanced portraiture of love—that we, as human beings, long for meaning in our lives and that this longing ennobles us."[30]

For what, in the end, are these dreams if not longings?

notes

INTRODUCTION

1. Ellison, "Golden Age, Time Past," in *Collected Essays*, 241.
2. I borrow the term *audiobiography* from multi-instrumentalist Rahsaan Roland Kirk. For more on Kirk's work, see especially Josh Kun's discussion of it in *Audiotopia* (135). See also a related use of the term in Leal, "*Wild Tongue.*"
3. Here I follow Walton Muyumba's example in *The Shadow and the Act*.
4. For more on the perception of acceleration in and of history, see Koselleck, "Does History Accelerate?" See also Greif, *Age of the Crisis of Man*.
5. Exec. Order No. 9066, February 19, 1942, General Records of the United States Government, Record Group 11, National Archives. See also Mai Ngai's important remarks on war nationalism: "The nation-state at war generates nationalism of the highest order in order to mobilize its citizens to arms and sacrifice. . . . Drawn in stark terms and heavily dependent upon symbol and ritual, [war nationalism] resists complexity and nuance." Ngai, *Impossible Subjects*, 171.
6. Rasberry, *Race and the Totalitarian Century*, 32. See also Kaplan, "'Left Alone with America.'"
7. See especially Kun, *Audiotopia*, 29–47.
8. Ellison, "Golden Age, Time Past," in *Collected Essays*, 241.
9. Iyer, "Beneath Improvisation." The phrase "loose and dreamlike" comes from Baldwin, "Sonny's Blues," 126.
10. Iyer, "Beneath Improvisation."
11. Kun, *Audiotopia*, 13.
12. Le-Khac, *Giving Form*, 14.
13. Stewart, *Ordinary Affects*, 56.
14. See Daphne Brooks on related issues in her *Liner Notes for the Revolution* (425–26).
15. For an example of a dream ethnography, see Garcia, *Skins of Columbus*; as well as Wang, *Sunflower Cast a Spell*.
16. Z. Jackson, *Becoming Human*, 4.

17 E. Alexander, *Black Interior*, 4–5.
18 Kelley, *Freedom Dreams*, 8, 10.
19 Brooks, *Liner Notes for the Revolution*, 314.
20 Radano, *Lying Up a Nation*, 16.
21 Iyer, "What's Not Music."
22 I join a number of scholars in ethnomusicology and musicology in this regard. For work mapping the friction produced by "music" as an analytic category, see Wong, "Sound, Silence, Music."
23 For a history of relationships between continental philosophy and critical theory via dialectics, see A. Cole, *Birth of Theory*.
24 Lewis, "Improvised Music after 1950."
25 As Mark Greif puts it, "Re-enlightenment writers conceived the whole of Western history as, once again, a long progress, but one in which something has gone wrong; and behaved as if by running through the entire history of the mind, man, faith, or ideas of human nature, developmentally, they might find the flaw and figure out how to repair it" for lasting, universal benefit. Greif, *Age of the Crisis of Man*, 53; see also especially 22–24.
26 See Gilroy, *Black Atlantic*.
27 This contrasts with a Baudrillardian sense of the postmodern, which saw in juxtaposition and play the abandonment of meaning altogether. For more, see especially Hall and Grossberg, "On Postmodernism and Articulation"; and Jameson, *Postmodernism*, 151.
28 As activity, theory is speculation, hypothesis, suggestion, and modeling *within a medium*; it is content that, by definition, requires material-conceptual form to give it shape and significance. By suggesting that musicking offers both, I maintain alongside others that thought and articulation are not exclusive to the linguistic field. Articulating the content of musical thought linguistically, however, is a deeply complex translational process that, as with all translation, involves productive approximation, both loss and gain. For a remarkable (and in some ways contrasting) analysis of the relationship between the musical and the figurative in the context of Black musicking, specifically see Anthony Reed's *Soundworks*:

> The figurative tendencies . . . tend to be analogical (this aesthetic gesture is like a similar gesture in the physical world), metaphorical (the aesthetic gesture is symbolic action), allegorical (the ensemble models ideal sociality), metonymical (the aesthetic is juxtaposed with supposedly determining context), or some combination of these. Black sound, in these accounts, becomes an indicator of the radically emergent, a harbinger or emblem of utopian possibilities or at least the establishment of separate spaces for being and deliberating together. While I'm sympathetic to those ways of arguing (and inevitably argue that way myself at times), I practice listening as a historically grounded orientation toward the event with the understanding that no "pure" listening to music's "interior" aspects is possible because each—pitch, tonality, harmony, rhythm, duration, melody—already participates in a symbolic economy (3–4).

29 Quoted in Gillespie, *To Be, or Not . . . to Bop*, 142.
30 Iton, *In Search of the Black Fantastic*, 16.
31 Gilmore, *Golden Gulag*, 27.
32 There is no doubt: bebop's *speed*—its structural rapidities, affective urgencies, and unrelenting pace—marked it as a sprinter's music. The tradition maintained an asymptotic relationship to destruction, flirting with the possibility of spontaneous combustion, though never quite getting there. Perhaps this formal feature offered a template, a way in to some way out. As Toni Morrison puts it in *Home*, "After Hiroshima, the musicians understood as early as anyone that Truman's bomb changed everything and only scat and bebop could say how" (108).

Indeed, in addition to the activisms in and around bebop in the 1940s, also present was an antiatomic fever: a fear of a bomb that could easily be turned in any direction. As Vincent Intondi and Jacqueline Foertsch have written, the birth of atomic weaponry rippled through arts circles even before the start of the Cold War proper; songs like Dexter Gordon's "Bikini" (1947) and Clarence "Gatemouth" Brown's "Atomic Energy" (1949), notable for their mix of humor, threat, and sex, became emblematic of an apprehension over this exponential spike in state power. Somehow, the splitting of the atom coincided with the splitting of the long tone: the birth of bebop, in that sense, can be heard as a counterspell against annihilation. For more, see Foertsch, *Reckoning Day*, 205. See also Intondi, *African Americans against the Bomb*.
33 And unlike with word-driven political communication, what was conveyed via sound among musicking agents (listeners and sounders alike) wasn't direct, linear argumentation about the ideal reorganization of a society, nor cleanly transcribable manifestos, but instead sound-driven feelings and affects, *felt states* that refuse naming, a sense that new arguments and social arrangements were indeed possible, desirable, and necessary. James Gordon Williams reminds us, "Musical information—relative to performance, composition, and improvisation—is an open form of symbolism, and the interpretation of musical events depends on who is doing the work of analytical listening." J. Williams, *Crossing Bar Lines*, 11–12. So while midcentury Black musicians created Black musical space via improvisation, there were of course no fixed or essential meanings in the sounds they produced but rather a plurality of possible meanings, a wide set of potentialities for listeners and performers, an invitation to activate and extend those possibilities in unforeseen and urgent ways. Bebop, like many forms of musicking, didn't speak its oppositions literally—its solos and accompaniments were largely wordless; the primary practitioners were complex living beings with inconsistent and contradictory goals from performance to performance, moment to moment. As Williams again reminds us, "You cannot hear or see a hip chord voicing and say that that chord voicing is intersectionality" (99); instead, it offered a dense and radical soundworld that, in the postwar moment, proved a generative revelation. See also Leal, review of *Crossing Bar Lines*.
34 Gillespie, *To Be, or Not . . . to Bop*, 297.
35 Iyer, "Deft, Quiet Shout," 94.

36 Trouillot, *Silencing the Past*, 27; and White, *Metahistory*, 1–42.
37 Edwards, "Taste of the Archive," 961.
38 Clifford, "Among Histories," in *Returns*, 13–49.
39 Legitimating bodies often don't know what to do with people who cut across categories and experience local successes: they often don't easily fit a narrative or discourse that already has its leading figures in place, and they also don't necessarily demand any radical refashioning of a canon, no formation of a new discourse with its own gestures and hierarchies. This is an intellectual and political hindrance.
40 If *reading* for minorness in fiction involves attending to overlooked, subordinated details and then mapping the structures they index in narrative discourse and society, then *listening* for minorness involves much of the same: striving to hear the background, the scaffolding, and, at every turn, the web of relation. As drummer Kenny Washington once put it, "When you listen to jazz you have to go beneath the surface. . . . You have to go beneath all that and find out *why* the drummer is playing like he's playing." Quoted in Monson, *Saying Something*, 64. For work on minorness and narrative, see Woloch, *One vs. the Many*; Hong, *Minor Feelings*; and Hartman, *Wayward Lives, Beautiful Experiments*. See also James Gordon Williams's listening for musicians' breathing (and effectively his disruption of the Cartesian epistemologies still undergirding much musicological study) in *Crossing Bar Lines*.
41 Ben Ratliff, "The Sideman Moves out of History's Shadows," *New York Times*, April 5, 1998, https://www.nytimes.com/1998/04/05/theater/jazz-view-the-sideman-moves-out-of-history-s-shadows.html.
42 This is an iteration of what historian Marcus Rediker terms a "history from below": a type of history that would "explore the experiences and history-making power of working people who had long been left out of elite, 'top-down' historical narratives." Such histories, becoming steadily more common, involve telling "a big story within a little story"; for Rediker the "big story" has often been "the violent, terror-filled rise of capitalism and the many-sided resistance to it from below," including, for example, the "common sailor who mutinied and raised the black flag of piracy," the "runaway former slave who escaped the plantation for a Maroon community in a swamp," and the "enslaved African woman trapped in the bowels of a fetid slave ship." Here the big story is the violent global realignment of the postwar years, the types of resistances it generated from below, and the ways those ideas traveled and modulated through largely minor individuals. See Rediker, "Poetics of History from Below."
43 Nelson, *On Freedom*, 28.
44 Lepore, "Historians Who Love Too Much," 141.
45 Moya, *Social Imperative*, 32–34. See also Le-Khac, *Giving Form*, 56.
46 Butler, *Gender Trouble*, 140.
47 Wade, "Racialized Masculinity," 922.
48 Wynter, "Unsettling the Coloniality of Being," 260.
49 Baldwin, "Sonny's Blues," 104.

50 On this historiographical front, Vanessa Blais-Tremblay's work has been clarifying, particularly her arguments about how racialized masculinities shape the collection of oral histories, the analysis of data, and the presentation of findings. For more, see Blais-Tremblay, "'Where You Are Accepted, You Blossom.'"
51 Massey, *Space, Place, and Gender*, 179.
52 On coloniality and race, see Quijano and Wallerstein, "Americanity as a Concept"; and Mignolo, *Darker Side of Western Modernity*. On race and representation, see Fanon, *Black Skin, White Masks*; Hall, "Work of Representation"; and Said, *Orientalism*. On dynamic racial formations, see Omi and Winant, *Racial Formation in the United States*.
53 On the Asian American category and its related discourses, see Lowe, *Immigrant Acts*; and Chuh, *Imagine Otherwise*. On Mexican American/Chicano discourses, see R. Saldívar, *Chicano Narrative*; Varon, *Before Chicano*; and J. Saldívar, *Border Matters*. On mixed-race discourses, see Elam, *Souls of Mixed Folk*; and Roberts, *Resounding Afro Asia*.
54 While the visual field plays a crucial role in the racial imagination, race has never been an exclusively visual phenomenon. Rather, as Jennifer Stoever notes, "Aural and visual signifiers of race [have always been] thoroughly enmeshed; sounds never really lose their referent to different types of bodies despite being able to operate independently of them." Stoever, *Sonic Color Line*, 12. Because of this sonic connection, experiences and understandings of "music," that narrower (and in many ways constricting) category, are always mediated by existing conceptions of racialized bodies and their positions in nested hierarchies (local, more than local, etc.). Ronald Radano and Philip Bohlman make this case clearest in their expansive "Music and Race, Their Past, Their Presence," in which they argue in part that the racial imagination "not only informs perceptions of musical practice but is at once constituted within and projected into the social through sound." Radano and Bohlman, *Music and the Racial Imagination*, 5. Because racial ideas are circulated through social fields via music and musical experience (just as visual and textual representations are circulated, a phenomenon classic works like Toni Morrison's *Playing in the Dark* and Edward Said's *Orientalism* get to the heart of quickly), music "may provide one of the most powerful media for listening to and understanding what it is that racism continues to do on a global scale." Radano and Bohlman, *Music and the Racial Imagination*, 37.

For at least the past two decades, humanities scholars across a range of (inter)disciplines have worked from precisely this starting point (the present work included). Josh Kun, in developing his concept of the "audio-racial imagination," has argued across a broad range of material (and in a wide variety of media forms) that the histories of race and popular music in the United States have always been coconstitutive. Kun, *Audiotopia*. T. Carlis Roberts, in studies of the production of the Afro-Asian category in and with music, has in their work remained adeptly attuned to "the organization of sound into taxonomies based on racialized conceptions of bodies," a process they call "sono-racialization." Roberts, *Resounding*

Afro Asia, 4. Further, Stoever, using sound (not necessarily music) as an organizing unit, has theorized the concept of "the sonic color line," making clear that understandings and representations of race are much more multisensory, multimodal, and relational than is often assumed in frequently "oculocentric" critical discourses, as Jonathan Sterne puts it in *The Audible Past*. An increasing number of studies in the United States devoted to the triangulation (and permutations) of race, music, and literary arts have essentially this shared question in mind: How and why are "certain bodies expected to produce, desire, and live amongst particular sounds" over others? Stoever, *Sonic Color Line*, 7.

55 As Aníbal Quijano and Immanuel Wallerstein argue in their influential 1992 essay, "Americanity as a Concept, or the Americas in the Modern World-System"—and as Walter Mignolo expounds with a difference in *The Darker Side of Western Modernity*—the modern world-system was made possible precisely *because* of the Americas: the colonial encounter, the subsequent razing and subjugation of indigenous peoples and their knowledges, and the eventual instantiation of a new capitalist world-economy.

56 "Ontological plasticity" is from Z. Jackson, *Becoming Human*, 59.

57 Lipsitz, *Possessive Investment in Whiteness*, 3.

58 Lipsitz, *Possessive Investment in Whiteness*, 4.

59 Lipsitz et al., "Race as a Relational Theory," 23. See also Molina, "Understanding Race as a Relational Concept," 101–2; and Emirbayer, "Manifesto for a Relational Sociology." As Mustafa Emirbayer notes, "Sociologists today are faced with a fundamental dilemma: whether to conceive of the social world as consisting primarily in substances or in processes, in static 'things' or in dynamic, unfolding relations" (281).

60 Fanon, *Black Skin, White Masks*, 193. I am also reminded here of Gayatri Chakravorty Spivak's notion that the most revolutionary research gestures may be precisely those that prompt us "to recognize agency in others, not simply to comprehend otherness." See Spivak, "Teaching for the Times," 473.

61 Iyer, "Beneath Improvisation."

62 Diawara, "One World in Relation," 9; and Iyer, "Beneath Improvisation."

63 Redmond, *Everything Man*, 8.

64 Center for Jazz Studies, Columbia University, "double-time," Jazz Glossary, accessed September 1, 2021, https://ccnmtl.columbia.edu/projects/jazzglossary/d/doubletime.html.

65 Center for Jazz Studies, Columbia University, "double-time."

66 By focusing many of the "slower" narratives on improvisatory invention and (co)creation during recording sessions, I effectively frame the studio, per Fred Moten, as a site of study and practice (rather than solely a place of commodification, exploitation, and erasure); by constructing the "faster" narratives via (audio) biographical portraiture, music analysis, literary criticism, and cultural history, I work to show how these different analytic modalities can converge and reveal stories otherwise overlooked. And again, by braiding these two speeds together, by constructing a history in double time, I work to offer a sense of contrasts, to pro-

vide a feeling of multiscalar, multitemporal interrelation, to show how even the smallest musical gestures can have broad historical resonances. See Abdurraqib and Moten, "Building a Stairway."

67 Brooks, *Liner Notes for the Revolution*, 7.
68 Some early questions for this project included: Can the word *musician* name a literary sensibility? Can the word *writer* name a musical disposition?
69 Baldwin, "World I Never Made."
70 This interpretive sensibility draws on examples set in recent years by scholars in literary theory, musicology, ethnomusicology, American studies, performance studies, and art practice. Brent Hayes Edwards's and Daniel Albright's calls to "hear across media" in productively analogical ways (that is, beyond metaphorical suggestion); Ana María Ochoa Gautier's and Jennifer Stoever's examples of doing so with different sonic repertoires; Shannon Jackson's and Philip Auslander's insights on performance historiography; Georgina Born's work on musical mediation, creativity, and historical inquiry; Anna Schultz's historical ethnomusicological theories and examples, including her writing on the relationship between archival study and fieldwork; and Josh Kun's writing on music, encounter, and the audio-racial imagination have all guided my own dreaming across a number of discourses, media, and histories. So, too, has the work of artist-theorists including Michiko Theurer, Claire Chase, Matana Roberts, Esperanza Spalding, Tyshawn Sorey, Vijay Iyer, Kwami Coleman, Steven Feld, and George Lewis, whose intellectual work rigorously connects scholarly inquiry with music making.

See Edwards, "Hearing across Media," in *Epistrophies*, 253–67; Albright, *Panaesthetics*; Ochoa Gautier, *Aurality*; Stoever, *Sonic Color Line*; S. Jackson, "When 'Everything Counts'"; Auslander, "Performativity of Performance Documentation"; Born, "On Musical Mediation"; Schultz, "Music Ethnography and Recording Technology"; Iyer, "Exploding the Narrative"; Feld, introduction to *Jazz Cosmopolitanism in Accra*; and Lewis, "Improvised Music after 1950."

71 My efforts in this chapter are indebted to two earlier biographical writings on Araki: Satoko, *Suwingu Japan*; and Atkins, *Blue Nippon*, 180.
72 This includes a song Wing cowrote with Ella Fitzgerald, "I Wonder What Kind of Guy You'd Be," that slipped by J. Wilfred Johnson's authoritative *Ella Fitzgerald: An Annotated Discography*: "Research on this title reveals no information whatever, not even its authors" (236). See Fitzgerald, "I Wonder What Kind of a Guy You'd Be," Decca Records 28930, 1953, 7-inch single, 45 rpm.
73 Ellison, *Collected Essays*, 243.

CHAPTER 1. AFTER-HOURS

1 Many scholars over the past few decades have contributed significantly to such efforts. Ingrid Monson, in *Saying Something* (1996), combined ethnography, transcription, and historicization to highlight the importance of the rhythm

section in modern jazz combos, intervening in soloist-dominated jazz historical discourses and thus pursuing "a more cultural music theory and a more musical cultural theory" (3). Scott DeVeaux, in *The Birth of Bebop* (1997), blended music analysis, archival research, and social historicization to provide a deeply nuanced look at bebop's development, focusing on the specific contributions of a number of musicians to the style, including Coleman "Bean" Hawkins, Dizzy Gillespie, Charlie Parker, and Thelonious Monk. Eric Porter, in *What Is This Thing Called Jazz?* (2002), took a different methodological and reportorial approach, reading and listening to jazz musicians as intellectuals who articulated critical ecumenical visions and politics through music and, when possible, the media. Walton Muyumba, in *The Shadow and the Act* (2009), uncovered connections between midcentury Black American improvisatory aesthetics and American philosophical pragmatism through the sound-soaked writings of James Baldwin, Ralph Ellison, and Amiri Baraka. Brent Hayes Edwards, in *Epistrophies* (2017), explored the often orphic relationships between literary writing and jazz culture, examining jazz literary mythmaking and, in one chapter, the importance of Mary Lou Williams to bebop's histories. And Guthrie P. Ramsey Jr., in *The Amazing Bud Powell* (2013), extended important arguments he makes in *Race Music* (2003) about the Afromodernity of midcentury Black musical invention and reception by focusing on the life and music of bebop pianist Bud Powell and the alienating concept of musical genius.

Too, many of these works, as well as others including Nichole Rustin-Paschal and Sherrie Tucker's important edited volume, *Big Ears* (2008), and Rustin-Paschal's *The Kind of Man I Am* (2017), have underscored how gender, and specifically racialized masculinities, have been a central, though irregularly addressed, part of bebop's stories, both in the popular press and in scholarly work. As Porter writes, once their new music left the Harlem underground, "beboppers quickly became seen by black and nonblack observers alike as symbols of a serious, politicized, and sometimes pathological black male creativity," ultimately marking "the emergence of the figure of the modern black jazzman as a defiant, alternative, and often exotic symbol of masculinity, an image that is common in postwar American arts and letters." E. Porter, *What Is This Thing?*, 79. Central to that exoticism was, as Ramsey notes, a sense that young, Black, predominantly male jazz musicians striving for a new idiom under American racial democracy posed "sexual threats to white superiority," for bebop was "a style that challenged many assumptions about black male creativity and the power of pop and mass culture in the making of 'art.'" Ramsey, *Amazing Bud Powell*, 130. So, too, was it a sonic arena, as Richard Brent Turner has argued, with the "potential to construct redemptive iterations of black masculine identities through critical reflection, new sounds, discipline, study, creativity, and self-improvement." Turner, *Soundtrack to Movement*, 83. To listen to recordings of it today, with the patience called for by its structures, is, in my view, to hear in its shimmers a working through of countermodern Black masculinities in the context of midcentury nationalist fervor. To listen with big ears, that is, is "to situate specific ideologies of musicality, masculinity, femininity, tonality, and 'the popular' in terms that are historically and socially specific to jazz in general and have some resonance with cultural values in American musical communities particularly." Ramsey, *Amazing Bud Powell*, 141.

These recent studies, in concert with foundational ones like Amiri Baraka's *Blues People* (1963), highlight the importance of bebop in the broader cultural history of the United States as well as the ever-shifting present tense of historical study. "History is not the passive imprint of the past," DeVeaux reminds us, "but an active search for meaning, a creative reading of the past to suit the needs of the present." DeVeaux, *Birth of Bebop*, 443. That creative reading might lead us back to a still-resonant (if condemning) passage from Ellison's classic essay on Minton's, "The Golden Age, Time Past": "Of those who came to Minton's . . . no one retained more than a fragment of its happening. Afterward the very effort to put the fragments together transformed them—so that in place of true memory they now summon to mind pieces of legend." Ellison, *Collected Essays*, 437. Piecing these fragments together today, listening almost a century after these musical experiments were conducted, for me means hearing improvisatory navigations of localized difference and constraint, hearing how an interplay of race, gender, and nation shaped an underground's broken rhythms.

2 Key to my thinking in this chapter are personal interviews I conducted with musicians and historians, as well as archival research pursued at the Institute of Jazz Studies at Rutgers University in Newark and Stanford University. Through these materials and more, my aim is to recover some of bebop musicians' reach in the postwar years, to listen for what their intimate dreaming inspired.

3 E. Porter, *What Is This Thing?*, 57.

4 For more, see DeVeaux, *Birth of Bebop*, especially 1–31.

5 An added bonus of this shift from the bass to the cymbals was a frequency change: the mid- and lower frequencies of the bass drum were freed up for more of the time, allowing other instrumentalists, particularly bassists, to explore that space more freely.

6 Gillespie, *To Be, or Not . . . to Bop*, 140.

7 Gillespie, *To Be, or Not . . . to Bop*, 140.

8 Gillespie, *To Be, or Not . . . to Bop*, 141.

9 E. Porter, *What Is This Thing?*, 54.

10 Giddins, *Celebrating Bird*, 46.

11 Muyumba, *Shadow and the Act*, 26. See also Borge, *Tropical Riffs*, 131–61.

12 Quoted in Shapiro and Hentoff, *Hear Me Talkin' to Ya*, 350.

13 Reed, *Soundworks*, 75.

14 Radano, *Lying Up a Nation*, 100.

15 Here I'm referencing Houston Baker's notable phrase, which Ronald Radano later elaborated in relation to critical, speculative methods in the historical study of Black musics. See Baker, "Dream of American Form," in *Blues, Ideology, and Afro-American Literature*, 113–99; and Radano, *Lying Up a Nation*, 304.

16 Peterson, "Sound Work."
17 DeVeaux, *Birth of Bebop*, 251.
18 E. Porter, *What Is This Thing?*, 85.
19 See Gilroy, *Against Race*, 308. See also Lott, "Double V, Double-Time."
20 Macías, *Mexican American Mojo*, 67.
21 Alvarez, *Power of the Zoot*, 16.
22 Alvarez, *Power of the Zoot*, 4–5.
23 Alvarez, *Power of the Zoot*, 85, 12.
24 R. Porter, *There and Back*, 67.
25 Greif, *Age of the Crisis of Man*, 61–63.
26 "Salt Peanuts," a reworking of George and Ira Gershwin's "I Got Rhythm," was recorded on January 9, 1945, for the Manor label; Gillespie was accompanied by Don Byas (tenor), Trummy Young (trombone), Clyde Hart (piano), Oscar Pettiford (bass), and Irv Kluger (drums).
27 "Ko-Ko" was recorded on November 26, 1945, for the Savoy label; Parker was accompanied during that session by a young Miles Davis (trumpet), Dizzy Gillespie (trumpet, piano), Sadik Hakim (Argonne Thornton) (piano), Curley Russell (bass), and Max Roach (drums).
28 Meanwhile, as Marc Myers notes, major labels including "RCA, Columbia, and Decca, plus Capitol on the West Coast, largely ignored bebop . . . viewing it as quirky and unsellable to postwar audiences that clung nostalgically to swing instrumentals and vocals." Myers, *Why Jazz Happened*, 32.
29 As one writer in *Metronome* put it, the publication championed those "musicians who stand for the most emphatic experimentation, for the most courageous investigations of new sounds, for musical daring and integrity." "Jazz Looks Ahead," *Metronome*, October 1945, 10. For an excellent survey of the critical reception of bebop in the New York jazz press, see Gendron, "Short Stay in the Sun."
30 The musicians' own memories of the early days of this Black altermodernist praxis are, as Ingrid Monson once wrote, "singularly devoid of the sensationalism found in the popular press, which tended to stress the fashion, language, and substance abuse associated with bebop. Instead the conviviality and environment of musical exploration are recalled." Monson, "Problem with White Hipness," 409. This gap between the facts and feelings of lived experience and the representations of Harlem's underground sounds in the media is one that writers and scholars have for decades worked to redress.
31 Baraka, "Swing from Verb to Noun," in *Blues People*, 142–65.
32 Mackey, "Other," 52.
33 Mackey, "Other," 52.
34 Reed, *Soundworks*, 18.
35 Quoted in Gillespie, *To Be, or Not . . . to Bop*, 149–50.
36 Gillespie, *To Be, or Not . . . to Bop*, 279.
37 Quoted in Shapiro and Hentoff, *Hear Me Talkin' to Ya*, 350.
38 Ramsey, *Amazing Bud Powell*, 8.

39 Abdul-Jabbar, "I Hear," 1.
40 Duersten, "When Charlie Parker Came to L.A."
41 Quoted in "The Bebop Feud," *Metronome*, April 1944, 44.
42 Gillespie, *To Be, or Not . . . to Bop*, 279.
43 "Be-Bop Be-bopped," *Time*, March 25, 1946, 52. As Bernard Gendron notes, it's interesting that this *Time* article drew primarily on California musicians, including pianist Harry Gibson and guitarist Slim Gaillard, whose work and scenes were distinct from those of the New Yorkers. See Gendron, "Short Stay in the Sun," 140–41.
44 Quoted in Shapiro and Hentoff, *Hear Me Talkin' to Ya*, 397.
45 Monson, "Problem with White Hipness," 414.
46 Kun, *Audiotopia*, 34.
47 See, too, Shipton, *Art of Jazz*, 124.
48 Barry Ulanov, "Band Reviews: Dizzy Gillespie," *Metronome*, November 1947, 22.
49 Gillespie, *To Be, or Not . . . to Bop*, 314.
50 Ellison, *Collected Essays*, 241.
51 Jackson, *Becoming Human*.
52 As Eric Lott notes, bebop was one of the "great modernisms": a project of critical effort and intentional refashioning that related to "earlier styles" via a mixture of demonstrable appreciation and "calculated hostility." "The social position of this modernism," Lott continues, "distanced from both the black middle class and the white consensus . . . gave aesthetic self-assertion political force and value." Lott, "Double V, Double-Time," 602. And it was, of course, not the only jazz modernism. As Gendron notes, "Faced with a bebop movement dominated by African-American musicians, the virtually all-white jazz journals seemed always to be in search of 'great white hopes'—white modernists, like Tristano and Kenton, with whom a mostly white readership would feel more at home. There may indeed have been a racial code operating in the white critics' expressed desire for a more cerebral and European modern jazz, as well as a jazz purified of any association with life-styles, argots, or dress." Gendron, "Short Stay in the Sun," 147.
53 Bebop's stylistic mechanics and complexity, combined with the fact that its inventors were primarily Black men (with important exceptions, including Mary Lou Williams), made it all too easy for white male listeners as well as more conservative, upwardly mobile African Americans to dismiss it as "noise"—unwanted sound by unwanted people. By extension, it was easy, before bebop became profitable (and, later, in its seeming decline), to suggest that the music was somehow either anti- or pseudointellectual.

Concerning noise, I'm relying especially on Mary Douglas's notion of dirt as "matter out of place": undesired material that implies "a set of ordered relations and a contravention of that order. . . . Where there is dirt there is system. Dirt is the by-product of systematic ordering and classification of matter, in so far as ordering involves rejecting inappropriate elements. This idea of dirt takes us straight

into the field of symbolism and promises a link-up with more obviously symbolic systems of purity." Douglas, *Purity and Danger*, 44. See also Attali, *Noise*.
54 L. Jones, *Blues People*, 188; Bruce, *How to Go Mad*, 12.
55 Quoted in Giddins, *Celebrating Bird*, 15.
56 Smith, "Gatekeepers."
57 Bruce, *How to Go Mad*, 6.
58 Gendron, "Short Stay in the Sun," 154–57.
59 Dave Dexter, quoted in Barry Ulanov, "Who's Dead, Bebop or Its Detractors?," *Metronome*, June 1947, 50.
60 Edward Said's influential essay "Traveling Theory"—and James Clifford's helpful complication of it in "Notes on Travel and Theory"—comes to mind here.
61 See Wilson, "'He Was a Force.'"
62 See especially Amezcua, "On the Outer Rim of Jazz."
63 See Kun and Madrid, "Exceptional Matters, Exceptional Times."
64 See Armbruster, *Before Seattle Rocked*, 167–68.
65 See Denning, *Noise Uprising*.
66 Kaldewey, *People's Music*, 59.
67 E. Porter, *What Is This Thing?*, 56. See also Stowe, *Swing Changes*, 230–33, 239, 243–44.
68 Gillespie, *To Be, or Not . . . to Bop*, 302.
69 See George Yoshida, interview by Alice Ito and John Pai, Seattle, February 18, 2002, Densho ıt: denshovh-ygeorge-01-0035, Densho Visual History Collection, Digital Archive, Densho Archives. See also Atkins, *Blue Nippon*.
70 Raúl R. Salinas Papers, Stanford Special Collections, M774 Box 1, Folder 11, Salinas, "Music for the Masses."
71 Alvarez, *Power of the Zoot*, 144.
72 Henry Luce, "The American Century," *Life Magazine*, February 17, 1941, 61–65. See also Fredric Jameson's *Postmodernism*: "Non-North American readers will inevitably deplore the Americanocentrism of my own particular account, which is justified only to the degree that it was the brief 'American century' (1945–1973) that constituted the hothouse, or forcing ground, of the new system, while the development of the cultural forms of postmodernism may be said to be the first specifically North American global style" (xx).
73 For more on Paredes during these years, see especially R. Saldívar, *Borderlands of Culture*, 344–94; and J. Saldívar, "Outernational Origins of Chicano/a Literature."
74 The same was true for the Black servicemen Araki traveled with and performed for in those years (mostly in Yokohama, as Jim Crow–style segregation was in effect in occupied Japan, and most Black servicemen were stationed in Yokohama) as well as for the Japanese musicians Araki befriended. All were dealing with a similar question that had become newly estranging in the postwar moment, and particularly on Japanese land not far from the hellish birthplace of nuclear sublimity: What is democracy? For more on this, particularly the question itself, see

Ramón Saldívar's thoughts on Américo Paredes's postwar journalism in *Borderlands of Culture*.
75 See especially Von Eschen, *Satchmo Blows Up the World*. See also Muyumba, *Shadow and the Act*, 34–35.
76 Muyumba, *Shadow and the Act*, 34–35.
77 Such efforts emerged, as Vaughn Rasberry notes, in part because the world-stage facade of idyllic American democracy had been visibly cracked by Jim Crow segregation and racial strife. See Rasberry, *Race and the Totalitarian Century*.
78 Jameson, *Postmodernism*, xx.
79 L. Jones (Amiri Baraka), *Blues People*, 210.
80 This was not necessarily the same concern as some of the re-enlightenment views of historical recovery that sought to comb back through the intellectual transformations of the preceding centuries to discover at what point people had gone wrong—nor was it, as with the Frankfurt school's Max Horkheimer and Theodor Adorno, a totalizing critique of progress itself as history's own undoing—but instead a very real, palpable, experience-based fear of losing parts of one's cultural memory through state ideological and martial power, losing one's world through internment and stripped rights, through the atomic annihilation of cities one's very ancestors may have resided in. For more, see Greif, *Age of the Crisis of Man*.
81 Shortly before his death in 1991, Araki was awarded the Order of the Rising Sun, 4th Class, by the Japanese government "in recognition of his contributions as an author and translator of Japanese literature as well as in the field of jazz in Japan." "Death Notices," *Los Angeles Times*, January 6, 1992. The obituary also notes, "Professor Araki was born in Salt Lake City and was a veteran of World War II and the Korean War. After receiving his BA from UCLA and his MA and Ph.D. from UC Berkeley, he taught at UCLA and in 1965 joined the University of Hawaii faculty as Professor of Japanese Literature, retiring in 1988. He was also a professional musician with various recordings in Japan and with the Lionel Hampton Big Band."
82 Brodsky, *From 1989*, 20.
83 E. Alexander, *Black Interior*, 4–5; and Radano, *Lying Up a Nation*, 230.
84 Saul, *Freedom Is, Freedom Ain't*, xiii–xiv.

CHAPTER 2. LAYERED TIME

1 Araki's "Day Dream" is a version of Duke Ellington, Billy Strayhorn, and John La Touche's "Daydream." Tenor saxophonist Johnny Hodges recorded a version of it in 1940; the tune became a standard in the 1940s and was eventually recorded by musicians including Sarah Vaughan, Ella Fitzgerald, Charles Mingus, Toshiko Akiyoshi, Rashaan Roland Kirk, Max Roach, Spaulding Giddens, and others.
2 Nelson, *On Freedom*, 28; and Faulkner, *Requiem for a Nun*, 73.
3 Elizabeth Alexander, *Black Interior*, 5.

4   Fellezs, "Silenced but Not Silent," 72–73.
5   Fujita and Yoshida, liner notes in Jimmy Araki Trio, *Jazz Beat: Midnight Jazz Session, Nippon Victor JV-5006, 1959*, LP.
6   Stanyek and Piekut, "Deadness," 21.
7   Leal, "Decorating Time with Tyshawn Sorey."
8   Fujita and Yoshida, liner notes in Jimmy Araki Trio, *Jazz Beat: Midnight Jazz Session*.
9   When I look closely at *Midnight Jazz Session*'s album cover, I find that its visual composition evokes the music's formal quirks and recording processes. Split into four rectangular areas, the image is a tableau of times that draws the eye toward strong vertical and horizontal layers, toward some of the many different moments arranged into this piece of relational, overdubbed studio art. The topmost layer, larger than the rest, features three contrasting photos of Araki playing saxophone, each manipulated slightly; below that is a photo of drummer Kawaguchi, his right stick in midair; below that, one of bassist Ono, his fingers curled around the neck of his instrument; and below that, another shot of Araki, seated at a piano, smiling over his shoulder, his visage forming the base of a vertical pillar of gazes and actions. Together, these shots, perhaps staged, perhaps not, form a temporal tapestry, just like the music the cover introduces.
10 "The Sheik of Araby," recorded by Sidney Bechet's One Man Band in 1941 without the use of multitrack technology, was the first overdubbed jazz record, and the American Federation of Musicians, "outraged," "banned overdubbing for years." "As for multitrack recording, it was invented by a jazz musician, Les Paul, whose most famous overdubbed recording was his absolutely wild 1947 'Lover,' featuring eight guitars recorded at various speeds." As Yuval Taylor relays, Lennie Tristano's "Line Up" (1955) is another example:

> Miles Davis's 1957 masterpiece *Miles Ahead* relied extensively on overdubs. There's the ebullient "I Don't Wanna Be Kissed (by Anyone but You)." As Loren Shoenberg explains, "During the taping of the orchestral track for 'I Don't Wanna Be Kissed,' Davis unexpectedly played a few random portions of his solo. Months later at the overdub session, he had to tailor new passages to lead in and out of what he had already played on the prerecorded track. During five attempts, Davis used a variety of rhetorical devices (many borrowed from his mentor, Lester Young) to solve a musical problem." In other words, the Miles Davis playing you hear was stitched together from six different takes, five of which were overdubs.

Quotations are from Taylor, "Does the Overdub Undercut Jazz?" See also Sasha Geffen's excellent work on contemporary overdubbing practices, including "Glitching the Gendered Voice."
11 As Barry Ulanov said of the tune in the album's liner notes, "The times will probably be as hard for the listener to follow as they were at various times for drummers: one track proceeds from 7/8 to 7/4, another from 5/8 to 5/4, the last from 3/8 to 4/4." "But one need not attempt to sort out the arithmetical delicacies,"

Ulanov adds somewhat apologetically, "to feel the exhilaration produced by the rhythmic point and counterpoint." Ulanov, liner notes in Lennie Tristano, *Lennie Tristano*, Atlantic Records 1224, 1955, LP.

12   Ulanov, liner notes in Lennie Tristano, *Lennie Tristano*.
13   Ulanov, liner notes in Lennie Tristano, *Lennie Tristano*.
14   Bill Evans, "A Statement," liner notes for *Conversations with Myself*, by Bill Evans, Verve Records V6-8526, 1963, LP.
15   Yoshida, *Reminiscing in Swingtime*, 114–15.
16   Lewis, "Too Many Notes," 37.
17   J. Williams, *Crossing Bar Lines*, 58.
18   Campbell, "Beautiful, Shining Sound Object," 123.
19   J. Williams, *Crossing Bar Lines*, 58.
20   James Araki, interview by Dr. George Akita, June 15, 1981, Oral Histories of Japanese Studies Scholars, 1960s–1980s, Special Collections, University of Hawaii at Manoa.
21   Weglyn, *Years of Infamy*, 281.
22   In *Jim and Jap Crow*, scholar Matthew Briones synthesizes over 100,000 pages of Charles Kikuchi's diaries into a unique cultural history and individual biography. This short section on the internment period is inspired by the example his work sets. See Briones, *Jim and Jap Crow*, 2.
23   Briones, *Jim and Jap Crow*, 3.
24   Dewitt, *Final Report* (emphasis added).
25   Chuh, *Imagine Otherwise*, 64.
26   Weglyn, *Years of Infamy*, 281.
27   Satoko, *Suwingu Japan*, 32.
28   Leong, "Gila River."
29   Araki, precocious, was often featured in the newsletter. See "Seven Graduate from Butte Hi," *Gila News-Courier*, February 3, 1944, 3 ("Seven seniors, among them Jim Araki, past president of the associated student body, have been listed as winter graduates of the Butte high school"); "High School Prom to Honor Seniors," *Gila News-Courier*, May 27, 1943, 5; and "Butte Elects School Officers: Araki Is President," *Gila News-Courier*, June 22, 1943, 4. For more on this publication's history, see Wakida, "*Gila News-Courier*."
30   J. Araki, interview by George Akita.
31   Dale Araki, interview by Jonathan Leal, September 24, 2020.
32   J. Araki, interview by George Akita.
33   Robertson, "Ballad for Incarcerated Americans," 287. See also Waseda, "Extraordinary Circumstances, Exceptional Practices."
34   Kajikawa, "Sound of Struggle," 192.
35   J. Araki, interview by George Akita. Too, as indicated in a 1944 issue of the *Gila News-Courier*: "Thirty-three telegrams were received by Gilans informing them that they are to go on active duty in the service of the United States Army effective June 7. The telegrams read: 'Active duty orders effective seventh June 1944

being mailed direct you comply end SPRPE.' Preparations are being made by the USO in Butte to hold a farewell dance for the inductees. They are meeting tonight to make final plans. The men who received their notices [include] . . . Jim Tomamasa Araki." "Thirty Three Gilans Will Go on Active Duty June 7," *Gila News-Courier*, June 1, 1944.

36   MISLS Registry, 1941–1946, compiled by Seiki Oshiro, Paul Tani, and Grant Ichikawa, James T. Araki. Class / Year: Snel44-09; Army Serial Number: 30117173.

37   "At Fort Snelling, there were a bunch of musicians, and we decided on organizing a dance band," Araki says. "I played the lead alto sax. We rehearsed and rehearsed, and then began playing dances at the field house. Eventually, it expanded and I became the leader. By then, I was an instructor and we had a 17-piece dance band. It was a mammoth group for those days: five saxes, five trumpets, four trombones, piano, guitar, bass, drums, and a vocalist." J. Araki, interview by George Akita.

Too, George Yoshida, a Japanese American cultural historian and Araki's friend, recalled of that time: "I recall seeing him practicing the piano, all alone, on the huge stage of the Ft. Snelling Field House back in 1945. (He was probably memorizing chord changes to an Ellington tune.) Nobi Nakamura, while stationed at Ft. Snelling, wandered into a recreation room one night where a jukebox was blasting out a swinging jazz tune. To Nakamura's great surprise, he discovered a young Nisei cat comping on the piano—accompanying, with great energy and skill, the jazz streaming from the jukebox. It was Jim Araki. Nakamura couldn't believe his ears." Yoshida, *Reminiscing in Swingtime*, 208. See also "Pictorial Review of the MISLS," *Yaban Gogai*, December 1945, 9.

38   At that point, bebop recordings were relatively hard to come by; owing to an overlap in the development of the music and the musicians' union ban on new recordings from 1942 to 1944, bebop musicians like Charlie Parker, Dizzy Gillespie, and others were largely unable to record and distribute their work until 1945. To know bop in the early to mid-1940s, then, was to have experienced the work live or heard of it by word of mouth. That Araki experienced both at just the right moment is notable in its own right: a stroke of luck cast in the evolving "cult," as Eric Lott famously put it, "of smack and the sixteenth note." Lott, "Double V, Double-Time," 603. See also "One Year of the Record Ban," *The Billboard Music Yearbook: 1943*; as well as Peterson, "Sound Work."

39   Geffen, *Glitter Up the Dark*, 15. Just a few months later, that same year, Araki's older brother, David, wrote a difficult letter to Edward J. Ennis in Washington, DC: "I admit I made a mistake in renouncing my citizenship," David Araki writes.

> Ever since the start of this war I've been kicked around. . . . I had just finished paying for my furniture, frigidaire, and car. Had just gotten promoted to the position of salesman at the wholesale produce company where I was employed. Everything was going as well as could be expected when orders came for evacuation. I was forced to sell all of our belongings, that I had worked so hard to pay for, at a third of their worth. . . . We were then thrown into an

internment camp like we were dangerous enemies.... On top of all that, our room was a stinking horse-stall at Santa Anita Assembly Center.... To think that my own people did this to me.... As far back as I could remember, from grammar school days, I had pledged my allegiance to the flag of the United States of America, and I meant and believed every word of it.... I'm very anxious to relocate with my family to Salt Lake City, Utah ... I'll do anything you suggest to get my citizenship back. (David Araki to Edward J. Ennis, Director, US Department of Justice, Alien Enemy Control Unity, Washington, DC, August 13, 1945, "Copies of correspondence, from renunciants to Edward J. Ennis, Ernest Besig, and others, notes," Bancroft MSS 67/14 c., folder R 9.05, Bancroft Library, University of California, Berkeley)

Writing this after having been sent to the notorious Tule Lake camp after answering "no" to questions 27 and 28 on the infamous loyalty questionnaire, David Araki was grappling with the realities of state power and foreclosed possibilities; his younger brother, meanwhile, was confronting that same state power, albeit from a very different angle: as a translator for the very armed forces that his older brother had earlier renounced. As Nisei, both brothers were thinking through what it meant to be othered men, provisional citizens; both brothers were seeking models to understand that marking and to navigate their relationships to a flag that, as James Baldwin once put it, "had pledged no allegiance to [them]." See Baldwin, "Price of the Ticket," in *Collected Essays*, 836.

40 J. Araki, interview by George Akita.
41 Atkins, *Blue Nippon*, 172.
42 Atkins, *Blue Nippon*, 172.
43 Atkins, *Blue Nippon*, 177.
44 Baldwin, "Price of the Ticket," in *Collected Essays*, 836.
45 Atkins, *Blue Nippon*, 171.
46 Or, restated: to hear jazz as possessing positive potential is to already occupy a certain position in social space; to hear it as imposing is to live in a different position. It is important to keep this tension alive—that jazz was not a completely benevolent sonic presence in Japan, nor was it simply the soundtrack to a new imperialism: jazz was iridescent on those Japanese shores, making Américo Paredes's oblique criticisms of swing's popularity in Tokyo all the more intriguing. For more, see R. Saldívar's discussion of Paredes's postwar journalism in *Borderlands of Culture*, 344–94.
47 To my ear, "A.P.O. 500" makes sense as an "address" in two senses of the word: at once a physical location for GHQ (General Headquarters) and an act of communication. (Araki presumably arranged it after clocking out of his army job at the Allied Translator and Interpreter Section [ATIS] NYK Building: Second Floor, Interpretation and Translation Division, G2.) The tune, quirky and light, is also part of an important story about the local musical ecosystem. As Araki put it, "After the war ... there was a specific function that I performed. Jazz could not be recorded in postwar Japan because the Japanese were not allowed to record

copyrighted American tunes. They needed originals. My friends wanted to record with Japan Victor. I would say, of the first seven or eight, or ten jazz records that were issued after the war, all of them are my compositions and arrangements."

Some of these efforts remain preserved in recordings of the Victor Hot Club's other Araki-arranged works: "The Tokyo Riff," a cheery, mischievous tune tapping into what Hiromu Nagahara identifies as a bundle of sonic Tokyo interpellations in *Tokyo Boogie-Woogie*; "In the Melancholy Mood," an arrangement evocative of Duke Ellington's 1935 work "In a Sentimental Mood"; "Loch Lomond," a version of a Scottish folk song popularized in 1937 by singer Maxine Sullivan; and "Night in Pakistan," an original that, like the others, features Araki's talents as a soloist and arranger (too: "East Side Boogie" and "Serenade to a Morning Star" by Jimmy's Trio, featuring Araki on piano; and "Swing in Orange," which Araki composed for musician Hiroshi Watanabe). And Araki's midnight oil was well spent: as documented by George Yoshida, Araki "managed to convey the most current jazz concepts and techniques to native Japanese musicians." In effect, he earned a reputation as "the great alto sax player who first introduced bebop to Japan," as a talented serviceman fondly remembered by Japanese jazz heavyweights like Toshiko Akiyoshi who, before embarking on successful careers in Japan and the United States, played with Araki in groups like the Victor Hot Club.

Araki's work with the Victor Hot Club as well as with other performing outfits like Hiromi Watanabe's Ensemble announced a young talent's musical acumen and sensibilities to a country in flux. As with the work of other servicemen like Sergeants Isaac K. Joseph and David Stacey, who participated in the Japanese arts scene via Tokyo's Ernie Pyle Theater, Araki's works were widely consumed, "leading," as Yoshida relays, "the jukebox parade in Tokyo." This consumption, while also catalyzed by the "occupational overtones" of the US armed forces' radio stations, like WVTR, highlights Araki's unusual musical and instrumental fluencies. By the end of his four-year stay in Japan, playing with musicians in Tokyo and Yokohama, taking important translation assignments, getting his bearings in a home in which he was at once an insider and an outsider, he'd been a performing musician for less than a decade.

See J. Araki, interview by George Akita; various artists, *Jazz in Japan: 1947–1963*, Victor Japan 60722, 2001, 7 CDs (many thanks to percussionist Kenji Okubo for sending me a copy of this out-of-print box set all the way from Higashinada); Yoshida, *Reminiscing in Swingtime*, 114; A. Paredes, *Pacific Stars and Stripes*, March 24, 1946; A. Paredes, *Pacific Stars and Stripes*, May 26, 1946; and Mas Manbo, "He Blows High . . . He Blows Low," *Nippon Times Magazine*, March 4, 1948. For more details on Akiyoshi's and Araki's experiences in the Ichiban Octet in 1948, consult Toshiko Akiyoshi and Anthony Brown, interview, June 29, 2008, Archives Center, National Museum of American History, Smithsonian Institution, transcript, 18–23. For more on music in postwar Japan, see Dower, *Embracing Defeat*; and Nagahara, *Tokyo Boogie-Woogie*.

48 Yoshida, *Reminiscing in Swingtime*, 114.

49 J. Araki, interview by George Akita.
50 Araki composed and recorded "East Side Boogie" and "Serenade to a Morning Star" with Jimmy's Trio as well as "Pastime in Pastels" and "Jimmy's Bop" with Victor Gay Bop.
51 These performers include J. Beesmer on trumpet, J. Araki on alto sax, Y. Atsumo on tenor sax, R. Conde on alto sax, J. Baker on piano, T. Tsunoda on guitar, H. Lewelle on bass, and G. Kawaguchi on drums. Victor Gay Bop, "Jimmy's Bop," Victor (JPN) V-40265A, 1949.
52 Ramsey, *Amazing Bud Powell*, 55.
53 On a pragmatic level, this is functional; it makes sense that an improvising musician and blues aficionado, particularly one performing at quick speeds, would outline chord changes through arpeggios and seek tonal possibility through chromatic ascension and descension. Yet on a more affective level, the oscillation between arpeggiation and chromatic lines is also a focus on space and directionality: both improvisatory, musical gestures sketch available tonal and technological space by moving upward and downward through the alto sax's register.
54 Muyumba, *Shadow and the Act*, 26.
55 "He said it was a war for volition and against the commodification of sadness." Plascencia, *People of Paper*, 53.
56 Atkins, "Localizing Jazz and Globalizing Identities," 6–7 (emphasis added).
57 I'm thinking here of a piece entitled "The Dance Hall." See "The Dance Hall," 1946, Benson Latin American Collections, Américo Paredes Papers, box 4, folder 6, University of Texas at Austin (the authorship is ambiguous, though most likely Horst Delacroix was the author).
58 See "The Dance Hall."
59 As with Mexican American intellectual Américo Paredes, it also happened that he did so while wearing a US Army uniform in Occupation-era Japan—significant, considering the Allied Occupation's pivotal role in defining Japanese music and popular culture "well into the 1990s." See also Matsue, *Music in Contemporary Japan*, 47.
60 "To articulate the past historically does not mean to recognize it 'the way it really was' (Ranke). It means to seize hold of a memory as it flashes up at a moment of danger." Benjamin, *Illuminations*, 255.
61 Haraway, *When Species Meet*, 88.
62 "I've got a child," said Charlie Parker in August 1950, "and I don't want that child to die. I would like to take the plans of the H and A bombs and make sure they were destroyed. The power to decide whether humanity is destroyed or lives lies in the hands of the people—all of the people—not the political few." That same year, Parker, teaming up with legendary arranger Chico O'Farrill, cut *The Afro-Cuban Jazz Suite*, one expression among many that's not only contemporaneous with his antinuclear stance and emblematic of bop's transnational roots and routes in the Caribbean but also representative of the urgency of response and invention among those we might now identify, following literary critic Steven Lee, as part of

an ethnic American avant-garde. For more on this, see Lee, *Ethnic Avant-Garde*. For Parker's remarks, see Intondi, *African Americans against the Bomb*, 33.

63 Gilroy, *Small Acts*, 141.
64 Solis, "Black Pacific." The term "Black Pacific" has in recent years grown in popularity; a variety of scholars have used it to explain, as Heather Smyth summarizes brilliantly, "the unexpected cultural connections and commitments we can witness when diasporas grow in their respective locations." Smyth, in a manner resonant with Solis, uses it "to indicate black diasporic culture that is shaped by a Pacific location such that it looks not just East in the imagination to Africa—across the Atlantic and the Middle Passage—but also West to Asia and the Pacific rim, and is shaped by the geography of the Pacific as well as the confluence, friction, and sometimes coalition of African, Asian, South Asian, First Nations, and European cultures in British Columbia." Smyth, "Black Atlantic Meets the Black Pacific," 390. Smyth offers a fairly comprehensive review of Black Pacific scholarship.
65 Wong, *Speak It Louder*, 162.
66 Wong, *Speak It Louder*, 162.
67 Coleman, "Dozens."
68 Dyer, *But Beautiful*.
69 Also notable is a tune on the record entitled "Blues for Bach." On a first listen, a listener might notice some surface similarities between Araki's "Blues for Bach" and the third-stream releases of the Modern Jazz Quartet in the 1950s. (The Modern Jazz Quartet did, after all, release a record called *Blues on Bach*.) Yet the more apt comparison would instead be to bebop pianist Bud Powell, who in 1957 recorded his own Bach-inspired jazz tune: a striking work entitled "Bud on Bach." Powell's tune—a blues grounded in a breakneck rendition of C. P. E. Bach's "Solfeggietto"—demonstrates a nuanced desire "to signif(y) on the classical tradition," as Ramsey puts it. "To play in the 'musical dark,'" "to stomp some pop"—not just to perform "musical mastery," but also to "creatively lay claim to a complex social identity." Ramsey, *Amazing Bud Powell*, 86. That Araki's version has more in common, structurally and energetically, with Powell's version than the Modern Jazz Quartet's efforts speaks not only of his admiration of Powell's musical insight—"My Dad always kept up with the latest trends in music," Araki's son, Dale, told me—but also of his own experiences, layers, and identities. D. Araki, interview by Jonathan Leal. For Powell, signif(y)ing on the classical tradition at once meant refuting dehumanizing, anti-Black cosmologies; for Araki, improvising out of the space between Japanese and American experiences, Black signif(y)ing radical imaginations and postwar, postinternment Nisei identities, live music making, through composition, and studio overdubbing—all of that was its own new articulation.
70 L. Hughes, *Collected Poems*, 387.
71 See here Monson, *Saying Something*; and Iyer, "Exploding the Narrative in Jazz Improvisation."
72 The two musicians never trade fours, for instance.

73 And by 1959 mambo had become a firmly established Afro-Cuban musical and dance practice in the United States and abroad; arrangers like Perez Prado and Chico O'Farrill had helped create the angular, rich compositions that blended the density of bop, the volume and numbers of big bands, and the rhythmic intricacy of Afro-Cuban musics into something fresh. That "Broken Rhythm" would contain a mambo—the only one of Araki's recorded tunes to do so—interests me in the ways it maps yet another circulation of musics across the Pacific; Araki brings mambo with him, tucking it inside his possessions as a bundle of lead sheets, nestling it into the heart of the tune itself.

For more on the relationship between mambo and bebop—and, in particular, how the influence of Afro-Cuban music on bebop is both profound and profoundly unsung—see Jason Borge's analyses and critiques in *Tropical Riffs* (especially "The Hazards of Hybridity: Afro-Cuban Jazz, Mambo, and Revolution," 131–62).

74 As much as this record highlights Araki's own individual musicianship, it also testifies to the sociality of his practice, his close relationships with his bandmates and recording engineer. His project brings to mind a line of John Ashbery's poetry: "an LP record of all your favorite friendships." Ashbery, *Collected Poems*, 466.

75 Z. Jackson, *Becoming Human*, 66.

76 In the profile Manbo also reiterates that many of Araki's peers considered him a prodigy: "Musicians declare that Araki on saxophone is far superior to any Japanese player, which includes jazz men who were blowing horns while he was still in rompers. . . . Araki has been playing music only since 1943 when he acquired a cheap clarinet at the Gila River, Arizona, relocation center." Manbo, "He Blows High . . . He Blows Low." For more on the LA scene, see Mike Amezcua's excellent article "On the Outer Rim of Jazz." See also especially Macías, *Mexican American Mojo*. See also Satoko, *Suwingu Japan*, 204.

77 J. Araki, interview by George Akita.

78 *Pacific Citizen*, March 10, 1951. Too, interestingly enough: this group actually makes a cameo in famed guitarist and music producer Ry Cooder's postwar noir short-story collection, *Los Angeles Stories* (2011): "I knew the place, the Zenda Ballroom, on Seventh and Figueroa. Tetsu Bessho and his Nisei Serenaders played there every Monday night. Jimmy Araki, the sax player, he was sharp." See Cooder, *Los Angeles Stories*, 277.

79 J. Araki, interview by George Akita.

80 Lionel Hampton and His Big Orchestra, "Airmail Special," Clef Records 89153X45-B, 1955, 7-inch single, 45 rpm. Many of the musicians Araki recorded with in Hampton's group went on to become well-known figures—Dwike Mitchell and Willie Ruff, for instance, who later formed an important duo; Bob Plater, who accomplished a great deal and, coincidentally, came from the same music scene Harold Wing grew up in in Newark, New Jersey, playing with musicians and in groups Wing would have heard, including the Savoy Dictators.

81 See also Von Eschen, *Satchmo Blows Up the World*.

82 J. Araki, interview by George Akita.
83 J. Araki, interview by George Akita.
84 Teju Cole, "Pictures in the Aftermath," *New York Times*, April 11, 2017, https://www.nytimes.com/2017/04/11/magazine/pictures-in-the-aftermath.html.
85 Díaz, *Brief Wondrous Life*, 236. See also Horkheimer and Adorno, *Dialectic of Enlightenment*, 1. Theorist Steven Feld also expresses as much in his haunting sound piece featuring bells and cicadas: "Hiroshima: The Last Sound," *The Time of Bells, 4*, VoxLox, 2006, CD.
86 I'm thinking here of andré m. carrington's insights on who has been "allowed" to imagine futures. See carrington, *Speculative Blackness*.
87 Araki's research interest in historical Japanese literature and folklore first found form in a master's thesis on Ueda Akinari and the *Ugetsu monogatari*, a thesis completed in 1958 at the University of California, Berkeley, that involved close reading, cultural and literary history, translation, and biographical portraiture; then as a 1961 dissertation on *kōwaka*, a long-standing ballad-performance tradition unique for its multimedia attributes and threatened at numerous instances since Japan's feudal era; and later as a number of detailed articles in *Monumenta Nipponica* and translations of novels from Japanese into English. Translation, as a practice and a research theme, slowly became a guiding idea across his scholarship, informed as it was by his experiences between countries, languages, and aesthetic traditions.

Reading Araki's dissertation and monograph now, with the clarities of retrospection, it's clear that Araki gravitated toward a tradition—the *kōwaka*—featuring performers who were also themselves translators, animating aged narratives through modes of interpretation that looked beyond the strictly linguistic (or even intersemiotic); they worked to ferry, as literary theorist Brent Hayes Edwards puts it in a related context ("Taste of the Archive," 952), "content from one instance into another" by pushing the echoes of past conflict into the domain of live, lived experience. That which they could not carry over—the heartache, the physical pain, the magnitude of loss, the passage of centuries—became the anchor of their art and the subject of Araki's early research. His interest in the *kōwaka*'s overlapping components and historical importance indicates that, as a translator of text, sound, and history, he was concerned not only with description, taxonomy, and notation but also with evocation, with feeling.

See Edwards's thoughts on Roman Jakobson's "three ways of interpreting a verbal sign" in "The Taste of the Archive," 952–59. See also J. Araki, "Study of Ueda Akinari"; J. Araki, "Kōwakamai"; J. Araki, *Ballad-Drama of Medieval Japan*; and J. Araki, "Japanese Literary Studies."
88 Yaffe, *Fascinating Rhythm*, 45.
89 Brodsky, *From 1989*, 45.
90 Quoted in Burns and Ward, *Ken Burns' Jazz*.

CHAPTER 3. QUARTERED NOTES

1. "Raúl Salinas. Un Trip through the Mind Jail, 1973. Chicano Poetry #2. 1973," reel, Raúl R. Salinas Papers, M774, box 17, folder 6, Special Collections and University Archives, Stanford University, Stanford, CA; Salas and Salinas, "Jazz Jaunts," 3.
2. Again, for more on the histories and historiographies of bebop's musical and social development, consult DeVeaux, *Birth of Bebop*. For a creative take on bebop's movement westward, see also Chisholm, *Chasin' the Bird*.
3. As Ben Olguín puts it, "A Trip through the Mind Jail" "literally facilitated [Salinas's] release from prison by attracting the attention of a cadre of activist literary critics who successfully campaigned for his release based on arguments that Salinas had received an unusually harsh sentence . . . and, more importantly, had become a writer of world-class caliber who exhibited profound political values and personal ethics." Olguín, *La Pinta*, 131–32.
4. Redmond, "Song Uncaged," 231.
5. Redmond, "Song Uncaged," 233.
6. Redmond, "Song Uncaged," 232.
7. Dillon, "Prisoner's Dream," 168.
8. Rivera Garza, *Restless Dead*, 9.
9. As Miguel Samano writes, each repetition of the word "frames the speaker's recollections" as "always at risk of being lost in time." Samano, "Subjects of Display," 73.
10. Raúl Salinas, "Trip through the Mind Jail," in *Trip through the Mind Jail*, 55.
11. The quotations here are from "Trip through the Mind Jail," except for the quotes "Chicano jazz enthusiast" and "quiz each other," which are from "Jazz Jaunts." See Salas and Salinas, "Jazz Jaunts," Raúl R. Salinas Papers, M774, box 27, folder 8, 2.
12. Mendoza, "Raúl Salinas."
13. Olguín, *La Pinta*, 133.
14. Olguín, *La Pinta*, 133. For another deft reading of Salinas's poem, see Hames-Garcia, *Fugitive Thought*, 202–3.
15. Mendoza, "Raúl Salinas."
16. I am grateful here for Olguín's reading of the printed work, which highlights the pictograph as a sign of an embodied poetics and thus a rejection of the still-dominant Western belief, as poet-semiotician Edgar Garcia puts it in *Signs of the Americas*, that somehow "literature begins with letters" and that "anything otherwise" "is treated as a relic of a preliterate and preliterary past." Garcia, *Signs of the Americas*, 1.
17. Salinas, *Memoir of un Ser Humano*, 32–33.
18. Salinas, *Memoir of un Ser Humano*, 32–33. Too, as with Ralph Ellison's narrator in *Invisible Man*, in that moment, Salinas, amid a drug trip, begins to hear through that musical contact zone the layered time and "lower frequencies" of the moment's broken rhythms, its experiential "breaks"; unlike Ellison's narrator, though, what was on the turntable wasn't the smooth trumpet playing and gruff voice of

Louis Armstrong but rather the knotty, searing improvisations of Dizzy Gillespie, whose playing offered a different kind of break, a different dreamlike vocabulary. See Ellison, *Invisible Man*, 8.

19   Salinas, *Memoir of un Ser Humano*, 28.
20   Lipsitz, *Time Passages*, 64.
21   Mendoza, "Raúl Salinas."
22   For Salinas, the hot spots were East Austin's thriving jazz clubs, bolstered as they were in the years following World War II: Charlie's Playhouse, 7th St. Club, Cherry Inn, 1300 Club, Sam's Showcase, La Spañada, Ernie's Inn, and others. Many of these clubs, as Jonathan Jay Meyers and the curators at the Texas Music Museum have observed, "were vital parts of the Chitlin' Circuit, the chain of small, black Southern venues where R&B and Soul singers," including "Etta James, Bobbie 'Blue' Bland, Joe Tex, Big Joe Turner, Johnny Taylor, and Freddie King," played in the 1950s, 1960s, and 1970s. Salinas, thoroughly tapped in, frequented for his lessons "La Petit Maison, Carlin's at Lydia and 11th Streets, Tony Von's Black Cat, The Oak Tree Lounge," "the New Orleans," and "the Jade Room." He also frequented one of the most famous of these clubs during its golden years: Victory Grill. "Contributions of East Austin African-American Musicians to Texas Music," wall text at Texas Music Museum, Austin, Texas, July 2018; and Salas and Salinas, "Jazz Jaunts," 3.

Victory Grill—originally Victory Café—was opened by Austin local Johnny Holmes on August 15, 1945 (Victory over Japan Day). Responding to segregationist policies that "prevented African American servicemen from enjoying most civilian restaurants and recreational facilities," Holmes converted an icehouse on East Eleventh Street into a vibrant, inclusive establishment for good dining and quality blues and jazz. "A lot of the musicians that were playing at Charlie's and Victory Grill," Salinas once said, "were studying at Huston–Tillotson on the G.I. Bill after they had been in the Army. They were guys like Walter Green, a trumpet player who stayed here after his tour of duty . . . another guy called Wimp who also worked at J.R. Reed music store. And then there was the quintessential James Polk." All of them Austin staples, each artist had a hand in contributing to what Holmes and his supporters helped create: sites for the celebration of Black music and the cultivation of a new postwar community ethos. "Victory Grill," Texas Historical Commission Historical Site Marker, Austin, Texas; and Salas and Salinas, "Jazz Jaunts," 3. See also Myers, "GI Bill and Cool," in *Why Jazz Happened*, 48–69; and Meyers, "Black Music Spaces and Subjectivity."

23   "Contributions of East Austin African-American Musicians to Texas Music," wall text.
24   Aldama and Aldama, "Decolonizing Latinx Masculinities," 5.
25   Varon, *Before Chicano*, 135.
26   Aldama and Aldama, "Decolonizing Latinx Masculinities," 5.
27   In late 1949, when Salinas was all of sixteen, he met surrogate big brother Richard "Chuy" Zapata—a fellow Austinite and music lover who served as Salinas's

first "jazz shepherd." In Chuy, Salinas "had a teacher who took [him] back to the 1940s with swing and be-bop in order to bring [him] back into the 50s." Lessons included scouring liner notes, repeating records like Charlie Parker's *Crazeology* ad infinitum, carefully considering rhythm sections and soloists at local clubs, and traveling frequently to larger venues and nearby cities to catch headliners. "One of my first live shows I'd ever saw," Salinas once told scholar Abel Salas, "was Gene Ammons and Sonny Stitt at the Carver Library in San Antonio." Another, as he recalled, was the Prez: "[I remember] The thrill of seeing/hearing Lester Young at Gregory Gym/Austin/UT." Each lesson offered its own singular truth while contributing to an emergent, strengthening connection between Salinas and a thriving Mexican American jazz scene in segregation-era Austin. The first two quotes are from Salas and Salinas, "Jazz Jaunts," 2; the third is from Salinas, "The Jazz Years," Raúl R. Salinas Papers, M774, box 1, folder 9. For more on what tended to constitute a jazz education, see Paul Berliner, "Hangin' Out and Jammin': The Jazz Community as an Educational System," in *Thinking in Jazz*.

28 Salas and Salinas, "Jazz Jaunts," 3.
29 Mendoza, "Raúl Salinas"; and Salas and Salinas, "Jazz Jaunts," 3.
30 Salas and Salinas, "Jazz Jaunts," 4.
31 Salinas, "Jazz Years." Too, during the early to mid-1950s, these last three men of color were all tapped into jazz scenes in the Bay Area and Southern California. For more on Araki, see chapter 2; for more on Gordon, see Britt, *Dexter Gordon*.
32 Macías, *Mexican American Mojo*, 6.
33 Amezcua, "On the Outer Rim," 424. See also Kun, *Tide Was Always High*.
34 Amezcua, "On the Outer Rim," 412.
35 Salinas, *Memoir of un Ser Humano*, 59.
36 Salinas, *Memoir of un Ser Humano*, 59.
37 Salinas, *Memoir of un Ser Humano*, 59. As it happens, he began that difficult journey in downtown Los Angeles near tenor saxophonist Dexter Gordon, one of his early jazz idols, who was himself battling drug addiction. "Dexter was a trusty in the Narco Tank (11–A–2) while I was there," Salinas once mentioned. Gordon, himself plagued by an increasingly debilitating habit and enduring his second incarceration, was beginning to realize how much of his art and life were succumbing to his injections. In jail, no amount of happy distraction could shake that deeply unsettling truth: if something did not change for them both, they, like Fats Navarro, Charlie Parker, Sonny Berman, and Bill Evans, might also succumb to that looming chemical void. For Gordon, long established and supported, this change would come through new music, increased travel, and renewed opportunity; for Salinas— distanced from family and friends, newly confined to unforgiving quarters—it would come instead through reflection and diligence, unfolding slowly, through a series of sketches, of dreams. Salinas, "Jazz Years." See also Stan Britt's biography of Gordon, in which he explains that the tenor giant had been struggling during the years leading up to this second major arrest, slowly fading from the jazz spotlight at a time when he should have surged. Britt, *Dexter Gordon*, 76–77.

38 Wang, *Carceral Capitalism*, 69.
39 Remnick, "Mass Incarceration in America."
40 Nellis, "Color of Justice."
41 M. Alexander, *New Jim Crow*, xxviii.
42 Fleetwood, *Marking Time*, 39.
43 M. Jones, *Muse Is Music*.
44 See Fredric Jameson's "Nostalgia for the Present," in *Postmodernism*, 279–96; and Ford, *Dig*, 87.
45 Ford, *Dig*, 87.
46 Erik Redling has explored such metaphorical "overlays" in great detail. See Redling, *Translating Jazz into Poetry*.
47 Salinas's jazz-focused written work also prepares us for the jazz poetry he would later record with other musicians, transforming his voice and verse, literally, into a solo instrument in ways that go beyond surface-level resemblance.

   Here I draw on Ingrid Monson's notion of an "intermusical" citation, one in which "aural references are conveyed primarily through instrumental means," without explicit, real-time linguistic signification. Distinguished from intertextuality in tack and shade, "intermusical" describes the "aurally perceptible musical relationships that are heard in the context of particular traditions." Monson, *Saying Something*, 127–29.
48 Salinas, "Did Charlie Have a Horn?," Raúl R. Salinas Papers, M774, box 2, folder 2.
49 Salinas, "Music for the Masses," Raúl R. Salinas Papers, M774, box 1, folder 11.
50 Salinas, "Music for the Masses."
51 Charlie Parker and His Orchestra, *Night and Day*, Verve Records MGC-5003, 1956, LP (recorded March 25, 1952).
52 Salinas, "Music for the Masses."
53 Salinas, "Music for the Masses."
54 Newspaper clipping, Raúl R. Salinas Papers, M0774, box 6, folder 15.
55 Salinas, "Prison Journals," Raúl R. Salinas Papers, M774, box 1, folder 14; and Salinas, "Jazz Jaunts and East Side Haunts," Raúl R. Salinas Papers, M774, box 27, folder 8.
56 Salinas, "Prison Journals."
57 See Littlejohn and Ford, *"The Enemy Within Never Did Without."*
58 Salinas, "Prison Journals."
59 Salinas, *raúlrsalinas and the Jail Machine*, 7.
60 Raúl Salinas, "Jazz: A Nascence," in *Trip through the Mind Jail*, 43.
61 See Ford, *Dig*, ch. 3.
62 Salinas, *raúlrsalinas and the Jail Machine*, 7.
63 As Salinas mentioned in different interviews, Gleason was a critical early model. See Salinas, "Jazz Jaunts and East Side Haunts." See "Una plática con Raúl Salinas: An Interview by Ben Olguín and Louis Mendoza," in Salinas, *raúlrsalinas and the Jail Machine*, 305–34. See also the video recording of that interview: Raúl Salinas, interview by Ben Olguín and Louis Mendoza, Stanford, CA, May 5, 1994,

Stanford University Video Collection, 1934–2016, Digital Archive, https://purl.stanford.edu/qy544qy8912.
64 Gennari, *Blowin' Hot and Cool*, 170.
65 Gennari, *Blowin' Hot and Cool*, 170.
66 For what it's worth, as Gennari points out, some of these critics, including Gleason and Hentoff, were conscious of this fact and largely worked through writing and activism to stand in solidarity with the marginalized. See Gennari, *Blowin' Hot and Cool*, 165–206.
67 Baraka, *Black Music*, 11.
68 Salinas, *raúlrsalinas and the Jail Machine*, 318. See also the recorded interview with Salinas by Olguín and Mendoza.
69 Iyer, "Deft, Quiet Shout," 94.
70 Raúl R. Salinas, Quartered Notes, *Huntsville Echo*, November 1964; and Raúl R. Salinas, Quartered Notes, *Huntsville Echo*, April 1964, both from reel 1998/038-369 (MF #3634), January 1964–August/September 1984, *The Echo*, Texas Department of Criminal Justice, Archives and Information Services Division, Texas State Library and Archives Commission.
71 "Jazz: The Loneliest Monk," *Time*, February 28, 1964.
72 Raúl R. Salinas, Quartered Notes, *Huntsville Echo*, March 1964, reel 1998/038-369 (MF #3634), January 1964–August/September 1984, *The Echo*, Texas Department of Criminal Justice. I'd be remiss not to mention Michel Foucault's thoughts on prison here: "The prison, that darkest region in the apparatus of justice, is the place where the power to punish, which no longer dares to manifest itself openly, silently organizes a field of objectivity in which punishment will be able to function openly as treatment and the sentence be inscribed among the discourses of knowledge." Foucault, *Discipline and Punish*, 256.
73 Edwards, "Evidence," 53.
74 Salinas, Quartered Notes, *Huntsville Echo*, March 1964.
75 Richard O. Boyer, "Profiles: Bop," *New Yorker*, July 3, 1948, 31. See also Eric Porter's *What Is This Thing Called Jazz?*, especially "Dizzy Atmosphere," 54–100.
76 As Edwards's work clarifies, there may well have been a surprising structural link there, too: "Monk is well known for his witty and evocative titles ('Straight No Chaser,' 'Trinkle Tinkle,' 'Gallop's Gallop'), but 'Evidence' is particularly noteworthy because it suggests the methodology of the music's abstraction. 'Just You, Just Me' became 'Just Us' when Monk first started playing the tune around 1947. Then he took the phrase sideways and began calling it 'Justice.' . . . And then another hop, diagonally, taking the word into another register through metonym—for how can one attain 'justice' under the law without 'evidence'?" Edwards, "Evidence," 52–53. Salinas didn't write about Monk's "Evidence" for his Quartered Notes column, but he did stick with the implications of Monk's music and aesthetics throughout his writing life.
77 I draw inspiration here from the sonic ambiguity in the title of Claudia Rankine's *Just Us*: "justice," "just us."

78 Edwards, "Evidence," 53–54.
79 Scrap with quotation of Thelonious Monk, Raúl R. Salinas Papers, M774, box 1, folder 9.
80 I understand retrospective music writing to be a mode of descriptive notation that focuses primarily on a listener's experience of a musical event. And while literary theories of representation and musical semiotics are useful for understanding this, I've lately found theories of cartography to be more immediately lucid. See especially Kitchin, Perkins, and Dodge, "Thinking about Maps."
81 In March 1965 Salinas wrote his last article for Quartered Notes, on the subject of jazz and religion, drawing on the work of musicians including Mary Lou Williams, Eric Dolphy, Ed Summerlin, and others to tease out the institutional and affective connections between jazz, spirituality, and religious experience. In April 1965 writer and musician Carmen Scoleri took over the column after Salinas's departure from Huntsville: "Since Roy Salinas is on Harlem 2 waiting to go home, I have been asked to do this column. First let me say: 'The best of luck to you Roy,' from all the musicians here in the walls. You and your column will be missed." Scoleri ends the article with this: "This writing a Jazz column is hard work. You gotta think. And then there's the wise guys peeking over your shoulder." See Quartered Notes, April 1965, reel 1998/038-369 (MF #3634), January 1964–August/September 1984, *The Echo*, Texas Department of Criminal Justice.
82 Newspaper clippings, Raúl R. Salinas Papers, M774, box 9, folder 4.
83 Ray Reece, "Busting out of the Mind Jail," Raúl R. Salinas Papers, M774, box 27, folder 9, 6.
84 Mendoza, "Raúl Salinas."
85 Reece, "Busting out of the Mind Jail," 7.
86 Mendoza, "Introduction," 10–11.
87 Salinas, "Prison Journals."
88 Among Salinas's interlocutors was Américo Paredes, by then an established professor at the University of Texas at Austin. See the letter from Paredes to Salinas, Raúl R. Salinas Papers, M774, box 5, folder 23.
89 Kun, *Audiotopia*, 169.
90 Mendoza, "Raúl Salinas."
91 Salas, liner notes in Salinas, *Los Many Mundos of raúlrsalinas: Un Poetic Jazz Viaje con Friends*, Calaca Press/Red Salmon, 2000, CD.
92 Salinas, liner notes in Tomás Ramírez, *Téjazz*, Vireo Records, 1995, CD.
93 Salinas, liner notes in Ramírez, *Téjazz*.
94 Ramírez, "Interview."
95 Salinas also recorded this poem for his second record, *Beyond the BEATen Path*. The two performances bear subtle variations; my transcription is based on the first of the two. Raúl R. Salinas, "Riffs I," on *Los Many Mundos of raúlrsalinas*; and Raúl Salinas, "Riffs I," on *Beyond the BEATen Path*, liner notes by Stephen Bruton, Red Salmon Press, 2002, CD.

96   Bruton, liner notes in Salinas, *Beyond the BEATen Path*.
97   "If there is any 'tradition' [in 'jazz']," Ho once wrote, "it is the continual exploding of time and pitch in quest of greater human expressiveness and a deeper spiritualizing of the music that is fundamentally rooted in the struggle to end all forms of exploitation and oppression and to seek a basic 'oneness' with life and nature." Ho, "What Makes 'Jazz' the Revolutionary Music," 96. Having grown up in the 1970s being "profoundly drawn to and inspired by African American music as the expression of an oppressed nationality"—as a high school student, Ho studied with saxophonist Archie Shepp, who was himself "daring to dream of a liberated society" through radical Black sounding—Ho found in Black improvisatory, critical praxis a way of understanding the relationship between biography and history, individual and community, self and other, imprisoned and liberated. Fujino, "Revolutionary Dreaming and New Dawns," 18. "As a non-African American, but a person of color (oppressed nationality in the United States), I was drawn to and inspired and revolutionized by the music's musical and—possibly more profoundly—extramusical qualities." . . . "I identified with its pro-oppressed, anti-oppressor character: with the militancy the musician displayed, with its social history of rebellion and revolt, and with its musical defiance to not kow-tow to, but challenge and contest, Western European 'classical' music and co-opted, diluted, eviscerated commercialized forms that became American pop music." Ho, "What Makes 'Jazz' the Revolutionary Music," 100, 93. It's perhaps no surprise, then, that Ho and Salinas, as kindred, revolutionary spirits, eventually gravitated toward one another, on the page and the stage.
98   "Review: *Red Arc*" in the *Texas Observer*, reproduced in Raúl Salinas and Fred Ho, *Red Arc: A Call for Liberación con Salsa y Cool*, liner notes by Alejandro Murguia, Raúl Salinas, and Fred Ho, Wings Press, 2005, CD.
99   Among the tracks that Salinas and Ho recorded in 2004 was a tribute to yet another musician who "stood the world on its ears"—or, rather, who saw the world through his ears, as a blind musician and theorist: Rahsaan Roland Kirk. As Josh Kun has written, Kirk, an audio-theorist of "Blacknuss," of "blackness as sound," was one of a great many intellectuals who "rebuke[d]" the "traditional notion that jazz musicians can only be spoken for (usually by white critics), that as musicians they are not also activists, writers, thinkers, and philosophers who speak for themselves and articulate their own artistic and political visions and agendas." "Kirk's blindness," Kun continues, "forced him to generate meanings and knowledge about social experience through his ear, and as a result he possessed a finely tuned comprehension of just how central sound and music have always been to racial formation, racial struggle, and social movements in the United States." Kun, *Audiotopia*, 133, 137. For Kirk, thinking and dreaming in sound meant grappling with constrictive patterns and harmful logics, rendering the unseen of American racial democracy audible, changeable.

When Salinas and Ho listened to Kirk in the 1970s, thousands of miles apart from one another, they heard what Kirk saw with his mind's ear. For Ho, Kirk's

"Black classical music"—a concept that rejected the word *jazz* and its terminological connection to racial capitalism (as a race-music genre label invented by white marketers)—amplified the revolutionary ethos of improvisatory creative praxis. "With marathon-like stamina," Ho writes in the album's liner notes, "Kirk played several horns simultaneously and reclaimed obscure woodwind horns such as the manzello and stritch." He was an "'inside' and 'outside' player steeped in blues and gospel traditions." He was a "great master," an "iconoclast." Ho, liner notes in Salinas and Ho, *Red Arc*.

For Salinas, Kirk's music, like that of Black altermodernists Parker and Gillespie, Monk and Powell, was similarly powerful, affirming—so much so that in 1979, nearly a decade after finally being released from prison, Salinas funneled his admiration for Kirk into a "song" in "a minor blues mode": a poem entitled "Song for Roland Kirk." See Salinas, *Trip through the Mind Jail*, 178–80.

In the poem, Salinas reflects:

RAHSAAN.
Shit!
You spoke
in spirit tongues
& things,
gave (some) folks
irritating feelin'
wid yo' jokes
of
Hurt & Pain
Raining
Jazz
Tears
dispelling fears
of
being
Sane....
Ballads / Bullets
Blown!
RAT-A-TAT-TATTING
in the battle of
Struggling Saxophones
(nose flute/ manzello & Stritch,
instruments to befuddle the rich!)
SOUNDS
that somehow
made it
RIGHT
for

US.
Blind Man
(seeing all)
calling to heed
1950s Austin
crowds of jazz
leading
to good direction
helping those not blind
to
SEE.

Kirk's sounds, for Salinas—his "spirit tongues" and "jokes / of / Hurt & Pain," his "Jazz / Tears / dispelling fears / of / being / Sane"—spoke to the structural and spiritual deficiencies of American racial democracy, rendering them loud and insistent enough to give "(some) folks / irritating feelin.'" And the way Salinas heard Kirk's music—the way he heard and recalled those "battle[s] of / Struggling Saxophones / (nose flute/ manzello & Stritch, / instruments to befuddle the rich!)"—captured how the relationality at the core of listening itself can, at its best, contain within it new keys for unlocking local experiences, new agendas for revolutionary struggle, new seeds for communities of difference:

SOUNDS
that somehow
made it
RIGHT
for
US.
Blind Man
(seeing all)
calling to heed
1950s Austin
crowds of jazz
leading
to good direction
helping those not blind
to
SEE.

As with the ways Salinas heard Parker, Monk, and Gillespie—those Black theorists of relation and music whose music was eventually labeled "bebop" by a white establishment—next-generation figures like Kirk, Charles Mingus, John Coltrane, and others helped Salinas hear his relation to others in a new way, helped him articulate radically liberatory Xicanindio visions uncoupled from the West's futurities.

In 2004 Salinas and Ho collaborated on their version of "Song for Roland Kirk": a trio, one might say, between Salinas's voice and text, and all the layers contained therein; Ho's baritone saxophone and improvisations, rich in tone and historical import; and Kirk's own spirit, animated by the space between a Xicanindio jazz poet and an Asian American jazz musician.

Red Arc's "Song for Roland Kirk" begins with an extended baritone sax introduction from Ho: trills, multiphonics, momentary modulations. It relies on two musical motifs—a rising one based on a trill, as well as a bluesier one to end phrases—and the general melodic and affective shape resembles an ocean wave: a build, a crash, a fizzle. At 1:08, as the introduction's first section ends, Ho interpolates the melody of Kirk's "Volunteered Slavery," a dense, swirling song Kirk recorded at Regent Sound Studios in New York in July 1969. (The repeated lyric in Kirk's original song all but echoes in Ho's solo: "Volunteered slavery has got me on the run.") At 1:33, the vamp of "Song for Roland Kirk" begins—"a combination," Ho explains "of a fast [200 BPM] 7/4 and 11/4 meter with some additives thrown in." Ho, liner notes in Salinas and Ho, *Red Arc*. Soon after, Salinas's voice sounds, intoning his poem's title and dedication before leaping into the verse.

As one listens, one might notice that the combination of Salinas and Ho's two instrumental voices—the regularity, drive, and metronomic precision of Ho's syncopated, looping baritone sax vamp; the temporal ebb and flow of Salinas's gusty vocal performance—creates a feeling of "twoness": a sense of two temporalities superimposed, audible and literary, producing a polyrhythm greater than the sum of its parts. This is significant. As Salinas performs his written text—stretching printed words into half-sung sustains in his signature way, improvising out of the space between speech and song—and as Ho starts modifying his saxophone vamp, creating contrasting affects by exploring timbre, range, and harmonic variation, together, they begin transforming their memories and admiration of Kirk's music into a moving cultural exchange, into a revolutionary meditation, a set of shared dreams.

See Salinas and Ho, *Red Arc*; and Salinas, "Jazz: A Nascence," in *Trip through the Mind Jail*, 43.

100 Gillespie, *To Be, or Not . . . to Bop*, 321.
101 Borge, *Tropical Riffs*, 132–33.
102 Ho, liner notes in Salinas and Ho, *Red Arc*.
103 Ho, "Fred Ho: Free New Africa! Boogaloo."
104 Salinas, "Loud and Proud," 53–54.
105 Salinas, "Loud and Proud," 53–54.
106 Salinas, "Loud and Proud," 53–54.
107 Salinas, "Loud and Proud," 53–54.
108 Salinas, "Loud and Proud," 53–54.
109 Salinas, "Solidarité," in *East of the Freeway*, 44.
110 Salinas, "Solidarité," 44.
111 Salinas, "Solidarité," 45.

112 Ho, "What Makes 'Jazz' the Revolutionary Music," 100.
113 The phrase "loose and dreamlike" comes from Baldwin, "Sonny's Blues," 126. The "clues" come from Edwards, "Evidence," 53–54.
114 E. Alexander, *Black Interior*, 4–5.
115 Kun, *Audiotopia*, 170.
116 Distinctions between prose and poetry often include shape, meter, and lineation. And different instances of prose and poetry approach language's mimetic function differently—on one hand, the sense of "directness"; on the other, the sense of "turning" or "warping"; and, between them, the diagonal. Or differently: the prosaic proposes a one-to-one similarity/correspondence while the poetic leans into difference/comparison (metaphor). Poetic language draws our attention to language as an apparatus, making us aware of language at work. In effect, it reminds us, following Friedrich Nietzsche, Karl Marx, Fredric Jameson, and others, that language is, at its core, metaphorical: linguistic signs *stand in* for feelings, objects, and processes. See especially Nietzsche's "On Truth and Lying in an Extramoral Sense."
117 Pollock, "Performing Writing," 80.
118 Albright, *Panaesthetics*, 212. Additionally, Brent Hayes Edwards's reading of this in relation to African American letters is magnificent. See Edwards, *Epistrophies*.
119 Fleetwood, *Marking Time*, 7.
120 In a cultural materialist sense, the production and distribution of a periodical in 1960s Huntsville Prison helped make this possible, carving an important opening for self-representation and reconstitution via local publishing.

Too, the appearance of Salinas's work in the *Echo*—and its subsequent overlooking by jazz historians—is part of something larger, something that John Gennari identifies in his study: too often, critics "writing for regional newspapers, college newspapers, jazz appreciation society newsletters, and the like" have gone unrecognized beyond local readerships for reasons of comparatively limited distribution and notably reduced cultural cachet. See Gennari, *Blowin' Hot and Cool*, 14.
121 Salinas, *raúlrsalinas and the Jail Machine*, 318. See also the recorded interview by Olguín and Mendoza.
122 Salinas, *raúlrsalinas and the Jail Machine*, 319. See also the recorded interview by Olguín and Mendoza.
123 Salinas, *raúlrsalinas and the Jail Machine*, 317. See also the recorded interview by Olguín and Mendoza.
124 Salinas, "Music for the Masses."
125 One wonders, What might it have meant for a formerly incarcerated Xicanindio poet to release a book of jazz critical, ethnographic, biographical, historical, poetic, and fictional writings in the late 1970s? In the years after he recited poems at the first Festival de Flor y Canto at the University of Southern California alongside others including Juan Felipe Herrera, Oscar Acosta, and Alurista? In the years in which he was beginning to relate revolutionary Chicano politics and poetics to the American Indian Movement? How might such a literary and musical release by

the author of "A Trip through the Mind Jail" have been received—among Black and Chicano readers? Among potentially interested jazz critics and musicians? For more, see Mendoza, "Introduction to Raúl Salinas," xii; and Salinas, "Music for the Masses."

126 Fischlin, Heble, and Lipsitz, *Fierce Urgency of Now*, xii.
127 Ybarra-Frausto, "Introduction," 7.

CHAPTER 4. AMONG OTHERS

1 Reed, *Soundworks*.
2 Writer Amiri Baraka, in his essay "Jazz and the White Critic: Thirty Years Later," included in *Digging*, names Wing as part of a cadre of Newark musicians who have gone overlooked, omitted from the jazz historical record in ways congruent with Newark itself. See Baraka, *Digging*, 153. Newark reporter and historian Barbara Kukla, in numerous studies to combat her city's erasure, also mentions Wing's importance to Newark's scenes, especially in the postwar and postrebellion years. See especially Kukla, *Swing City*. Poet Raúl Salinas, too, deeply admired Wing, having met him on a few occasions after live performances.
3 Brief profile of Wing in "Music Master: In N.J. and N.Y.," *New Jersey After Hours: The Weekly Guide to Entertainment*, February 8, 1950, 9–10.
4 Etta Jones, *'75*, Westbound Records W-203, 1975, LP; Horn, *Where Are You Going*, Perception Records PLP 31, 1972, LP; and Junior Mance, *That Lovin' Feelin'*, Milestone Records MSP 9041, 1972, LP.
5 Lordi, *Meaning of Soul*, 11.
6 Michiko Theurer, quoted in Long, *Performing Knowledge*, 12–14.
7 Sorey, "Allowing Things to Happen."
8 See a 1911 map of Newark's enclaves, "A Map of Newark with Areas Where Different Nationalities Predominate," Newark Public Library Digital Collection, https://www.digital.npl.org/islandora/object/newarkmaps%3Aa40ed90c-3dd2-4694-8773-3cf081e7dd36. As the archival notes on this map indicate, this is an imperfect document, as it doesn't include census data for the populations it depicts, but it remains one of the widely circulated visualizations of racial, ethnic, and spatial overlap in Newark during this early twentieth-century period.
9 Eugene "Goldie" Goldston, interview by Jonathan Leal at Chateau of Spain, Newark, NJ, August 7, 2018.
10 Moody, "James Moody."
11 Ellison, *Collected Essays*, 257. See also Skipper, "Nicknames, Folk Heroes and Jazz Musicians."
12 Lalami, *Moor's Account*, 7.
13 Godrej, "Spaces for Counter-narratives," 111.

14 I'm reminded here, too, of what Maggie Nelson writes in *The Argonauts*: "That is what reclaimed terms do—they retain, they insist on retaining, a sense of the fugitive" (29).
15 The phrases "barbed challenge" and "exhilarating invitations" come from Saul, *Freedom Is, Freedom Ain't*, xiii–xiv; see also Baldwin, "Sonny's Blues."
16 Quoted in Barbara Kukla, "Friends to 'Wing It' at Essex County College for a Tribute to a Music Pro," *Newark Star-Ledger*, February 19, 1985.
17 Kukla, *Encyclopedia of Newark Jazz*, 39.
18 Goldston, interview by Jonathan Leal.
19 C. Alan Simms, "Chink Wing Joins Jam at JFK: Jazz Star Tells Young His Secrets: Study and Work," *Information*, May 1975, 2.
20 Kukla, *Encyclopedia of Newark Jazz*, 8.
21 Quoted in Kukla, "Friends to 'Wing It.'"
22 Kukla, *Swing City*, 226–27.
23 Berliner, *Thinking in Jazz*, 41.
24 Quoted in Kukla, "Friends to 'Wing It.'"
25 Kukla, "Friends to 'Wing It'"; and Simms, "Chink Wing Joins Jam."
26 Green, "'Art for Life's Sake,'" 28.
27 Wing's time as a student at the Henry Street Settlement is interesting. "Early in its existence," as scholar Shannon Louise Green puts it, "the School distinguished itself by having a strong and committed support from such renowned musicians as Aaron Copland, George Gershwin, and Jascha Heifetz, who were members of the School's advisory committee." The faculty aimed to cultivate overlooked musical talent and, more broadly, to invest in an ideal of musical literacy and enrichment for all residents; however, the curriculum was narrowly defined, promoting almost exclusively the study of canonical Western art musics. "The 'good' music taught in the settlements did not include jazz or popular styles of music," Green remarks. Green, "'Art for Life's Sake,'" 47.
28 As musicologist Paul Berliner has put it, "As a consequence of formal training, instrument selection, and performance participation, youngsters acquired different kinds of knowledge, including musical exercises, tunes, and different parts from band arrangements of compositions. Such knowledge reflected the youngsters' characteristically diverse, polymusical environment, spanning sacred and secular African American and Western classical traditions, among others." Berliner, *Thinking in Jazz*, 27. For more on musical improvisation and formalized education, see Suechting and Leal, "Jam Sessions."
29 Kukla, "Friends to 'Wing It.'"
30 Billie Smith, "This Is It," *New Jersey Herald News*, April 20, 1946.
31 Billie Smith, "This Is It," *New Jersey Herald News*, May 11, 1946.
32 This contrasts with more avant-garde experimentation in jazz that would highlight in musical performance and form what James Clifford has observed of some "big-enough histories": that they include elements that are "simultaneous but not synchronous." Clifford, *Returns*, 8.

33 Iyer, "What's Not Music."
34 Quoted in Kukla, "Friends to 'Wing It.'"
35 In 1948 and 1949, Wing recorded professionally for one of the first times as part of an act called Joseph August's "Mr. Google Eyes" with Billy Ford and his Musical v8s. August, marketed as "the world's youngest blues singer," had just signed a contract with Columbia Records after living and working in New Orleans; the record he was recording with this Newark band was set to help catapult him into a new tier of fame. Wing, notable for his versatility and familiar by then with a variety of genres, provided August and the band solid rhythmic support, demonstrating musical maturity on songs that, through their lyrical content, drew attention to an unsettling discontinuity: youth and loss. See the rerelease of this material via Joseph "Mr. Google Eyes" August, *Rock My Soul*, Route 66 Records KIX-32, 1986 reissue, LP. See also Simms, "Chink Wing Joins Jam."
36 Ellison, *Collected Essays*, 229.
37 Ramsey, *Amazing Bud Powell*, 86.
38 Gillespie, *To Be, or Not to . . . Bop*, 287.
39 Brief profile of Wing in "Music Master: In N.J. and N.Y.," *New Jersey After Hours: The Weekly Guide to Entertainment*, February 8, 1950, 9–10.
40 Brief profile of Wing in "Music Master: In N.J. and N.Y."
41 Ramsey, *Amazing Bud Powell*, 128.
42 See especially Ramsey, *Amazing Bud Powell*, 128. Too, for excellent discussions of how such approaches to musical rhythm were further developed by Black artist-technologists like J Dilla, see Charnas, *Dilla Time*.
43 Ramsey, *Amazing Bud Powell*, 128.
44 Ramsey, *Amazing Bud Powell*, 128.
45 Ramsey, *Amazing Bud Powell*, 123.
46 Quoted in Monson, *Saying Something*, 64.
47 Sorey, "Tyshawn Sorey."
48 "Harold (Chink) Wing, Top Newark Musician," *Newark Star-Ledger*, December 21, 1993.
49 Kukla, "Friends to 'Wing It.'"
50 Erroll Garner, *The Greatest Garner*, liner notes by Whitney Balliet (1956) and Bob Porter (2003), Atlantic Records 1227, 2003 reissue, CD.

   In late February 1950, the trio played a set at the Blue Note in Chicago, which Jerry Hammes has documented, including a nice anecdote about Wing being friendly to Hammes and his friends, as well as a photograph of an autograph Wing signed. See Hammes, "Blue Note Nightclub—1950."

   Weeks later, the band returned to the Windy City, as Jack Tracy of *Downbeat* notes: "Chicago . . . Garner rambled through some familiar standards, tossed in a few up-tempo originals in his portions of the show. He was backed by bassist John Simmons and drummer Harold Wing." See Jack Tracy, "Capsule Comments: Tristano-Garner," *Downbeat* 17, no. 8 (April 21, 1950), 5. See also the brief profile of Wing in "Music Master: In N.J. and N.Y."

51 Quoted in Simms, "Chink Wing Joins Jam."
52 That first session also came at a moment of career transition: Garner was signing with a new manager (Martha Glaser) and a new record label (Columbia); Simmons was learning to better navigate his by-then long-standing performance relationship with Garner; Wing was breaking into the New York scene while still living and performing in Newark; and the group already had more tour dates lined up. (Such tours allowed Wing and Raúl Salinas to meet on a few occasions. As Kukla wrote in the *Star-Ledger*, this lineup of the Erroll Garner Trio "toured the country with side trips to Mexico and Canada." Kukla, "Friends to 'Wing It.'") With their tour-born sleep deficit, late-night local sessions, and upcoming travel plans, the trio worked efficiently and feverishly, playing with few breaks, practically recording songs with duffels on their backs.

All the songs recorded that day featured Garner's stylistic signatures: a penchant for rich melodies, a theory of innovative chord voicings, a prevailing sense, ultimately, of the novel promise of old material. All the songs, including the two that Wing wrote, featured Garner's rhythmic acumen, his penchant for syncopations, polyrhythms, and phasing, both between his hands and against his rhythm sections. See the Erroll Garner Trio, *Garnering*, Mercury Records MG 36026, 1955, LP.

53 On the Jazz Discography Project, Doc West is erroneously listed as the drummer on the April 1950 session—understandable, given that West played and recorded with Garner regularly. The labels and liner notes of multiple releases clear this up, however. See "Erroll Garner Discography."

Some of the confusion about Wing's work with Garner might be traced back to a simple name slip: John Simmons, in an oral history interview, accidentally used the name "Harold West" to refer to Wing. (He clarifies afterward that he was referring to a drummer who was "half Chinese and Negro. And we called him Chink.") Because there was indeed a famous jazz drummer by the name of Harold "Doc" West," songs recorded during those April and May 1950 sessions have in some places been misattributed to the more famous of the two drummers, including in James Doran's extensive discography in *Erroll Garner: The Most Happy Piano* (1985). See Patricia Willard's interview with John Simmons, reprinted in Doran, *Erroll Garner*, 73–75.

54 In his liner notes essay for Garner's *Piano Solos Vol. II*, jazz critic Ralph Gleason wrote the following of "Perpetual Emotion": "A Garner nightclub performance of any tune lasts as long as the spirit moves him. Sometimes he plays a melody for only one chorus, sometimes for an entire 'set,' as improvisation inspires re-improvisation. Here on 'Perpetual Emotion,' with time restrictions lifted by understanding recording directors, we have a full 10 minutes of the most exciting Garner ever waxed! Idea tumbles upon idea in a seemingly endless cascade of delightful variations."

Gleason also praised Wing's and Simmons's accompanimental work, stating that "the remarkable foundation of the rhythm of John Simmons on bass and

Harold Wing on drums," combined with "Erroll's hesitant, almost stuttering treatment of the [Summertime] melody" and "his slow, swinging beat," gives "this grand number the tender treatment it deserves." See Gleason, liner notes in Erroll Garner, *Piano Solos Vol. II*, Atlantic Records ALR 135, 1952, LP.

55 T. Hughes, "Groove and Flow," 17.
56 T. Hughes, "Groove and Flow," 15.
57 An Easter egg: Garner's idea is seven bars long the first time around (at 2:45) and six bars the second time (at 2:53); Wing, likely assuming the idea would be the same length on the repeat, plays seven bars to Garner's six, then realizes "where Garner is."
58 Butterfield, "Variant Timekeeping Patterns" (emphasis added).
59 Ramsey, *Amazing Bud Powell*, 55.
60 Ramsey, *Amazing Bud Powell*, 55 (emphasis added).
61 It is telling that with each new version, Garner explores his jazz historicity ("Erroll at the Philharmonic"), his musical fallibilities ("Margin for Erroll"), and his studies and theorems ("Garnerology.") For more on Garner's discography, see Doran, *Erroll Garner*, 215.
62 Tomlinson and Lipsitz, "American Studies as Accompaniment," 11.
63 Goldston, interview by Jonathan Leal.
64 Halberstam, *Female Masculinity*, 2.
65 E. Porter, *What Is This Thing?*, 79.
66 Ramsey, *Amazing Bud Powell*, 29.
67 Ramsey, *Amazing Bud Powell*, 130.
68 Matthew Salesses, "'Good-Looking for an Asian': How I Shed White Ideals of Masculinity," *Guardian*, October 23, 2020.
69 Salesses, "'Good-Looking for an Asian.'"
70 Fellezs, "Silenced but Not Silent," 72–73.
71 The road manager and occasional vocalist for the group until 1954 was bop vocalist (and fellow Newarker) Babs Gonzales.
72 Baldwin, "Discovery of What It Means," in *Collected Essays*, 137. See also Rashida Braggs's study of Black American musicians in postwar Paris, *Jazz Diasporas: Race, Music, and Migration in Post–World War II Paris*.
73 This perhaps comes as no surprise: Moody truly got his start by playing in Gillespie's now-famous big band bebop group in 1946, taking his first recorded solo on a track called "Emanon" (No Name). Moody left the band and the United States in 1948 to live with his uncle in Paris; in 1951, after achieving some fame with his hit "Moody's Mood for Love," which singer King Pleasure recorded in the United States, Moody returned to the United States and promptly formed his septet, of which Harold Wing was a key member. For the wailing, check out 2:15. James Moody, *Moody's Home*, EmArcy Records EP-1-6010, 1951, EP.
74 While impressive and useful on occasion, raw instrumental athleticism has a short shelf life as a physical and stylistic default.
75 This exemplifies yet another principle that has long been standard among drummers; as Ingrid Monson puts it, "Professional drummers think about melody, har-

mony, and timbre, just as the other members of the jazz ensemble do. They are not interested in timbre and tone merely as decorations for their primary rhythmic function either, for they see that rhythm, pitch contrast, and timbre interact in interesting ways in building a performance." Monson, *Saying Something*, 62. The performance built with "Moody's Home," full of rich, energetic comping from the entire rhythm section and an elated set of sax solos, is anchored by a drummer whose windows to solo were informed by a sense of the whole.

76 Moody, "James Moody."
77 See Theurer and Leal, "Reach"; and Theurer and Leal, "Sonic Offering."
78 Paul Quinichette All Stars, *Moods*, liner notes unsigned, EmArcy Records MG 36003, 1954, LP.
79 Kun, *Tide Was Always High*.
80 It's difficult to say with certainty what the story behind the name is. "Pablo" is Paul in Spanish; "Roonie" is a nonsense word often used by vocalist Slim Gaillard. As Bill Crow writes, "Slim Gaillard invented a lot of nonsense words that he sprinkled liberally throughout his songs and conversation. 'Roonie' and 'voutie' seem to be basic forms from which sprang words like 'o-voutie,' 'o-roonie,' 'vouse-o-roonie-mo,' 'reetie-voutie,' etc." Crow, *Jazz Anecdotes*, 231.
81 By this point in his career, Wing was used to performing a variety of styles. And, as with drummers even today, going about matters otherwise wasn't exactly a choice: a certain degree of what Monson has called *polymusicality* is required for many musicians (especially drummers) who find work primarily as accompanists. Wing, long used to bebop but here playing a kind of mambo, went with the flow, providing only what was necessary to help the music succeed. See Monson, *Saying Something*.
82 Brown, "Modern Jazz Drumset Artistry," 39.
83 For more in this vein, see Schultz and Gopinath, "Sentimental Remembrance and the Amusements of Forgetting."
84 Charles Fox of the *Gramophone* reviewed the record as follows in July 1957: "There are lengthy solos, hard-toned and laconic, by Paul Quinichette on both sides of this EP. With Quinichette sounding, as usual, very like Lester Young, and 'Sir Charles' Thompson adding nimble, brisk touches at the piano, Shorty George takes on quite a Basie flavour. Jerome Darr is heard in good solos and playing rhythm guitar, Barry Galbraith being used as an extra voice in the ensembles. Jazz flautists are beginning to bore me and Sam Most's solo (in Plush Life) is not particularly enterprising. But on the whole this is a record full of unpretentious and swinging jazz." Charles Fox, "Jazz and Swing: Reviews," *Gramophone*, July 1957. Curiously, there is no mention of "Pablo's Roonie" at all.
85 Quoted in Palmer, *Mr. P.C.*, 30.
86 L. Jones (Baraka), *Blues People*.
87 Rasberry, *Race and the Totalitarian Century*, 32.
88 Von Eschen, *Satchmo Blows Up the World*.
89 Colleen O'Dea, "Newark before the Comeback: A City Marked by White Flight, Poor Policy," *New Jersey Spotlight*, September 4, 2019, https://www.njspotlight

.com/2019/09/19-09-02-newark-before-the-comeback-a-city-marked-by-white-flight-and-poor-policy/.

90   Skeete-Laessig, *When Newark Had a Chinatown*, 257.
91   The 1968 report of the National Advisory Commission on Civil Disorders (the Kerner Commission), completed at the request of President Lyndon B. Johnson, underscored "white racism" as the base condition and catalyzing agent for the events in Newark and elsewhere. As the report's writers noted, "White racism is essentially responsible for the explosive [ad]mixture which has been accumulating in our cities since the end of World War II. Among the ingredients of this mixture are: pervasive discrimination and segregation in employment, education, and housing," "Black in-migration and white exodus," "a climate that tends toward approval and encouragement of violence," "the frustrations of powerlessness," and a new "self-esteem" and "enhanced racial pride" among disenfranchised residents no longer tolerant of their corrosive environs. See National Advisory Commission on Civil Disorders, *Report*, 5.
92   Curvin, *Inside Newark*, 101.
93   J. Chang, "Future Aesthetics."
94   Goldston, interview by Jonathan Leal.
95   Malee Wing, interview by Jonathan Leal by phone, September 2018. See also "Newark Recreation Sponsors Jazz Festival," *Information*, November 1978, 16.
96   Kukla, "Friends to 'Wing It.'"
97   In September 1972, for instance, Doug Johnson, a writer for the *Crusader*, wrote up a story on Wing's efforts:

> [This week,] eleven prisoners from the U.S. Federal Penitentiary at Lewisburg will present "The Evolution of Jazz." . . . The men, most of whom were professional musicians "on the street," have been playing jazz together for some time at the institution and are led by Harold ("Chink") Wing, Mercury records songwriter and arranger, as well as one of the prisoners. "The Evolution of Jazz" is an interpretation in music and song of the development of this original American art form from Southern Gospel, through the war periods, up to today. Some rarely heard songs favored by early jazz fans are included along with many new arrangements of the foundation melodies of the genre. (Johnson, "Prisoners to Sing a Few Bars," *Crusader*, September 21, 1972)

Wing also played regularly for students, introducing them to local musicians, supplying entertainment, and presenting a broad spectrum of musical possibilities while continuing his efforts to help prisoners. An example, as written up in the *Crusader* in 1976:

> It isn't often that you get the chance to hear a composer play his own works, and to donate toward a worthwhile cause at the same time, but that is exactly what will be happening on Friday night. . . . Chink Wing, a versatile composer, arranger, drummer, and pianist, is bringing his Newark, New Jersey–based nightclub act band, "Music on Wings," to the area for a Prison Visitors Service

Benefit Concert/Dance.... All proceeds from this Concert/Dance will be turned over to the Prison Visitors Service, a non-profit volunteer organization that provides special services to the families of inmates at the U.S. Northeastern Penitentiary at Lewisburg.

The performances, like the funds they generated, were warmly welcomed; as student reporter Richard Boehret noted, "True jazz lives on!" See Richard Boehret, "Chink Brings On the Blues," *Crusader*, October 15, 1976.

98 Simms, "Chink Wing Joins Jam." As an educator, Wing helped young artists, including singer Tisha Campbell, get early performance experience by coaching youth bands.

99 A pair of these songs, "Clean Up Newark" and "Join the Newark Block Clubs," were city commissions. As is mentioned in a 1979 piece in *Information*: the "Summer '79: Cleanest Summer of All Time" rally featured "the first public performance of Newark's Clean City campaign song, 'Clean Up Newark,' composed and arranged by Harold 'Chink' Wing. It was performed by a group of professional musicians and students from Maple Avenue School." "'Cleanest Summer' in Full Swing," *Information*, July 1979, 3.

These two commissions were also released on vinyl: Harold "Chink" Wing and Co., featuring Ann Bailey, "Join the Newark Block Clubs" and "Clean Up Newark," Newark Block Club and Tenant Council NE-72079-1, 7-inch single, 45 rpm.

100 "Consequences of a Drug Addict Role" appears on Shirley Horn, *Where Are You Going*, Perception Records PLP 31, 1972, LP.

101 Dyer, *But Beautiful*, 195.

102 See a short write-up of Wing's court appearance in "'Let Me Break Dope Habit,' Begs N.J. Drummer," *Jet Magazine*, May 15, 1958.

103 Rainy Smith, quoted in Richard Harrington, "The Wonder of the Way She Sings," *Washington Post*, October 18, 1992.

104 See "Dope Addiction and the Jazz Musician," *Playboy Magazine*, November 1960.

105 Baraka, *Digging*, 101.

106 For ease of access, these are the songs Wing copyrighted in order of registration: "Love from Your Mother," "That's What I'm Looking For," "Spare a Moment!," "But I Was Sure That She'd Be Gone," "Drifting along Down Broadway," "All Cities and All Countries to Be Free!," "That's the Way They Send Their Love," "Black People!," "An African Girl Is Queen of the World," "Educate Your Mind," "It's Time for Us," "They Make It All Worth While," "Are the Rumors True?," "Harolyn's Lovely" (for his daughter, Harolyn Wing), "Life Will Be No Bore in Music," "Catch a Ton of Fun, Pun, Fun," "Lois," "Martin Luther King, a Black American King," "Pray I'll Be in Heaven One Sweet Day," "The Same from Which We Came," "Pattern of Life," "The World Will Set Love Free," "God, Wake Me from This Dream," "Nisa!," "The Love of My Woman," "The Fare to Heaven," "The Cherry Picker," "New York City," "While Listening to the Music!," "Give the Credit to God," "Compensation," "Can I Have You?," "Search for the Love Door,"

"Long, Long Hair," "Don't You Try to Hold Us Back ('Cause We're Little)," and "Turn, Mister Fate, to Me."

I'm also reminded here of Brent Hayes Edwards's "micropoetics of the song title," specifically of understanding, per poet John Ashbery, a title as a keyhole, a small aperture that allows one to understand some of a work's shades. Yet what does a title become when it is all that remains of a song? See Edwards, *Epistrophies*, 181–96.

107   Goldston, interview by Jonathan Leal.
108   Barbara Kukla, interview by Jonathan Leal, August 30, 2020.
109   Tomlinson and Lipsitz, "American Studies as Accompaniment," 13.
110   Tomlinson and Lipsitz, "American Studies as Accompaniment," 12.
111   As many have noted, drummers are often implicitly (if not explicitly) subordinated to melodic soloists in many critical jazz discourses (unless, of course, those drummers happen to be bandleaders or national brands). As Ingrid Monson puts it in her classic study, "The drummer is generally the member of the band most underrated by the audience and least discussed in the jazz historical and analytical literature. Since drummers don't play harmonies and melodies in the same way as other instrumentalists, audience members and even some musicians have a tendency to deprecate the musical knowledge of the person sitting behind the drum set. Many mistakenly assume that the drummer just plays rhythm and therefore doesn't participate in the melodic and harmonic flow of the music." Monson, *Saying Something*, 51.
112   Ellison, *Collected Essays*, 227.
113   Woloch, *One vs. the Many*, 50.
114   An example: Wing never recorded his own songs as the "main" act. The songs of his that were recorded were always sung or played by others. So because the performance of each of Wing's tunes is always mediated through others' bodies, intentions, and aesthetics, one thus listens for his songwriting as one does for his drumming: with a sense of accompaniment in mind. That is: Wing's songwriting comes into view only in relation to the artists bringing his music to life. The takeaway: by necessity more than convention, one is forced to talk about the ways musicians elaborate each other's visions and personalities.
115   Salinas, "Music for the Masses."
116   Reed, *Soundworks*, 64.
117   Reed, *Soundworks*, 64.
118   Salinas, "Music for the Masses."
119   Goldston, interview by Jonathan Leal.
120   Elda María Román's scholarship explores such contentions brilliantly. See Román, *Race and Upward Mobility*.
121   See especially Brackett, *Categorizing Sound*.
122   Fanon, *Black Skin, White Masks*, 192.

EPILOGUE. AFFINITIES

1   Late in his life, as an emeritus professor of literature, Araki both performed and wrote about music actively, collaborating with and covering local groups as a musician and as a critic for Honolulu publications. One article for the *Honolulu Advertiser*, "A Lot of Jazz," offers concert reviews alongside general, if quietly prickly, thoughts on jazz, its global reception, and the United States:

> Jazz music in all its variety—Dixieland, traditional mainstream plus bebop, cool, and modern, fusion of jazz and rock, and avant-garde—might well be the only native product of the United States that is welcome and esteemed throughout the world. While jazz has been this country's most effective ambassador of good will around the world, at home it's been treated with relative indifference, even disdain, during the past quarter of a century. But today, jazz is suddenly very much alive in the United States, rekindling the interest of those who were once among its appreciative audience and attracting youngsters surfeited with rock. (See James T. Araki, "A Lot of Jazz," *Honolulu Advertiser*, February 24, 1980.)

Too, like the other figures in this book, by the time he reached his final years, Araki had also left lasting impressions on those around and after him. Saxophonist Gabe Baltazar, reflecting in his autobiography on his career and politely complicating his press label as "the first Asian-American jazz player," noted that "prior to my notoriety in the jazz scene, there were others, and I think they played great.... Jim Araki worked with Hampton's band. The late Jim Araki." Robert Huey, a scholar of Japanese literature and one of Araki's former colleagues, told me via correspondence that Araki was not only "kind," "soft-spoken," and humble, speaking about his jazz career only after being asked about it directly, but also well regarded for his research, service, and teaching among his academic peers. Fred Kavanagh, one of Araki's former dissertation advisees, mentioned that Araki "was one of the most amazing people I have ever known (and I've known a few)." Mas Manbo of the *Nippon Times*, writing some thirty years after first profiling Araki in 1948, reflected, "It was early in 1948 when Japanese musicians told me about this amazing young fellow who would sit in with Japanese bands and play all kinds of instruments well.... Jim Araki, a 22-year-old lieutenant attached to the Allied Translator and Interpreter Section." And George Yoshida, in an oral history interview conducted by Alice Ito and John Pai in Seattle, Washington, reflected fondly:

> [There was this] outstanding musician . . . Jimmy Araki. Jimmy, he was a little bit younger than I was, and he was—let's see. Where did he go now? What camp? Oh, Gila in Arizona. And when he was there, he was maybe high school or junior high school, but he learned how to play, play the clarinet in camp. Pretty soon he's moved into the saxophone. And soon enough he's playing the saxophone in the dance band. Well, there aren't too many people like

that. And he was so proficient that when he, when eventually he was inducted in the Army and he ended up at Fort Snelling, and I don't think he knew—well, he may have knew, known some Japanese, but eventually he became an instructor. I mean that was, he was so sharp musically and language-wise, too. And I think he was the leader of the band at Fort Snelling. But he was so good. I mean he loved music. He had, all by himself, every so often I'd see him in the auditorium all by himself, he was playing his saxophone or playing the piano, self-taught, playing the piano. He—I said goodbye to him after, when I graduated Fort Snelling. I mean, next thing I knew, years later he ends up in Hawaii as a professor, and he's teaching Japanese language, translating Japanese, these classical Japanese plays, songs into English so forth, there. So it's—Professor Araki, University of Hawaii. And he plays—during the occupation, he taught bebop to Japanese musicians. . . . That's so far out.

"My dad was serious," Araki's son told me. "He was interested in music, interested in literature, interested in what it meant to be an American. He enjoyed living with all of that." Baltazar, *If It Swings, It's Music*, 205; Robert Huey, email message to author, May 19, 2019; Fred Kavanagh, email message to author, August 13, 2019; Mas Manbo, "When Douglas MacArthur 'Reigned' in Japan," *Pacific Citizen*, New Year Special, January 5–12, 1979; George Yoshida, interview by Alice Ito (primary) and John Pai (secondary), Seattle, February 18, 2002, Densho Visual History Collection, Densho Digital Archive, Densho IT: denshovh-ygeorge-01-0035; and Dale Araki, interview by Jonathan Leal via Zoom, September 24, 2020. For a Japanese-language retrospective on Araki's career, see *Asahi Shimbun*, December 13, 1984, Evening Publication No. 03.

2 Adams, *Epic of America*, 404.
3 L. Hughes, *Collected Poems*, 387.
4 L. Hughes, *Collected Poems*, 396.
5 E. Alexander, *Black Interior*, 4–5.
6 Z. Jackson, *Becoming Human*.
7 Ramsey, *Amazing Bud Powell*, 56.
8 L. Hughes, *Collected Poems*, 390.
9 Matthews, "1995: Mariah Carey, *Daydream*."
10 As Ramón Saldívar writes, "Private lives can only be apprehended in their social terms. And the opposite also holds true. The ultimate efficacy and import of social movements can only be reckoned in personal histories." R. Saldívar, *Borderlands of Culture*, 434.
11 Le-Khac, *Giving Form to an Asian and Latinx America*, 50.
12 Molina, "Understanding Race as a Relational Concept," 101–2.
13 Molina, "Understanding Race as a Relational Concept," 104–5.
14 Lipsitz et al., "Race as a Relational Theory," 23.
15 Molina, HoSang, and Gutiérrez, "Theorizing Race Relationally," 19. See also Lipsitz, Sánchez, and Hernández with HoSang and Molina, "Race as a Relational Theory: A Roundtable Discussion."

16 Fanon, *Black Skin, White Masks* (2008), 193.
17 See especially Alexander Weheliye's *Habeas Viscus: Racializing Assemblages, Biopolitics, and Black Feminist Theories of the Human*.
18 Moten, *In the Break*, 1.
19 See G. Chang, "Eternally Foreign." See also Fujii, "What a Japanese-American Artist Inherited."
20 Shelemay, "Musical Communities," 373.
21 Ben Ratliff, "The Sideman Moves out of History's Shadows," *New York Times*, April 5, 1998, https://www.nytimes.com/1998/04/05/theater/jazz-view-the-sideman-moves-out-of-history-s-shadows.html.
22 Alvarez, *Power of the Zoot*, 244.
23 As Tyshawn Sorey puts it, "Improviser-composers within the African American creative music tradition who reject 'jazz musician' as a totalizing label inspire me. Following the pathways forged by these predecessors, I have long resisted generic labeling and racially essentialized, social categorizations of my own work. I renounce the label of 'jazz composer' or 'jazz arranger' for this composition. This overly suggestive term, which is often incorrectly applied to my music by critics, does not describe the realization of the music itself. For these reasons it is crucial for me as a Black creative improviser-composer . . . to define my terms of creative music making." Sorey, "Perle Noire," 44–45.
24 Inada, *Legends from Camp*, 57.
25 Gene Oishi, another Nisei writer and music enthusiast, shared similar visions. For more, see Oishi, *In Search of Hiroshi*, 98–99.
26 Baldwin, "Sonny's Blues," 126.
27 My thinking on these contemporary matters has been informed by recent work by Paul Gilroy, Shoshana Zuboff, Byung-Chul Han, Ramón Saldívar, Jia Tolentino, Joanna Demers, and others. See especially Gilroy, "Agonistic Belonging"; Zuboff, *Age of Surveillance Capitalism*; Han, *Psychopolitics*; R. Saldívar, "Historical Fantasy"; Tolentino, *Trick Mirror*; and Demers, *Drone and Apocalypse*.
28 For more on Jafa's film and career, see "Arthur Jafa."
29 See E. Alexander, *Black Interior*, 4–5.
30 Moraga, "'Holla' from the West Side," 97.

bibliography

ARCHIVES

Archive of Recorded Sound, Stanford University, Stanford, CA
Archives Center, National Museum of American History, Smithsonian Institution,
    Washington, DC
Bancroft Library, University of California, Berkeley, CA
    Digital Repository
    Theses and Dissertations Catalogue
    Yuen Ren Chao Papers
Benson Latin American Collections, University of Texas at Austin, Austin, TX
    Américo Paredes Papers
Densho Archives
    Digital Repository
Institute of Jazz Studies, Rutgers University, Newark, NJ
Music Library, Stanford University, Stanford, CA
    Metronome Magazine
Newark Public Library
    Digital Collections
Special Collections, University of Hawai'i at Mānoa, Honolulu, HI
    Oral Histories of Japanese Studies Scholars, 1960s–1980s
Special Collections and University Archives, Stanford University, Stanford, CA
    Juan Felipe Herrera Papers
    Raúl R. Salinas Papers
Stanford University Video Collection, 1934–2016. Digital Archive, Stanford, CA
Texas Music Museum Exhibits and Holdings, Austin, TX
    Huntsville Echo
    Texas State Library and Archives Commission

UC Santa Barbara Library, Department of Special Collections, University of California, Santa Barbara, Santa Barbara, CA
  José Montoya Papers
  Oscar Acosta Papers

SELECT UNPUBLISHED INTERVIEWS AND CORRESPONDENCE

Akiyoshi, Toshiko, and Anthony Brown. Interview. Archives Center, National Museum of American History, Smithsonian Institution, June 29, 2008. Transcript.
Araki, Dale. Interview by Jonathan Leal via Zoom. September 24, 2020.
Araki, James. Interview by Dr. George Akita. Conducted June 15, 1981. Oral Histories of Japanese Studies Scholars, Special Collections, University of Hawaii at Manoa.
Goldston, Eugene "Goldie." Interview by Jonathan Leal at Chateau of Spain, Newark, NJ, August 7, 2018.
Huey, Robert. Email message to author. May 19, 2019.
Kavanagh, Fred. Email message to author. August 13, 2019.
Kukla, Barbara. Interview by Jonathan Leal by phone. August 30, 2020.
Salinas, Raúl R. Interview by Ben Olguín and Louis Mendoza. Stanford, CA, May 5, 1994. Stanford University Video Collection, 1934–2016, Digital Archive. https://purl.stanford.edu/qy544qy8912.
Wing, Malee. Interview by Jonathan Leal by phone. September 2018.
Yoshida, George. Interview by Alice Ito (primary) and John Pai (secondary). Seattle, Washington, February 18, 2002. Densho IT: denshovh-ygeorge-01-0035. Densho Visual History Collection, Digital Archive, Densho Archives.

MULTIMEDIA

Abdurraqib, Hanif, and Fred Moten. "Building a Stairway to Get Us Closer to Something beyond This Place." *Millennials Are Killing Capitalism* (podcast), May 13, 2021. https://millennialsarekillingcapitalism.libsyn.com/website/hanif-abdurraqib-fred-moten-building-a-stairway-to-get-us-closer-to-something-beyond-this-place.
Ho, Fred. "Fred Ho: Free New Africa! Boogaloo." YouTube video, 3:41, March 30, 2011. https://youtu.be/kNZVn0KcGaU.
Moody, James. "James Moody: Forming My Own Band." YouTube video, 3:40, May 1, 2010. https://youtu.be/9-iB7zD7-Ks.
Remnick, David. "Mass Incarceration in America, Then and Now." *New Yorker Radio Hour* (podcast), December 3, 2021. https://www.newyorker.com/podcast/the-new-yorker-radio-hour/mass-incarceration-in-america-then-and-now.
Sorey, Tyshawn. "Tyshawn Sorey: A Reality Check with Dave Douglas." New Music USA. YouTube video, 3:50, October 1, 2019. https://www.youtube.com/watch?v=Qgv7ah3kFR0.

Theurer, Michiko, and Jonathan Leal. "A Sonic Offering: Michiko Theurer and Jonathan Leal on the Air/Light Podcast, Ep. 11." Interview by Aaron Winslow. *Air/Light Podcast*, episode 11, November 4, 2021. https://airlightmagazine.org/etc/podcasts/a-sonic-offering-michiko-theurer-and-jonathan-leal-on-the-air-light-podcast/.

NEWSPAPERS AND MAGAZINES

Araki, James T. "A Lot of Jazz." *Honolulu Advertiser*, February 24, 1980.
Asahi Shimbun, December 13, 1984. Evening Publication No. 03. Accessed via Kikuzo II Visual.
Boehret, Richard. "Chink Brings On the Blues." *Crusader*, October 15, 1976.
Boyer, Richard O. "Profiles: Bop." *New Yorker*, July 3, 1948, 31.
Cole, Teju. "Pictures in the Aftermath." *New York Times*, April 11, 2017. https://www.nytimes.com/2017/04/11/magazine/pictures-in-the-aftermath.html.
Fox, Charles. "Jazz and Swing: Reviews." *Gramophone*, July 1957.
Gila News-Courier. "Butte Elects School Officers: Araki Is President." June 22, 1943, 4.
Gila News-Courier. "High School Prom to Honor Seniors." May 27, 1943, 5.
Gila News-Courier. "Seven Graduate from Butte Hi." February 3, 1944, 3.
Gila News-Courier. "Thirty Three Gilans Will Go on Active Duty June 7." June 1, 1944.
Harrington, Richard. "The Wonder of the Way She Sings." *Washington Post*, October 18, 1992.
Information. "'Cleanest Summer' in Full Swing." July 1979, 3.
Information. "Newark Recreation Sponsors Jazz Festival." November 1978, 16.
Jet Magazine. "'Let Me Break Dope Habit,' Begs N.J. Drummer." May 15, 1958.
Johnson, Doug. "Prisoners to Sing a Few Bars." *Crusader*, September 21, 1972.
Kukla, Barbara. "Friends to 'Wing It' at Essex County College for a Tribute to a Music Pro." *Newark Star-Ledger*, February 19, 1985.
Los Angeles Times. "Death Notices." January 6, 1992.
Luce, Henry. "The American Century." *Life Magazine*, February 17, 1941, 61–65.
Manbo, Mas. "He Blows High . . . He Blows Low." *Nippon Times Magazine*, March 4, 1948.
Manbo, Mas. "When Douglas MacArthur 'Reigned' in Japan." *Pacific Citizen*, New Year Special, January 5–12, 1979.
Metronome. "The Bebop Feud." April 1944, 44.
Metronome. "Jazz Looks Ahead." October 1945, 10.
Newark Star-Ledger. "Harold (Chink) Wing, Top Newark Musician." December 21, 1993.
New Jersey After Hours: The Weekly Guide to Entertainment. "Music Master: In N.J. and N.Y." February 1950.
O'Dea, Colleen. "Newark before the Comeback: A City Marked by White Flight, Poor Policy." *New Jersey Spotlight News*, September 4, 2019. https://www.njspotlight.com/2019/09/19-09-02-newark-before-the-comeback-a-city-marked-by-white-flight-and-poor-policy/.
Pacific Citizen, March 10, 1951.
Pacific Stars and Stripes, March 24, 1946.

Pacific Stars and Stripes, May 26, 1946.

Playboy Magazine. "Dope Addiction and the Jazz Musician." November 1960.

Ratliff, Ben. "The Sideman Moves out of History's Shadows." *New York Times*, April 5, 1998. https://www.nytimes.com/1998/04/05/theater/jazz-view-the-sideman-moves-out-of-history-s-shadows.html.

Salesses, Matthew. "'Good-Looking for an Asian': How I Shed White Ideals of Masculinity." *Guardian*, October 23, 2020.

Salinas, Raúl, Carmen Scoleri, Herb Alexander, et al. Quartered Notes. *Huntsville Echo*, January 1964–March 1969.

Simms, C. Alan. "Chink Wing Joins Jam at JFK: Jazz Star Tells Young His Secrets: Study and Work." *Information*, May 1975, 2.

Smith, Billie. "This Is It." *New Jersey Herald News*, April 20, 1946.

Smith, Billie. "This Is It." *New Jersey Herald News*, May 11, 1946.

Smith, Michael Denzel. "The Gatekeepers." *Harper's Magazine*, November 21, 2018.

Time. "Be-Bop Be-bopped." March 25, 1946, 52.

Time. "Jazz: The Loneliest Monk." February 28, 1964. Tracy, Jack. "Capsule Comments: Tristano-Garner." *Downbeat* 17, no. 8 (April 21, 1950): 5.

Ulanov, Barry. "Band Reviews: Dizzy Gillespie." *Metronome*, September 1947, 22.

Ulanov, Barry. "Who's Dead, Bebop or Its Detractors?" *Metronome*, June 1947, 50.

Yaban Gogai. "Pictorial Review of the MISLS." December 1945, 9.

SELECTED DISCOGRAPHY

August, Joseph "Mr. Google Eyes." *Rock My Soul*. Route 66 Records KIX-32, 1986 reissue, LP.

Erroll Garner Trio. *Garnering*. Mercury Records MG 36026, 1955, LP.

Erroll Garner Trio. *The Greatest Garner*. Liner notes by Whitney Balliet (1956) and Bob Porter (2003). Atlantic Records 1227, 2003 reissue, CD.

See also Garner, Erroll

Evans, Bill. *Conversations with Myself*. Verve Records V6-8526, 1963, LP.

Feld, Steven. "Hiroshima: The Last Sound." *The Time of Bells, 4*. VoxLox, 2006, CD.

Fitzgerald, Ella. "I Wonder What Kind of a Guy You'd Be." Song written by Harold Wing, orchestra directed by Sy Oliver. Decca Records 28930, 1953, 7-inch single, 45 rpm.

Garner, Erroll. *Piano Solos Vol. II*. Liner notes by Ralph J. Gleason. Atlantic Records ALR 135, 1952, LP.

Horn, Shirley. *Where Are You Going*. Perception Records PLP 31, 1972, LP.

Jimmy Araki Trio. *Jazz Beat: Midnight Jazz Session*. Liner notes by Kiyoshi Fujita and Etsuzo Yoshida. Nippon Victor JV-5006, 1959, LP.

Jones, Etta. *'75*. Westbound Records W-203, 1975, LP.

Lionel Hampton and His Big Orchestra. "Airmail Special." Clef Records 89153X45–B, 1955, 7-inch single, 45 rpm.

Mance, Junior. *That Lovin' Feelin'*. Milestone Records MSP 9041, 1972, LP.

Moody, James. *Moody's Home*. EmArcy Records EP-1-6010, 1951, EP.

Parker, Charlie. *Night and Day*. Verve Records MGC–5003, 1956, LP.
Paul Quinichette All Stars. *Moods*. Liner notes unsigned. EmArcy Records MG 36003, 1954, LP.
Ramírez, Tomás. *Téjazz*. Liner notes by Raúl Salinas. Vireo Records, 1995, CD.
Salinas, Raúl R. *Beyond the BEATen Path*. Liner notes by Stephen Bruton. Red Salmon, 2002, CD.
Salinas, Raúl R. *Los Many Mundos of raúlrsalinas: Un Poetic Jazz Viaje con Friends*. Liner notes by Abel Salas and Raúl Salinas. Calaca Press/Red Salmon, 2000, CD.
Salinas, Raúl R., and Fred Ho. *Red Arc: A Call for Liberación con Salsa y Cool*. Liner notes by Alejandro Murguia, Raúl Salinas, and Fred Ho. Wings Press, 2005, CD.
Tristano, Lennie. *Lennie Tristano*. Liner notes by Barry Ulanov. Atlantic Records 1224, 1955, LP.
Various artists. *Jazz in Japan: 1947–1963*. Victor Japan 60722, 2001, 7 CDs.
Victor Gay Bop. "Jimmy's Bop." Victor (JPN) V-40265A, 1949, LP.
Wing, Harold "Chink" and Co., featuring Ann Bailey. "Join the Newark Block Clubs" and "Clean Up Newark." Newark Block Club and Tenant Council NE-72079-1, 7-inch single, 45 rpm.

BOOKS, JOURNALS, AND OTHER SOURCES

Abdul-Jabbar, Kareem. "I Hear." In *Chasin' the Bird: Charlie Parker in California*, by Dave Chisholm with Peter Markowski, 1. Seoul, South Korea: Z2 Comics, 2020
Adams, James Truslow. *The Epic of America*. Boston: Little, Brown, 1931.
Albright, Daniel. *Panaesthetics: On the Unity and Diversity of the Arts*. New Haven, CT: Yale University Press, 2014.
Aldama, Frederick Luis, and Arturo J. Aldama. "Decolonizing Latinx Masculinities: An Introduction." In *Decolonizing Latinx Masculinities*, edited by Frederick Luis Aldama and Arturo J. Aldama, 3–22. Tucson: University of Arizona Press, 2020.
Alexander, Elizabeth. *The Black Interior: Essays*. St. Paul, MN: Graywolf, 2004.
Alexander, Michelle. *The New Jim Crow: Mass Incarceration in the Age of Colorblindness*. New York: New Press, 2010.
Alvarez, Luis. *The Power of the Zoot: Youth Culture and Resistance during World War II*. Berkeley: University of California Press, 2009.
Amezcua, Mike. "On the Outer Rim of Jazz: Mexican American Jazzmen and the Making of the Modern Pacific Borderlands, 1950–1969." *Journal of Social History* 50, no. 2 (Winter 2016): 411–31.
Araki, James T. *The Ballad-Drama of Medieval Japan*. Los Angeles: University of California Press, 1964.
Araki, James T. "Japanese Literary Studies: The Trials and Rewards." *Educational Perspectives* 13, no. 1 (March 1974): 29–32.
Araki, James T. "The Kōwakamai: A Survey of Its Development as a Medieval Performed Art and a Study of Its Texts." PhD diss., University of California, Berkeley, 1961.

Araki, James T. "A Study of Ueda Akinari and the Ugetsu monogatari." Master's thesis, University of California, Berkeley, 1958.

Armbruster, Kurt E. *Before Seattle Rocked: A City and Its Music*. Seattle: University of Washington Press, 2011.

"Arthur Jafa: *Dreams Are Colder Than Death*." Liquid Blackness. Accessed September 15, 2021. https://liquidblackness.com/arthur-jafa-dreams-are-colder-than-death.

Ashbery, John. *Collected Poems: 1956–1987*. New York: Library of America, 2008.

Atkins, E. Taylor. *Blue Nippon: Authenticating Jazz in Japan*. Durham, NC: Duke University Press, 2001.

Atkins, E. Taylor. "Localizing Jazz and Globalizing Identities in Japan." Paper prepared for Triangle East Asia Colloquium, University of North Carolina at Chapel Hill, November 1, 2003.

Attali, Jacques. *Noise: The Political Economy of Music*. Minneapolis: University of Minnesota Press, 1985.

Auslander, Philip. "The Performativity of Performance Documentation." *Journal of Performance and Art* 28, no. 3 (September 2006): 1–10.

Baker, Houston. *Blues, Ideology, and Afro-American Literature: A Vernacular Theory*. Chicago: University of Chicago Press, 1985.

Baldwin, James. "The Artist's Struggle for Integrity." In *The Cross of Redemption: Uncollected Writings*, edited by Randall Kenan, 41–47. New York: Pantheon, 2010.

Baldwin, James. *Collected Essays*. Edited by Toni Morrison. New York: Library of America, 1998.

Baldwin, James. "Sonny's Blues." In *Going to Meet the Man*, 101–42. New York: Random House, 1995.

Baldwin, James. "The World I Never Made." Lecture, National Press Club Luncheon Speakers, Washington, DC, December 10, 1986. https://www.loc.gov/rr/record/pressclub/baldwin.html.

Baltazar, Gabe. *If It Swings, It's Music: The Autobiography of Hawai'i's Gabe Baltazar Jr.* With Theo Garneau. Honolulu: University of Hawai'i Press, 2012.

Baraka, Amiri [LeRoi Jones]. *Black Music*. New York: Akashi Classics, 2010.

Baraka, Amiri. *Digging: The Afro-American Soul of American Classical Music*. Berkeley: University of California Press, 2010.

Benjamin, Walter. *Illuminations*. Edited with an introduction by Hannah Arendt. New York: Schocken, 1968.

Berliner, Paul. *Thinking in Jazz: The Infinite Art of Improvisation*. Chicago: University of Chicago Press, 1994.

Blais-Tremblay, Vanessa. "'Where You Are Accepted, You Blossom': Toward Care Ethics in Jazz Historiography." *Jazz and Culture* 2 (2019): 59–83.

Borge, Jason. *Tropical Riffs: Latin America and the Politics of Jazz*. Durham, NC: Duke University Press, 2018.

Born, Georgina. "On Musical Mediation: Ontology, Technology, and Creativity." *Twentieth-Century Music* 2, no. 1 (March 2005): 7–36.

Brackett, Dave. *Categorizing Sound: Genre and Twentieth-Century Popular Music*. Berkeley: University of California Press, 2016.

Braggs, Rashida. *Jazz Diasporas: Race, Music, and Migration in Post–World War II Paris*. Oakland: University of California Press, 2016.

Briones, Matthew. *Jim and Jap Crow: A Cultural History of 1940s Interracial America*. Princeton, NJ: Princeton University Press, 2012.

Britt, Stan. *Dexter Gordon: A Musical Biography*. New York: Da Capo, 1989.

Brodsky, Seth. *From 1989, or European Music and the Modernist Unconscious*. Berkeley: University of California Press, 2017.

Brooks, Daphne. *Liner Notes for the Revolution: The Intellectual Life of Black Feminist Sound*. Cambridge, MA: Harvard University Press, 2021.

Brown, Anthony. "Modern Jazz Drumset Artistry." *Black Perspective in Music* 18, nos. 1/2 (1990): 39–58.

Bruce, La Marr Jurelle. *How to Go Mad without Losing Your Mind: Madness and Black Radical Creativity*. Durham, NC: Duke University Press 2021.

Burns, Ken, and Geoffrey C. Ward. *Ken Burns' Jazz: The Story of America's Music*. New York: Sony Music Entertainment, 2000. Documentary miniseries.

Butler, Judith. *Gender Trouble: Feminism and the Subversion of Identity*. London: Routledge, 1990.

Butterfield, Matthew W. "Variant Timekeeping Patterns and Their Effects in Jazz Drumming." MTO: *A Journal for the Society for Music Theory* 16, no. 4 (December 2010). https://www.mtosmt.org/issues/mto.10.16.4/mto.10.16.4.butterfield.html.

Campbell, Gregory Alan. "A Beautiful, Shining Sound Object: Contextualizing Multi-instrumentalism in the Association for the Advancement of Creative Musicians." DMA diss., University of Washington 2006.

carrington, andré m. *Speculative Blackness: The Future of Race in Science Fiction*. Minneapolis: University of Minnesota Press, 2017.

Chang, Gordon H. "Eternally Foreign: Asian Americans, History, and Race." In *Doing Race: 21 Essays for the 21st Century*, edited by Hazel Markus and Paula Moya, 216–33. New York: W. W. Norton, 2010.

Chang, Jeff. "Future Aesthetics." Lecture, Stanford University, January 20, 2016.

Charnas, Dan. *Dilla Time: The Life and Afterlife of J Dilla, the Hip-Hop Producer Who Reinvented Rhythm*. New York: MCD/Farrar, Straus & Giroux, 2022.

Chisholm, Dave. *Chasin' the Bird: Charlie Parker in California*. With Peter Markowski. Seoul, South Korea: Z2 Comics, 2020.

Chuh, Kandice. *Imagine Otherwise: On Asian Americanist Critique*. Durham, NC: Duke University Press, 2003.

Clifford, James. "Notes on Travel and Theory." Commentary in *Traveling Theories, Traveling Theorists*. Vol. 5 of *Inscriptions*, edited by James Clifford and Vivek Dhareshwar. Center for Cultural Studies, University of California, Santa Cruz, 1989. https://culturalstudies.ucsc.edu/inscriptions/volume-5/james-clifford/.

Clifford, James. *Returns: Becoming Indigenous in the Twenty-First Century*. Cambridge, MA: Harvard University Press, 2013.

Cole, Andrew. *The Birth of Theory*. Chicago: University of Chicago Press, 2014.
Coleman, Steve. "The Dozens: Steve Coleman on Charlie Parker." Edited by Ted Panken and Steve Coleman. M-Base, accessed November 15, 2020. http://m-base.com/the-dozens-steve-coleman-on-charlie-parker/.
Cooder, Ry. *Los Angeles Stories*. San Francisco: City Lights, 2011.
Crow, Bill. *Jazz Anecdotes: Second Time Around*. New York: Oxford University Press, 2001.
Curvin, Robert. *Inside Newark: Decline, Rebellion, and the Search for Transformation*. New Brunswick, NJ: Rutgers University Press, 2014.
Demers, Joanna. *Drone and Apocalypse: Exhibit Catalogue for the End of the World*. Alresford, Hants, UK: Zero, 2015.
Denning, Michael. *Noise Uprising: The Audiopolitics of a World Musical Revolution*. London: Verso, 2015.
DeVeaux, Scott. *The Birth of Bebop: A Social and Musical History*. Berkeley: University of California Press, 1997.
Dewitt, John L. *Final Report: Japanese Evacuation from the West Coast, 1942*. Washington, DC: US Government Printing Office, 1943. https://www.archive.org/details/japaneseevacuatioodewi.
Diawara, Manthia. "One World in Relation: Édouard Glissant in Conversation with Manthia Diawara." *Nka: Journal of Contemporary African Art* 2011, no. 28 (Spring 2011): 4–19.
Díaz, Junot. *The Brief Wondrous Life of Oscar Wao*. New York: Riverhead, 2007.
Dillon, Stephen. "The Prisoner's Dream: Queer Visions from Solitary Confinement." *Qui Parle* 23, no. 2 (Spring/Summer 2015): 161–84.
Doran, James M. *Erroll Garner: The Most Happy Piano*. Metuchen, NJ: Scarecrow / Institute of Jazz Studies, Rutgers University, 1985.
Douglas, Mary. *Purity and Danger: An Analysis of Concepts of Pollution and Taboo*. New York: Routledge Classics, 2008.
Dower, John W. *Embracing Defeat: Japan in the Wake of World War II*. New York: W. W. Norton, 2000.
Duersten, Matthew. "When Charlie Parker Came to L.A.: The Peaks and Valleys of a Jazz Genius." *LA Magazine*, March 25, 2014. https://www.lamag.com/culturefiles/when-charlie-parker-came-to-la-the-peaks-and-valleys-of-a-jazz-genius/.
Dyer, Geoff. *But Beautiful: A Book about Jazz*. New York: Farrar, Straus & Giroux, 2009.
Edwards, Brent Hayes. *Epistrophies: Jazz and the Literary Imagination*. Cambridge, MA: Harvard University Press, 2017.
Edwards, Brent Hayes. "Evidence." *Transition*, no. 90 (2001): 42–67.
Edwards, Brent Hayes. "The Taste of the Archive." *Callaloo* 35, no. 4 (Fall 2012): 944–72.
Elam, Michele. *The Souls of Mixed Folk: Race, Politics, and Aesthetics in the New Millennium*. Stanford, CA: Stanford University Press, 2011.
Ellison, Ralph. *The Collected Essays of Ralph Ellison*. Edited by John F. Callahan. New York: Modern Library, 2003.
Ellison, Ralph. *Invisible Man*. New York: Vintage, 1995.

Emirbayer, Mustafa. "Manifesto for a Relational Sociology." *American Journal of Sociology* 103, no. 2 (September 1997): 281–317.

"Erroll Garner Discography." Jazz Discography Project, accessed October 15, 2018. https://www.jazzdisco.org/erroll-garner/discography/.

Fanon, Frantz. *Black Skin, White Masks*. 1967. Translated by Richard Philcox. New York: Grove, 2008.

Faulkner, William. *Requiem for a Nun*. 1950. New York: Vintage, 2011.

Feld, Steven. *Jazz Cosmopolitanism in Accra: Five Musical Years in Ghana*. Durham, NC: Duke University Press, 2012.

Fellezs, Kevin. "Silenced but Not Silent: Asian Americans and Jazz." In *Alien Encounters: Popular Culture in Asian America*, edited by Mimi Thi Nguyen and Thuy Linh N. Tu, 69–110. Durham, NC: Duke University Press, 2007.

Fischlin, Daniel, Ajay Heble, and George Lipsitz. *The Fierce Urgency of Now: Improvisation, Rights, and the Ethics of Cocreation*. Durham, NC: Duke University Press, 2013.

Fleetwood, Nicole R. *Marking Time: Art in the Age of Mass Incarceration*. Cambridge, MA: Harvard University Press, 2020.

Foertsch, Jacqueline. *Reckoning Day: Race, Place, and the Atom Bomb in Postwar America*. Nashville, TN: Vanderbilt University Press, 2013.

Ford, Phil. *Dig: Sound and Music in Hip Culture*. New York: Oxford University Press, 2013.

Foucault, Michel. *Discipline and Punish: The Birth of the Prison*. Translated by Alan Sheridan. New York: Pantheon, 1978.

Fujii, Moeko. "What a Japanese-American Artist Inherited from the Atomic Bomb." *New Yorker*, December 9, 2018.

Fujino, Diane C. "Revolutionary Dreaming and New Dawns." In *Wicked Theory, Naked Practice: A Fred Ho Reader*, by Fred Ho, edited by Diane C. Fujino, 7–40. Minneapolis: University of Minnesota Press, 2009.

Garcia, Edgar. *Signs of the Americas: A Poetics of Pictography, Hieroglyphs, and Khipu*. Chicago: University of Chicago Press, 2020.

Garcia, Edgar. *Skins of Columbus: A Dream Ethnography*. Hudson, NY: Fence, 2019.

Geffen, Sasha. "Glitching the Gendered Voice." In *The Oxford Handbook of Electronic Dance Music*, edited by Luis Manuel García-Mispireta and Robin James. Oxford University Press, November 10, 2021. https://doi.org/10.1093/oxfordhb/9780190093723.013.25.

Geffen, Sasha. *Glitter Up the Dark: How Pop Music Broke the Binary*. Austin: University of Texas Press, 2020.

Gendron, Bernard. "A Short Stay in the Sun: The Reception of Bebop, 1944–1950." In *The Bebop Revolution in Words and Music*, edited by Dave Oliphant, 137–60. Austin: Harry Ransom Humanities Research Center, University of Texas at Austin, 1994.

Gennari, John. *Blowin' Hot and Cool: Jazz and Its Critics*. Chicago: University of Chicago Press, 2006.

Giddins, Gary. *Celebrating Bird: The Triumph of Charlie Parker*. New York: Beech Tree, 1987.

Gillespie, Dizzy. *To Be, or Not . . . to Bop*. With Al Fraser. Minneapolis: University of Minnesota Press, 2009.

Gilmore, Ruth Wilson. *Golden Gulag: Prisons, Surplus, Crisis, and Opposition in Globalizing California*. Berkeley: University of California Press, 2007.

Gilroy, Paul. *Against Race: Imagining Political Culture beyond the Color Line*. Cambridge, MA: Belknap Press of Harvard University Press, 2001.

Gilroy, Paul. "Agonistic Belonging: The Banality of Good, the 'Alt Right,' and the Need for Sympathy." *Open Cultural Studies* 3, no. 1 (2019): 1–14.

Gilroy, Paul. *The Black Atlantic: Modernity and Double Consciousness*. Cambridge, MA: Harvard University Press, 1993.

Gilroy, Paul. *Small Acts: Thoughts on the Politics of Black Cultures*. New York: Serpent's Tail, 1993.

Godrej, Farah. "Spaces for Counter-narratives: The Phenomenology of Reclamation." *Frontiers: A Journal of Women Studies* 32, no. 3 (2011): 111–33.

Green, Shannon Louise. "'Art for Life's Sake': Music Schools and Activities in U.S. Social Settlement Houses, 1892–1942." PhD diss., University of Wisconsin–Madison, 1998.

Greif, Mark. *The Age of the Crisis of Man: Thought and Fiction in America, 1933–1973*. Princeton, NJ: Princeton University Press, 2015.

Halberstam, Jack. *Female Masculinity*. Durham, NC: Duke University Press, 1998.

Hall, Stuart. "The Work of Representation." In *Representation: Cultural Representations and Signifying Practices*, edited by Stuart Hall, 13–74. Thousand Oaks, CA: Sage, 1997.

Hall, Stuart, and Lawrence Grossberg. "On Postmodernism and Articulation: An Interview with Stuart Hall." In *Stuart Hall: Critical Dialogues in Cultural Studies*, edited by David Morley and Kuan-Hsing Chen, 131–50. New York: Routledge, 1996.

Hames-Garcia, Michael Roy. *Fugitive Thought: Prison Movements, Race, and the Meaning of Justice*. Minneapolis: University of Minnesota Press, 2004.

Hammes, Jerry. "The Blue Note Nightclub—1950." Jerry Hammes.com, accessed October 1, 2018. https://jerryhammes.com/view/7/17/22.html.

Han, Byung-Chul. *Psychopolitics: Neoliberalism and New Technologies of Power*. New York: Verso, 2017.

Haraway, Donna. *When Species Meet*. Minneapolis: University of Minnesota Press, 2008.

Hartman, Saidiya. *Wayward Lives, Beautiful Experiments: Intimate Histories of Social Upheaval*. New York: W. W. Norton, 2019.

Ho, Fred. "What Makes 'Jazz' the Revolutionary Music of the Twentieth Century, and Will It Be Revolutionary for the Twenty-First Century?" In *Wicked Theory, Naked Practice: A Fred Ho Reader*, by Fred Ho, edited by Diane C. Fujino, 91–103. Minneapolis: University of Minnesota Press, 2009.

Hong, Cathy Park. *Minor Feelings: An Asian American Reckoning*. New York: One World, 2020.

Horkheimer, Max, and Theodor Adorno. *Dialectic of Enlightenment: Philosophical Fragments*. Translated by Edmund Jephcott. Stanford, CA: Stanford University Press, 2009.

Hughes, Langston. *The Collected Poems of Langston Hughes*. Edited by Arnold Rampersad and David Roessel. New York: Vintage, 1995.

Hughes, Timothy S. "Groove and Flow: Six Analytical Essays on the Music of Stevie Wonder." PhD diss., University of Washington, 2003.

Inada, Lawson Fusao. *Legends from Camp*. Minneapolis: Coffee House, 1993.

Intondi, Vincent J. *African Americans against the Bomb: Nuclear Weapons, Colonialism, and the Black Freedom Movement*. Stanford, CA: Stanford University Press, 2015.

Iton, Richard. *In Search of the Black Fantastic: Politics and Popular Culture in the Post–Civil Rights Era*. New York: Oxford University Press, 2008.

Iyer, Vijay. "Beneath Improvisation." In *The Oxford Handbook of Critical Concepts in Music Theory*, edited by Alexander Rehding and Steven Rings. New York: Oxford University Press, 2020. https://doi.org/10.1093/oxfordhb/9780190454746.013.35.

Iyer, Vijay. "The Deft, Quiet Shout of Her Hands: Geri Allen's Speculative Musicalities." *Jazz and Culture* 3, no. 2 (Fall–Winter 2020): 92–110.

Iyer, Vijay. "Exploding the Narrative in Jazz Improvisation." In *Uptown Conversation: The New Jazz Studies*, edited by Robert G. O'Meally, Brent Hayes Edwards, and Farah Jasmine Griffin, 393–403. New York: Columbia University Press, 2004.

Iyer, Vijay. "What's Not Music, but Feels Like Music to You?" *Behavioral and Brain Sciences* 44 (2021): e79. https://doi.org/10.1017/S0140525X20001740.

Jackson, Shannon. "When 'Everything Counts': Experimental Performance and Performance Historiography." In *Representing the Past: Essays in Performance Historiography*, edited by Charlotte M. Canning and Thomas Postlewait, 240–62. Iowa City: Iowa University Press, 2010.

Jackson, Zakiyyah Iman. *Becoming Human: Matter and Meaning in an Antiblack World*. New York: New York University Press, 2020.

Jameson, Fredric. *Postmodernism, or, The Cultural Logic of Late Capitalism*. Durham, NC: Duke University Press, 1991.

Johnson, J. Wilfred. *Ella Fitzgerald: An Annotated Discography*. Jefferson, NC: McFarland, 2010.

Jones, LeRoi [Amiri Baraka]. *Blues People: Negro Music in White America*. New York: W. Morrow, 1963.

Jones, Meta DuEwa. *The Muse Is Music: Jazz Poetry from the Harlem Renaissance to Spoken Word*. Chicago: University of Illinois Press, 2011.

Kajikawa, Loren. "The Sound of Struggle: Black Revolutionary Nationalism and Asian American Jazz." In *Jazz/Not Jazz: The Music and Its Boundaries*, edited by David Ake, Charles Hiroshi Garrett, and Daniel Goldmark, 190–216. Berkeley: University of California Press, 2012.

Kaldewey, Helma. *A People's Music: Jazz in East Germany, 1945–1990*. New York: Cambridge University Press, 2019.

Kaplan, Amy. "'Left Alone with America': The Absence of Empire in the Study of American Culture." In *Cultures of United States Imperialism*, edited by Amy Kaplan and Donald Pease, 3–21. Durham, NC: Duke University Press, 1993.

Kaufman, Bob. *Solitudes Crowded with Loneliness*. New York: New Directions, 1965.

Kelley, Robin D. G. *Freedom Dreams: The Black Radical Imagination*. Boston: Beacon, 2002.

Kitchin, Rob, Chris Perkins, and Martin Dodge. "Thinking about Maps." In *Rethinking Maps: New Frontiers in Cartographic Theory*, edited by Martin Dodge, Rob Kitchin, and Chris R. Perkins, 1–25. New York: Routledge, 2011.

Koselleck, Reinhard. "Does History Accelerate?" In *Sediments of Time: On Possible Histories*, edited and translated by Sean Franzel and Stefan-Ludwig Hoffman, 79–99. Stanford, CA: Stanford University Press, 2018.

Kukla, Barbara. *Encyclopedia of Newark Jazz: A Century of Great Music*. West Orange, NJ: Swing City, 2017.

Kukla, Barbara. *Swing City: Newark Nightlife, 1925–1950*. New Brunswick, NJ: Rutgers University Press, 2002.

Kun, Josh. *Audiotopia: Music, Race, and America*. Berkeley: University of California Press, 2005.

Kun, Josh. *The Tide Was Always High: The Music of Latin America in Los Angeles*. Berkeley: University of California Press, 2017.

Kun, Josh, and Alejandro L. Madrid. "Exceptional Matters, Exceptional Times: A Conversation about the Challenges of U.S. Music Scholarship in the Age of Black Lives Matter and Trump." In *Sounding Together: Collaborative Perspectives on U.S. Music in the Century*, edited by Charles Hiroshi Garrett and Carol J. Oja, 239–63. Ann Arbor: University of Michigan Press, 2021.

Lalami, Laila. *The Moor's Account*. New York: Vintage, 2015.

Leal, Jonathan. "Decorating Time with Tyshawn Sorey." *San Francisco Classical Voice*, August 30, 2021. https://www.sfcv.org/articles/artist-spotlight/decorating-time-tyshawn-sorey.

Leal, Jonathan. Review of *Crossing Bar Lines: The Politics and Practices of Black Musical Space*, by James Gordon Williams. *Jazz and Culture* 5, no. 1 (Spring/Summer 2022): 95–99.

Leal, Jonathan. "*Wild Tongue*: A New Record of Rio Grande Valley Expression." *Rio Bravo: A Journal of the Borderlands* 24 (Spring 2020). https://rbj-ojs-utrgv.tdl.org/rbj/article/view/37.

Lee, Steven. *The Ethnic Avant-Garde: Minority Cultures and World Revolution*. New York: Columbia University Press, 2015.

Le-Khac, Long. *Giving Form to an Asian and Latinx America*. Stanford, CA: Stanford University Press, 2020.

Leong, Karen J. "Gila River." *Densho Encyclopedia*, last updated July 14, 2020. https://encyclopedia.densho.org/Gila_River/.

Lepore, Jill. "Historians Who Love Too Much: Reflections on Microhistory and Biography." *Journal of American History* 88, no. 1 (June 2001): 129–44.

Lewis, George E. "Improvised Music after 1950: Afrological and Eurological Perspectives." *Black Music Research Journal* 16, no. 1 (Spring 1996): 91–122.

Lewis, George E. "Too Many Notes: Computers, Complexity and Culture in *Voyager*." *Leonardo Music Journal* 10 (December 2000): 33–39. https://doi.org/10.1162/096112100570585.

Littlejohn, Jeffrey L., and Charles Howard Ford. *"The Enemy Within Never Did Without": German and Japanese Prisoners of War at Camp Huntsville, 1942–1945.* Huntsville: Texas Review, 2015.

Lipsitz, George. *The Possessive Investment in Whiteness: How White People Profit from Identity Politics.* 3rd ed. Philadelphia: Temple University Press, 2018.

Lipsitz, George. *Time Passages: Collective Memory and American Popular Culture.* Minneapolis: University of Minnesota Press, 1990.

Lipsitz, George, George J. Sánchez, and Kelly Lytle Hernández with Daniel Martinez HoSang and Natalia Molina. "Race as a Relational Theory: A Roundtable Discussion." In *Relational Formations of Race: Theory, Method, and Practice*, edited by Natalia Molina, Daniel Martinez HoSang, and Ramón A. Gutiérrez, 22–42. Oakland: University of California Press, 2019.

Long, Daphne. *Performing Knowledge: Twentieth-Century Music in Analysis and Performance.* New York: Oxford University Press, 2019.

Lordi, Emily. *The Meaning of Soul: Black Music and Resilience since the 1960s.* Durham, NC: Duke University Press, 2020.

Lott, Eric. "Double V, Double-Time: Bebop's Politics of Style." *Callaloo*, no. 36 (Summer 1988): 597–605.

Lowe, Lisa. *Immigrant Acts: On Asian American Cultural Politics.* Durham, NC: Duke University Press, 1996.

Macías, Anthony. *Mexican American Mojo: Popular Music, Dance, and Urban Culture in Los Angeles, 1935–1968.* Durham, NC: Duke University Press, 2008.

Mackey, Nathaniel. "Other: From Noun to Verb." *Representations*, no. 39 (Summer 1992): 51–70.

Massey, Doreen. *Space, Place, and Gender.* Minneapolis: University of Minnesota Press, 1999.

Matsue, Jennifer Milioto. *Music in Contemporary Japan.* New York: Routledge, 2016.

Matthews, Wes. "1995: Mariah Carey, *Daydream*." SixtyEight2OhFive: A Playlist Project, accessed December 8, 2020. https://www.68to05.com/essays/1995-mariah-carey-daydream2.

Mendoza, Louis. "Introduction: Raúl Salinas and the Poetics of Human Transformation." In *raúlrsalinas and the Jail Machine: My Weapon Is My Pen: Selected Writings*, by Raúl Salinas, edited by Louis Gerard Mendoza, 3–24. Austin: University of Texas Press, 2006.

Mendoza, Louis. "Introduction to Raúl Salinas." In *Indio Trails: A Xicano Odyssey through Indian Country*, xi–xiv. San Antonio, TX: Wings, 2007.

Mendoza, Louis G. "Raúl Salinas." In *Oxford Research Encyclopedia of Literature*, February 28, 2020. https://oxfordre.com/literature/view/10.1093/acrefore/9780190201098.001.0001/acrefore-9780190201098-e-1148.

Meyers, Jonathan Jay. "Black Music Spaces and Subjectivity Formation: The Legacy of the Chitlin' Circuit, Juke Joints, and the Preservation of the Victory Grill." Master's thesis, University of Texas at Austin, 2007.

Mignolo, Walter. *The Darker Side of Western Modernity: Global Futures, Decolonial Options*. Durham, NC: Duke University Press, 2011.

Molina, Natalia. "Understanding Race as a Relational Concept." *Modern American History* 1, no. 1 (March 2018): 101–5. https://doi.org/10.1017/mah.2017.14.

Molina, Natalia, Daniel Martinez HoSang, and Ramón A. Gutiérrez, eds. *Relational Formations of Race: Theory, Method, and Practice*. Oakland: University of California Press, 2019.

Molina, Natalia, Daniel Martinez HoSang, and Ramón A. Gutiérrez. "Theorizing Race Relationally." In *Relational Formations of Race*, edited by Natalia Molina, Daniel Martinez HoSang, and Ramón A. Gutiérrez, 19–21.

Monson, Ingrid. "The Problem with White Hipness: Race, Gender, and Cultural Conceptions in Jazz Historical Discourse." *Journal of the American Musicological Society* 48, no. 3 (Autumn 1995): 396–422.

Monson, Ingrid. *Saying Something: Jazz Improvisation and Interaction*. Chicago: University of Chicago Press, 1996.

Moraga, Cherríe. "A 'Holla' from the West Side." In *Radical Hope: Letters of Love and Dissent in Dangerous Times*, edited by Carolina de Roberts, 92–101. New York: Vintage, 2017.

Morrison, Toni. *Home*. New York: Alfred A. Knopf, 2012.

Morrison, Toni. *Playing in the Dark: Whiteness and the Literary Imagination*. New York: Vintage, 1993.

Moten, Fred. *In the Break: The Aesthetics of the Black Radical Tradition*. Minneapolis: University of Minneapolis Press, 2003.

Moya, Paula M. L. *The Social Imperative: Race, Close Reading, and Contemporary Literary Criticism*. Stanford, CA: Stanford University Press, 2015.

Muyumba, Walton. *The Shadow and the Act: Black Intellectual Practice, Jazz Improvisation, and Philosophical Pragmatism*. Chicago: University of Chicago Press, 2009.

Myers, Marc. *Why Jazz Happened*. Berkeley: University of California Press, 2013.

Nagahara, Hiromu. *Tokyo Boogie-Woogie: Japan's Pop Era and Its Discontents*. Cambridge, MA: Harvard University Press, 2017.

National Advisory Commission on Civil Disorders. *Report of the National Advisory Commission on Civil Disorders*. Washington, DC: US Government Printing Office, 1968.

Nellis, Ashley. "The Color of Justice: Racial and Ethnic Disparity in State Prisons." The Sentencing Project, October 13, 2021. https://www.sentencingproject.org/publications/color-of-justice-racial-and-ethnic-disparity-in-state-prisons/.

Nelson, Maggie. *The Argonauts*. Minneapolis: Graywolf, 2015.

Nelson, Maggie. *On Freedom: Four Songs of Care and Constraint*. Minneapolis: Graywolf, 2021.

Ngai, Mai. *Impossible Subjects: Illegal Aliens and the Making of Modern America*. Princeton, NJ: Princeton University Press, 2004.

Nietzsche, Friedrich. "On Truth and Lying in an Extramoral Sense." In *The Portable Nietzsche*, edited and translated by Walter Kaufmann, 42–47. New York: Penguin, 1976.

Ochoa Gautier, Ana María. *Aurality: Listening and Knowledge in Nineteenth-Century Colombia*. Durham, NC: Duke University Press, 2014.

Oishi, Gene. *In Search of Hiroshi: A Japanese-American Odyssey*. Rutland, VT: Charles E. Tuttle, 1988.

Olguín, Ben V. *La Pinta: Chicana/o Prisoner Literature, Culture, and Politics*. Austin: University of Texas Press, 2010.

Omi, Michael, and Howard Winant. *Racial Formation in the United States*. New York: Routledge, 2015.

"One Year of the Record Ban." *Billboard Music Yearbook: 1943*.

Oshiro, Seiki, Paul Tani, and Grant Ichikawa, compilers. Military Intelligence Service Language School (MISLS) Registry, 1941–1946. James T. Araki. Class / Year: Snel44-09; Army Serial Number: 30117173.

Palmer, Rob. *Mr. P.C.: The Life and Music of Paul Chambers*. Bristol, CT: Equinox, 2012.

Parker, Chan, and Francis Paudras. *To Bird with Love*. Antigny, France: Wizlow, 1980.

Peterson, Marina. "Sound Work: Music as Labor and the 1940s Recording Bans of the American Federation of Musicians." *Anthropological Quarterly* 86, no. 3 (Summer 2013): 791–823.

Plascencia, Salvador. *The People of Paper*. New York: Harcourt, 2007.

Pollock, Della. "Performing Writing." In *The Ends of Performance*, edited by Peggy Phelan and Jill Lane, 73–103. New York: New York University Press, 1997.

Porter, Eric. *What Is This Thing Called Jazz? African American Musicians as Artists, Critics, and Activists*. Berkeley: University of California Press, 2002.

Porter, Roy. *There and Back: The Roy Porter Story*. With David Keller. Baton Rouge: Louisiana State University Press, 1991.

Quijano, Aníbal, and Immanuel Wallerstein. "Americanity as a Concept, or the Americas in the Modern World-System." *International Social Science Journal* 29 (1992): 549–57.

Radano, Ronald. *Lying Up a Nation: Race and Black Music*. Chicago: University of Chicago Press, 2003.

Radano, Ronald, and Philip V. Bohlman. *Music and the Racial Imagination*. Chicago: University of Chicago Press, 2000.

Ramírez, Tomás. "Interview with Tomás Ramírez." Interview by Dick Metcalf (Rotcod Zzaj). *Improvijazzation Nation*, no. 124 (April 2, 2012). http://rotcodzzaj.com/42-2/improvijazzation-nation-issue-124/issue-124-interview-with-tomas-ramirez/.

Ramsey, Guthrie P., Jr. *The Amazing Bud Powell: Black Genius, Jazz History, and the Challenge of Bebop*. Berkeley: University of California Press, 2013.

Ramsey, Guthrie P., Jr. *Race Music: Black Cultures from Bebop to Hip-Hop*. Berkeley: University of California Press, 2003.

Rankine, Claudia. *Just Us: An American Conversation*. Minneapolis: Graywolf, 2020.

Rasberry, Vaughn. *Race and the Totalitarian Century: Geopolitics in the Black Literary Imagination*. Cambridge, MA: Harvard University Press, 2016.

Rediker, Marcus. "The Poetics of History from Below." *Perspectives on History: The Newsmagazine of the American Historical Association*, September 1, 2010. https://www.historians.org/publications-and-directories/perspectives-on-history/september-2010/the-poetics-of-history-from-below.

Redling, Erik. *Translating Jazz into Poetry: From Mimesis to Metaphor*. Berlin: Walter de Gruyter, 2017.

Redmond, Shana L. *Everything Man: The Form and Function of Paul Robeson*. Durham, NC: Duke University Press, 2020.

Redmond, Shana L. "Song Uncaged: Prison Temporality and Black Pop Culture Escape." *Souls* 16, no. 3–4 (2014): 227–41. https://doi.org/10.1080/10999949.2014.968976.

Reed, Anthony. *Soundworks: Race, Sound, and Poetry in Production*. Durham, NC: Duke University Press, 2021.

Rivera Garza, Cristina. *The Restless Dead: Necrowriting and Disappropriation*. Translated by Robin Myers. Nashville, TN: Vanderbilt University Press, 2020.

Roberts, T. Carlis [Tamara]. *Resounding Afro Asia: Interracial Music and the Politics of Collaboration*. New York: Oxford University Press, 2016.

Robertson, Marta. "Ballad for Incarcerated Americans: Second Generation Japanese American Musicking in World War II Camps." *Journal of the Society of American Music* 11, no. 3 (August 2017): 284–312.

Román, Elda María. *Race and Upward Mobility: Seeking, Gatekeeping, and Other Class Strategies in Postwar America*. Stanford, CA: Stanford University Press, 2017.

Rustin-Paschal, Nichole. *The Kind of Man I Am: Jazzmasculinity and the World of Charles Mingus Jr*. Middletown, CT: Wesleyan University Press, 2017.

Rustin-Paschal, Nichole, and Sherrie Tucker, eds. *Big Ears: Listening for Gender in Jazz Studies*. Durham, NC: Duke University Press, 2008.

Said, Edward. *Orientalism*. New York: Pantheon, 1978.

Said, Edward. "Traveling Theory." In *The World, the Text, and the Critic*, 226–47. Cambridge, MA: Harvard University Press, 1983.

Saldívar, José David. *Border Matters: Remapping American Cultural Studies*. Berkeley: University of California Press, 1997.

Saldívar, José David. "The Outernational Origins of Chicano/a Literature: Paredes's Asian-Pacific Routes and Hinojosa's Cuban Casa de las Américas Roots." In *Trans-Americanity: Subaltern Modernities, Global Coloniality, and the Cultures of Greater Mexico*, 123–51. Durham, NC: Duke University Press, 2012.

Saldívar, Ramón. *The Borderlands of Culture: Américo Paredes and the Transnational Imaginary*. Durham, NC: Duke University Press, 2006.

Saldívar, Ramón. *Chicano Narrative: The Dialectics of Difference*. Minneapolis: University of Minnesota Press, 1990.

Saldívar, Ramón. "Historical Fantasy, Speculative Realism, and Postrace Aesthetics in Contemporary American Fiction." *American Literary History* 23, no. 3 (Fall 2011): 574–99.

Salinas, Raúl R. *East of the Freeway: Reflections de mi Pueblo (Poems)*. Austin, TX: Red Salmon Arts, 1995.

Salinas, Raúl R. *Indio Trails: A Xicano Odyssey through Indian Country*. Introduction by Louis Mendoza. San Antonio, TX: Wings, 2007.

Salinas, Raúl R. "Loud and Proud." In *A Latin@ Anthology on Language Experience*, edited by Louis G. Mendoza and Toni Nelson Herrera, 53–54. Austin, TX: Red Salmon, 2007.

Salinas, Raúl R. *Memoir of un Ser Humano: The Life and Times of raúlrsalinas*. Edited by Louis G. Mendoza. Austin, TX: Red Salmon, 2018.

Salinas, Raúl R. "Una Plática con Raúl Salinas: An Interview by Ben Olguín and Louis Mendoza." In *raúlrsalinas and the Jail Machine: My Weapon Is My Pen; Selected Writings*, edited by Louis Gerard Mendoza, 305–34. Austin: University of Texas Press, 2006.

Salinas, Raúl R. *raúlrsalinas and the Jail Machine: My Weapon Is My Pen; Selected Writings*. Edited by Louis Gerard Mendoza. Austin: University of Texas Press, 2006.

Salinas, Raúl R. *Un Trip through the Mind Jail y Otras Excursiones (Poems)*. Houston, TX: Arte Público, 1999.

Samano, Miguel I. "Subjects of Display: Retrospective Art Historiography and Chicano Identity Formation." Honors thesis, Stanford University, 2019.

Satoko, Akio. *Suwingu Japan: Nikkei beigunhei Jimī Araki to senryō no kioku*. Tokyo: Shinchōsha, 2012.

Saul, Scott. *Freedom Is, Freedom Ain't: Jazz and the Making of the Sixties*. Cambridge, MA: Harvard University Press, 2003.

Schultz, Anna. "Music Ethnography and Recording Technology in the Unbound Digital Era." With Mark Nye. In *The Oxford Handbook of Mobile Music Studies*, edited by Sumath Gopinath and Jason Stanyek, 1:298–313. New York: Oxford University Press, 2014.

Schultz, Anna, and Sumanth Gopinath. "Sentimental Remembrance and the Amusements of Forgetting in Karl and Harty's 'Kentucky.'" *Journal of the American Musicological Society* 69, no. 2 (Summer 2016): 477–524.

Shapiro, Nat, and Nat Hentoff. *Hear Me Talkin' to Ya: The Story of Jazz as Told by the Men Who Made It*. New York: Dover, 2012.

Shelemay, Kay Kaufman. "Musical Communities: Rethinking the Collective in Music." *Journal of the American Musicological Society* 64, no. 2 (Summer 2011): 349–90.

Shipton, Alyn. *The Art of Jazz: A Visual History*. Foreword by John Edward Hasse. Watertown, MA: Charlesbridge, 2020.

Simmons, John. Interview by Patricia Willard. Reprinted in *Erroll Garner: The Most Happy Piano*, by James M. Doran, 73–75. Metuchen, NJ: Scarecrow / Institute of Jazz Studies, Rutgers University, 1985.

Skeete-Laessig, Yoland. *When Newark Had a Chinatown: My Personal Journey*. Pittsburgh, PA: Dorrance, 2016.

Skipper, James K., Jr. "Nicknames, Folk Heroes and Jazz Musicians." *Popular Music and Society* 10, no. 4 (1986): 51–62. https://doi.org/10.1080/03007768608591259.

Slobin, Mark. *Subcultural Sounds: Micromusics of the West*. Hanover, NH: Wesleyan University Press, 2000.

Smyth, Heather. "The Black Atlantic Meets the Black Pacific: Multimodality in Kamau Brathwaite and Wayde Compton." *Callaloo* 37, no. 2 (Spring 2014): 389–403. https://doi.org/10.1353/cal.2014.0046.

Solis, Gabriel. "The Black Pacific: Music and Racialization in Papua New Guinea and Australia." *Critical Sociology* 41, no. 2 (March 2015): 297–312.

Sorey, Tyshawn. "Allowing Things to Happen: An Interview with Tyshawn Sorey." By Craig Morgan Teicher. *Paris Review*, September 29, 2021.

Sorey, Tyshawn. "Perle Noire: Meditations for Josephine; Aesthetics, Discussion, and Reception." DMA diss., Columbia University, 2017.

Spivak, Gayatri Chakravorty. "Teaching for the Times." In *Dangerous Liaisons: Gender, Nation, and Postcolonial Perspectives*, edited by Anne McClintock, Aamir Mufti, and Ella Shohat, 468–80. Minneapolis: University of Minnesota Press, 1997.

Stanyek, Jason, and Benjamin Piekut. "Deadness: Technologies of the Intermundane." *TDR: The Drama Review* 54, no. 1 (Spring 2010): 14–38.

Sterne, Jonathan. *The Audible Past: Cultural Origins of Sound Reproduction*. Durham, NC: Duke University Press, 2003.

Stewart, Kathleen. *Ordinary Affects*. Durham, NC: Duke University Press, 2007.

Stoever, Jennifer. *The Sonic Color Line: Race and the Cultural Politics of Listening*. New York: New York University Press, 2016.

Stowe, David. *Swing Changes: Big Band Jazz in New Deal America*. Cambridge, MA: Harvard University Press, 1994.

Suechting, Max, and Jonathan Leal. "Jam Sessions: Improvising across Disciplines." *Critical Studies in Improvisation/Études critiques en improvisation* 13, no. 1 (2020). https://doi.org/10.21083/csieci.v13i1.5795.

Taylor, Yuval. "Does the Overdub Undercut Jazz?" *Faking It* (blog), May 4, 2007. https://fakingit.typepad.com/faking_it/2007/05/does_the_overdu.html.

Theurer, Michiko, and Jonathan Leal. "Reach: A Correspondence." *Air/Light Magazine*, no. 2 (Winter 2021). https://airlightmagazine.org/airlight/winter-2021/reach/.

Tolentino, Jia. *Trick Mirror: Reflections on Self-Delusion*. New York: Random House, 2019.

Tomlinson, Barbara, and George Lipsitz. "American Studies as Accompaniment." *American Quarterly* 65, no. 1 (March 2013): 1–30.

Trouillot, Michel-Rolph. *Silencing the Past: Power and the Production of History*. Boston: Beacon, 1995.

Turner, Richard Brent. *Soundtrack to Movement: African American Islam, Jazz, and Black Internationalism*. New York: New York University Press, 2021.

Varon, Alberto. *Before Chicano: Citizenship and the Making of Mexican American Manhood, 1848–1959*. New York: New York University Press, 2018.

Von Eschen, Penny. *Satchmo Blows Up the World: Jazz Ambassadors Play the Cold War*. Cambridge, MA: Harvard University Press, 2004.

Wade, Jay C. "Racialized Masculinity." In *The SAGE Encyclopedia of LGBTQ Studies*, edited by Abbie E. Goldberg, 921–24. Thousand Oaks, CA: SAGE, 2016.

Wakida, Patricia. "*Gila News-Courier* (Newspaper)." In *Densho Encyclopedia*, last updated May 12, 2014. http://encyclopedia.densho.org/Gila_News-Courier_(newspaper).

Wang, Jackie. *Carceral Capitalism*. New York: Semiotext(e), 2018.
Wang, Jackie. *The Sunflower Cast a Spell to Save Us from the Void*. Illustrations by Kalan Sherrard. New York: Nightboat, 2021.
Waseda, Minako. "Extraordinary Circumstances, Exceptional Practices: Music in Japanese American Concentration Camps." *Journal of Asian American Studies* 8, no. 2 (June 2005): 171–209.
Weglyn, Michi. *Years of Infamy: The Untold Story of America's Concentration Camps*. New York: William Morrow, 1976.
Weheliye, Alexander. *Habeas Viscus: Racializing Assemblages, Biopolitics, and Black Feminist Theories of the Human*. Durham, NC: Duke University Press, 2014.
White, Hayden. *Metahistory: The Historical Imagination in Nineteenth-Century Europe*. Baltimore, MD: Johns Hopkins University Press, 1973.
Williams, James Gordon. *Crossing Bar Lines: The Politics and Practices of Black Musical Space*. Jacksonville: University of Mississippi Press, 2021.
Wilson, Matt. "'He Was a Force': Rene Sandoval—Renowned Musician from Valley—Dies at 86." *Monitor*, February 4, 2022. https://myrgv.com/featured/2022/02/04/he-was-a-force-rene-sandoval-renowned-musician-from-valley-dies-at-86/.
Woloch, Alex. *The One vs. the Many: Minor Characters and the Space of the Protagonist in the Novel*. Princeton, NJ: Princeton University Press, 2003.
Wong, Deborah. "Sound, Silence, Music: Power." *Ethnomusicology* 58, no. 2 (Spring/Summer 2014): 347–53.
Wong, Deborah. *Speak It Louder: Asian Americans Making Music*. London: Taylor & Francis, 2004.
Wynter, Sylvia. "Unsettling the Coloniality of Being/Power/Truth/Freedom: Towards the Human, after Man, Its Overrepresentation—an Argument." *New Centennial Review* 3, no. 3 (Fall 2003): 257–337.
Yaffe, David. *Fascinating Rhythm: Reading Jazz in American Writing*. Princeton, NJ: Princeton University Press, 2006.
Ybarra-Frausto, Tomás. "Introduction to the First Edition." In *Un Trip through the Mind Jail y Otras Excursions: Poems*, by Raúl R. Salinas, 7–14. Houston, TX: Arte Público, 1999.
Yoshida, George. *Reminiscing in Swingtime: Japanese Americans in American Popular Music, 1925–1960*. San Francisco: National Japanese American Historical Society, 1997.
Zuboff, Shoshana. *The Age of Surveillance Capitalism: The Fight for a Human Future at the New Frontier of Power*. New York: PublicAffairs, 2018.

index

Abdul-Jabbar, Kareem, 33
Acea, John, 132
Acosta, Oscar, 83, 193n125
Adams, James Truslow, 154
Addonizio, Hugh, 141
Adorno, Theodor, 173n80
affinity-mapping, Black radical music and, 158–59
"African Girl Is Queen of the World, An" (Wing), 146
Afro-Asian Americans: bebop music and, 21; music production of, 165n54; racial and gender stereotypes of, 131–32; racial democracy and, 5
Afro Asian Music Ensemble, 105
Afro-Caribbean music, 39, 159–60
Afro-Chinese Americans: biracial negotiation and, 5; in Newark, 117; Wing's identity as, 3
Afro-Cuban jazz: Araki's invocation of, 66–67, 181n73; "Manteca" project and, 105
Afro-Cuban Jazz Suite (album), 1, 62, 136, 179n62
Afrological music, creative praxes and, 48
after-hours sessions, bebop music and, 31–32, 130–32
"After You've Gone" (Parker & Gillespie), 33, 44
Akita, George, 57
Albany, Joe, 82, 102
Albright, Daniel, 110, 167n70
Aldama, Arturo, 82

Aldama, Frederick, 82
Alexander, Elizabeth, 7, 160
Alexander, Herbert, 93
Alexander, Michelle, 85
"All Cities and All Countries to Be Free!" (Wing), 146
Allied Translator and Interpreter Section (ATIA), Araki's work with, 61, 177n47
"Almost Like Being in Love," Araki's interpretation of, 66
Alvarez, Luis, 30, 158
Amazing Bud Powell (Ramsey), 167n1, 180n69
American dream, origins of, 154–55
American Federation of Musicians: overdubbing ban, 174n10; strike by, 29
American Indian Movement, 193n125
American Society of Composers, Authors, and Publishers (ASCAP), 144
Ammon, Eugene "Jug," 83, 102
Annotations of the Muses (album), 38
"Anthropology" (Parker), 62
anti-Blackness, postwar evolution of, 29
"A.P.O. 500" (Araki recording), 60–61, 177n47
Araki, Dale, 57
Araki, David, 176n39
Araki, James T., 3; academic scholarship of, 71–72, 182n87, 203n1; Baltazar and, 38; bebop in recordings by, 65–70; Black radical music and, 13–16; internment experiences of, 30, 39–41, 54–57, 175n29; in Japan, 39–41; jazz arrangements by, 177n47;

Araki, James T. (*continued*)
   Jazz Beat: Midnight Jazz Session recorded by, 46–51, 65–70, 174n9, 179n53; jazz performances in Japan by, 59–65, 177n47; legacy of, 72–73; life and work of, 20–21, 23, 39–44, 150, 183n81; military service of, 39–40, 44, 47, 56–60, 70, 175n35, 176n37; musical skills of, 56–57; Order of the Rising Sun awarded to, 173n81; overdubbing experiments by, 52–53, 65–70; post-military jazz career of, 70–71; rhythmic experiments of, 65–70; Salinas and, 40, 83
Armstrong, Albert, 122
Armstrong, Louis, 91, 94
"Artist's Struggle for Integrity, The" (Baldwin), 148–49
Asian Americans: exoticization of, 48; jazz by, 20; radical music by, 80; stereotypes of, 131–32. *See also* Chinese Americans; Japanese Americans
Atkins, E. Taylor, 59, 63
"Atomic Energy" (Brown), 163n32
atomic weaponry, 41, 173n80; bebop in context of, 163n32, 179n62; in Salinas's work, 107–9
audio-racial imagination, 165n54, 167n70
August, Joseph, 116, 122, 126, 196n35
Auslander, Philip, 167n70
avant-garde jazz experimentation, 195n32
Ayewa, Camae, 7
Aztlán (Leavenworth prison newsletter), 98–99

Bach, C. P. E., 180n69
Bach, Johann Sebastian, jazz music based on, 93, 180n69
Bailey, Anne, 147
Baker, Chet, 83
Baker, Houston, 169n15
Baldwin, James: on art, 148–49; on Black radical music, 14, 120, 167n1; on drug use, 35; on jazz criticism, 94; on race and music, 19, 132, 159
Balliet, Whitney, 93–94
Baltazar, Gabriel Ruiz Hiroshi, Jr., 38, 203n1

Baraka, Amiri (LeRoi Jones), 16, 36, 43, 94, 140, 146, 167n1, 194n2
Barker, Mickey, 93
Beats, 36, 40, 86–87, 92
bebop: Araki's recordings of, 60–70, 176n38; Black intellectualism and, 8–10; Black radical dreaming and, 14; commodification of, 31–32; competition and dominance among performers, 130–32; early performances and recordings of, 25–29, 176n38; history of, 3–4, 19–20; Hughes's writing on, 66; international recognition of, 38–39; interracial audience for, 38–39; in Los Angeles, 33–34; mambo and, 181n73; media stereotypes about, 34–37, 42; political communication in, 163n33; postwar mainstreaming of, 30–32; racial democracy and, 3–5, 118; racism and, 17–18, 22–24; recordings of, 29–30, 170n28; rhythms in, 124–26, 129–30; Salinas and, 75, 92–93, 102; scholarship on, 167n1; speed of, 163n32; US foreign affairs and, 42–43; Wing's involvement in, 118, 122–24
"Be-Bop Bebopped" (*Time* magazine), 34
Bechet, Sidney, 174n10
Benny Goodman Orchestra, 41
Berliner, Paul, 195n28
Berman, Sonny, 185n37
Berry, Leon Brown ("Chu"), 102
Beyond the BEATen Path (album), 99, 103–9
big bands, bebop recordings by, 38
"Big Red! (For Malcolm X and Mao Zedong)," 105
"Bikini" (Gordon), 163n32
Billy Eckstein Orchestra, 29
"Billy's Bounce" (Parker), 62
Bird and Diz, 1
Bird and Pres: Jazz at the Philharmonic (recording), 25–26
"Birdwatcher" (Ortega), 38
Birth of Bebop, The (DeVeaux), 167n1
Black Americans: incarceration rates for, 84–85; jazz aesthetics and, 167n1; military service of, 39–41, 172n74; in Newark, 141–42; postwar Japanese awareness of, 59–65
Black art, dreaming and, 7

Blackburn, John, 102
Black experimental/radical music: bebop and, 8–10, 59, 163n33; community and role of, 150; double time in, 53; dream space of, 6, 13–14, 24, 153–54; industry commodification of, 31–32; influence of, 2–5; international expansion of, 45, 47–48; Japanese Americans and, 20, 47–51, 54, 56–58, 63–65; legacy of, 158–59; media stereotypes about, 35–37; minoritization of, 12, 164nn39–40; nonwhite youth and influence of, 72–73; productive destabilization in, 53–54; race and, 15–18, 59; racial democracy and, 13, 22, 45, 104, 107, 110; reparative socialities and, 155–56; Salinas and, 13–16, 75–76, 79–84, 99–109; as subversion, 16–18, 59; Wing's engagement with, 119–24
Black intellectualism, bebop and, 8–10, 162n25, 162n27
Blackness: Blacknuss theory, 189n99; cultural investment in, 16–18; media stereotypes of, 35–37
Black Pacific, scholarship on, 65, 180n64
Black speculative musicalities, 10, 95
Blais-Tremblay, Vanessa, 165n50
Blakey, Art, 43, 83, 144
Blanton, Jimmy, 27
"Blues for Bach" (Araki arrangement), 180n69
blues idiom, bebop and, 9
Blues People (Baraka), 140, 167n1
Bohlman, Philip, 165n54
Borge, Jason, 105
Born, Georgina, 167n70
Boyer, Richard, 96
Bracero program, 4
Bradley, Herman, 120
"Brilliant Corners" (Monk), 18
Briones, Matthew, 55, 175n22
"Broken Rhythm" (Araki), 66–68, 181n73
Brooks, Daphne, 7, 12
Brown, Anthony, 138
Brown, Clarence "Gatemouth," 163n32
Bruce, La Marr Jurelle, 37
Bruton, Stephen, 103

Cabral, Amílcar, 92
Campbell, Gregory, 53
Cancel Miranda, Rafael, 97
carceral capitalism, 84
Cassady, Neal, 86
Césaire, Aimé, 7
Chaloff, Serge, 102
Chambers, Paul, 114, 136, 138–39
Chang, Jeff, 142
Charles, Ray, 90
Charlie Parker with Strings, 1
Chasin' the Bird (graphic novel), 33
"Cherokee" (Noble), 31
Chicano literary renaissance, 111–12; Salinas's participation in, 75–76, 80–81, 193n125
Chinese Americans: dreaming and, 157; in Newark, 118–19, 141
Christian, Charlie, 27
Chuh, Kandice, 55
"Chuy z." (Salinas), 113
Clarke, Kenny, 9, 26–27, 32, 59
class, jazz criticism and, 94–97
Clifford, James, 195n32
Clifford Brown's All Stars, 10–11
Cold War, bebop and, 42–43
Cole, Teju, 72
Coleman, Steve, 65
"Cologne" (Wing song), 126
colonialism, American racism and, 15–18, 166n55
Colony Club (Newark), 120
Coltrane, John, 43, 95, 136, 189n99
communal virtuosity, 117–18
"Compensation" (Wing), 146
complementarity, in drummers' work, 125–26
"Consequences of a Drug Addict Role" (Wing), 144–46
Conversations with Myself (Evans album), 51–52
Cooder, Ry, 181n78
Copland, Aaron, 195n27
'Crazeology' (Chaz Parker and his Pebon Boys), 81
criminal justice system: Mexican Americans and, 20; racism and, 20–21
"Cuando tocaban 'You Don't Know Me'" (Salinas), 90

culture: bebop's influence on, 167n1; ecosystems of, 142–44; jazz criticism and, 94–97; in postwar Japan, 60–65
Curvin, Robert, 142

"Dance of the Infidels" (Fats Navarro), 81
Darr, Jerome, 115, 135, 138
Davis, Miles, 3, 40, 43, 102, 116, 136
"Day Dream" (Ellington), 46–47, 73, 173n1
"Day Dream," Araki's version of, 66–67, 73, 173n1
Denning, Michael, 39
Desmond, Paul, 65
DeVeaux, Scott, 167n1
Dewitt, John, 55
Dexter, Dave, 37–38
"Dexterity" (Parker), 62
Diawara, Manthia, 17
Díaz, Junot, 72
"Did Charlie Have a Horn?" (Salinas), 87–88, 103
"Discovery of What It Means to Be an American, The" (Baldwin), 132
Dolphy, Eric, 188n81
double time in music, 18–19, 53; incarceral experience and, 75
Douglas, Mary, 171n53
Downbeat magazine, 42, 82, 95
dreaming: aspiration and imagination, 6; bebop and influence of, 44–45; jazz poetry and, 109–12; radical musicking and, 8–10; in Wing's music, 150–51
Dreams Are Colder Than Death (film), 160
drug use and distribution: Baldwin on, 35; media stereotypes about bebop and, 34–35; Parker's involvement in, 35, 83–84, 144, 185n37; Salinas's involvement in, 43, 75, 79, 83–84, 97–98; in Wing's music, 142–44
drummers: complementarity in work by, 125–26; rhythm perceptions of, 198n75, 202n11
Duersten, Matthew, 34

Earthling Studios, 100–101
Eason, Leon, 121
East Austin jazz clubs, history of, 184n22

East of the Freeway (Salinas), 101–2
Eckstine, Billy, 126
Edit Point Studios, 103
"Educate Your Mind" (Wing), 146
Edwards, Bart, 93
Edwards, Brent Hayes, 11, 96–97, 167n1, 167n70, 182n87, 201n106
"8 ríos to cross" (Ramírez), 101
Eisenhower, Dwight, 42
Ellington, Duke, 46, 177n47
Ellison, Ralph: bebop and, 35–36, 167n1; on capsule history, 119; *Invisible Man* by, 85–86, 183n18; on jazz, 94
Epic of America, The (Adams), 154
Epistrophies (Edwards), 167n1
Erroll Garner Trio, 41
Eurological music: bebop and, 8–10, 162n25; creative praxes and, 48
Evans, Bill, 51–52, 185n37
Evans, Herschel, 83, 102
"Evolution of Jazz, The," Wing's presentation of, 200n97
Executive Order 9066, 4, 39, 55–56, 161n5
Executive Order 9981, 141

Fanon, Frantz, 7, 17, 97, 166n60
Farlow, Joe, 83
Farmer, Art, 83
Fellezs, Kevin, 48
Fenton, Nick, 26
Fernandez, Vicente, 11
Festival de Flor y Canto, 99, 193n125
Figgins, Mikey, 100–102
Figueroa Cordero, Andres, 97
Fine Sound Studios, 135
Fischlin, Daniel, 112
Fitzgerald, Ella, 3, 40, 116, 126
Fleetwood, Nicole, 75, 85, 110
Flores Rodríguez, Irvin, 97
Foertsch, Jacqueline, 163n32
Ford, Phil, 86, 92
Ford, William "Billy," 122
Fort Snelling Dance Band, 58, 176n37
Foucault, Michel, 187n72
Fox, Charles, 199n84

Foxx, Red, 126
Frankfurt school, 173n80
Freedom Dreams (Kelley), 7
"Free New Africa! Boogaloo" (Ho), 105
Fuller, Gil, 105

Gaillard, Slim, 171n43, 199n80
Galbraith, Barry, 115, 135–36, 138
Garcia, Edgar, 183n16
Garner, Erroll, 3, 40, 116, 126–30, 196n50, 197nn52–53, 198n57
Geffen, Sasha, 12
Gems of Jazz (Japanese radio show), 59
gender: Black radical music and, 14–15, 167n1; jazz criticism and, 94–97; stereotypes about, 130–32
Gendron, Bernard, 171n43
Gennari, John, 94, 187n66, 193n120
Germany, bebop in, 38–39
Gershwin, George, 195n27
Getz, Stan, 27, 83
Giant Steps (Coltrane), 136
GI Bill, 40–41
Gibson, Dan, 120
Gibson, Harry, 171n43
Gibson, Ken, 142
Gila News-Courier, 56, 175n29, 175n35
Gila River War Relocation Center, 3, 39, 56
Gillespie, Dizzy, 1, 3, 10; Afro-Caribbean music and, 39; on bebop's expansion, 124; Cold War policy and, 43; early bebop and, 26–27, 31; influence on bebop of, 39, 167n1; jazz ambassador tours and, 141; in Los Angeles, 33–34; "Manteca" collaborative project and, 105–6; media coverage of, 35–37; Moody and influence of, 133; Newark jazz culture and, 126; Parker and, 32–33; public bravado of, 31; on racism and music, 124; in Salinas's jazz poetry, 102, 189n99; on stereotypes about bebop, 34; Wing's collaboration with, 40, 116, 124
Gilroy, Paul, 30, 64
Ginsberg, Allen, 86
Gleason, Ralph, 93–94, 187n66, 197nn54–55
Glissant, Édouard, 17

Godrej, Farah, 119
Goins, Larry, 132
"Golden Age, Time Past, The" 167n1
Golden Inn (Newark), 120
Goldston, Eugene "Goldie," 21, 116, 119–20, 130, 142–43, 147, 149–50
Gomez, Magdalena, 109
Gonzales, Babs, 3, 40, 82, 116, 126, 198n71
Gordon, Dexter, 38, 40, 83, 163n32, 185n37
Gottlieb, William, 35
Granz, Norman, 25, 34, 71
Green, Kevin P., 100–102
Green, Shannon Louise, 195n27
Greif, Mark, 162n25
Grennard, Elliott, 34–35
Griffin, Farah Jasmine, 12
Grims, John, 132
Guy, Joe, 26, 59

Hadnott, Billy, 25
Hall, Al, 136
Hamilton, Chris, 83
Hamilton, Denise, 147
Hampton, Lionel, 40–41, 71, 181n80
Harlem: early bebop performances in, 26–29; Newark jazz scene and influence of, 118
Harris, Ynomia, 122
Hartman, Saidiya, 7, 12
Hawes, Hampton, 38, 41, 144
Hawkins, Coleman "Bean," 167n1
Haygood, Pancho, 82
Heifetz, Jascha, 195n27
Henry Street Conservatory of Music, 121, 143, 195n27
Hentoff, Nat, 93–94, 187n66
Herrera, Juan Felipe, 193n125
Hill, Teddy, 26
Hiroshima, 41
Ho, Fred, 20, 80, 103–9, 189n97, 189n99
Hodges, Johnny, 46–47
Holiday, Billy, 126
Holiday Inn (Newark), 126
Holmes, Johnny, 184n22
Hong, Cathy Park, 12
Honshu Hayride (Japanese radio show), 59

Horkheimer, Max, 173n80
Horn, Rainy, 145
Horn, Shirley, 3, 116, 144–45
Hughes, Langston, 66, 99, 109, 154–55
Hughes, Timothy, 127
Huntsville Echo, 44, 93–97, 193n120

"I Can't Get Started" (song), 44
ideal Now, Beat fetishization of, 86
I'll Remember (album), 38
improvisation: Araki's work in, 65–70; Ho's discussion of, 189n97; studio music and, 69–70, 166n66
Inada, Lawson Fusao, 158
incarceration: Foucault on, 187n72; mass criminalization and racism linked to, 84–85; as microcosm, 111–12; Salinas's experience of, 40, 43, 75–77; US statistics on, 84–85
Indio Trails: A Xicano Odyssey through Indian Country (Salinas), 104
Information (newspaper), 143
Institute of Jazz Studies, 21
intermusical citation, 186n47; in Salinas's poetry, 87–89
"In the Melancholy Mood" (Araki arrangement), 177n47
Intondi, Vincent, 163n32
Invisible Man (Ellison), 85–86, 183n18
Iton, Richard, 7, 9
"It's Time for Us" (Wing), 146
Iyer, Vijay, 5, 10, 17

Jackson, Shannon, 167n70
Jackson, Zakiyyah Iman, 36, 70, 154–55
Jafa, Arthur, 160
James, Etta, 3
James, Harry, 59
Jameson, Fredric, 86, 172n72, 193n116
Jam Session (Clifford Brown All Stars album), 11
Japan: Araki's work in, 39–40, 44, 47; atomic bombing of, 41; bebop in, 3, 40, 172n74; internment in US of citizens from, 30, 39–41, 47, 54–56; jazz in, 47–51, 54, 59–65, 177n46; US occupation of, 41, 59–60

Japanese American Citizens League (JACL), 71
Japanese Americans: Black experimental music and, 50, 63–65, 158–59; dreaming and, 157; internment of, 4, 30, 39–41, 47, 54–58; jazz music and, 20, 47–51, 54, 56–58; military service by, 56; racial democracy and, 5, 70
"Jazz: A Nascence" (Salinas), 90–92, 102
Jazz at the Philharmonic (JATP) concerts, 25–26, 71
Jazz Beat: Midnight Jazz Session, 20, 47–51, 54, 65–70, 72–73, 174n9
jazz criticism, 93–97, 188n81, 193n120, 193n125
Jazz Discography Project, 197n53
Jazz Epistles, 39
Jazz Epistle Verse I (album), 39
"Jazz Jaunts" (Salinas), 40, 112–13, 149–50
jazz junkie stereotype, 36
"Jazzmanian Devil" (album), 100–101
jazz poetry, 20–21, 44, 74–81, 86–89, 98–103; dreaming in, 109–12; as resistance, 111–12
jazz scholarship, bebop and, 167n1
Jim and Jap Crow (Briones), 175n22
Jim Crow segregation, 4, 42; international image of, 42–43, 173n77; Latinx communities and, 81–82
"Jimmy's Bop" (Araki recording), 61–63
Jimmy's Trio (band), Araki's recording with, 61
John F. Kennedy Recreation Center, 143
Johnson, Buddy, 124
Johnson, Doug, 200n97
Johnson, J. J., 27
Jones, Elvin, 144
Jones, Etta, 116
Jones, Hank, 93
Jones, Jimmy "Chops," 136, 147
Jones, Quincy, 114, 126, 136, 139
Joseph, Isaac K., 177n47

Kajikawa, Loren, 58
Kaldewey, Helma, 39
Kaufman, Bob, 89
Kawaguchi, George, 46, 49, 66, 68, 174n9
Kelley, Robin D. G., 7
Kelly, Charles "Brother," 120–21
Kenton, Stan, 38–39

Kerouac, Jack, 86–87
Kikuchi, Charles, 175n22
Kind of Blue (Davis), 136
King, Martin Luther, Jr., 160
Kinney Club (Newark), 120
Kirk, Rahsaan Roland, 104–5, 156, 189n99
"Ko-Ko" (Parker), 31
Konitz, Lee, 65
Korean War, 41
Kukla, Barbara, 122, 147, 194n2, 197n52
Kun, Josh, 109, 165n54, 167n70, 189n99

"Lady Be Good" (song), 25, 44
Lalami, Laila, 119
"Lamento" (Salinas), 87–89
Latin jazz, 39, 81, 136–42
Latinx culture: dreaming and, 157; media coverage of, 81; in Newark, 141–42; racial democracy and, 82; Salinas's Xicanindio poetry and journalism and, 21
Lebrón, Lolita, 97
Lee, Steven, 179n62
Legends from Camp, 158
Leong, Karen J., 56
Lewis, George, 8, 53
Lewis, John, 93, 95
Lighthouse Club, 83–84
Liner Notes for the Revolution (Brooks), 7
Lippman, Joe, 89
Lipsitz, George, 81, 112, 147–48
literature: bebop stereotypes in, 34–35; jazz culture and, 85–89, 167n1; pictographs and, 183n16; prose vs. poetry in, 193n116; as resistance, 111–12
"Loch Lomond" (Araki arrangement), 177n47
Lopez, Tommy, 136
Lordi, Emily, 117
Los Angeles: Araki's return to, 70–71; bebop musicians in, 38, 171n43; early bebop in, 33–34; Salinas in, 82–84
Los Many Mundos of raúlrsalinas: Un Poetic Jazz Viaje con Friends (album), 99–103
Lott, Eric, 171n52, 176n38
"Loud and Proud" (Salinas), 104–9
Luce, Henry, 41

Machito and his Afro Cubans, 1, 136
Macías, Anthony, 83
Mackey, Nathaniel, 31–32
Malcolm X, 92, 97
mambo music, 136, 181n73
Man and His Horns, A (Ortega album), 38
Manbo, Mas, 70, 181n76
Mance, Junior, 116
"Mangetsu" (Araki song), 54
Mann, Herbie, 136
"Manteca" collaborative project, 105–6
Mao Zedong, 97
"Margie" (Wing's interpretation of), 132
Marsh, Warne, 65
"Martin Luther King, a Black American King" (Wing), 146
Marx, Karl, 97, 193n116
masculinities: bebop music and, 21, 130–32, 167n1; Black radical music and, 14–15, 165n50; in Latinx culture, 82–84
McGhee, Howard, 38
McLean, Jackie, 144
Meals, Donney, 103
media: bebop coverage in, 31, 170nn29–30; Latinx culture in, 81; stereotypes about bebop in, 34–37, 170nn29–30
Melodia Rhythmiker, 39
Memoir of un Ser Humano (Salinas), 185n37
Mendoza, Louis, 90, 98
Mendoza, Lydia, 11
Metronome magazine, 35–36, 42, 82, 95, 170n29
Mexican Americans: Black radical music and, 3, 13–16, 75–76, 83–84; racism experienced by, 5–6, 42
Midnight Jazz Session, 44
military desegregation, 141
Military Intelligence Service Language School, Araki's work with, 58
Mingus, Charles, 102, 189n99
minorization of Black experimental music, 12, 164n42, 164nn39–40
Minton, Henry, 26–27, 29
Minton's Playhouse, 26–28, 32, 37, 60, 167n1
Mitchell, Dwike, 181n80
modernism, bebop and, 69–70, 171n52

Modern Jazz Quartet, 180n69
Modern Sounds in Country and Western Music (Ray Charles album), 90
Moeketsi, Kippie, 39
Molina, Natalia, 156
Monk, Thelonius: bebop and, 27, 43, 158, 167n1; Black experimental music and, 18; Salinas and, 83, 95–96, 98, 103, 187n76, 189n99; *Time* magazine story on, 95
Monroe's Uptown, bebop performances at, 27–28, 37
Monson, Ingrid, 12, 35, 167n1, 186n47, 198n75, 199n81, 202n111
"Montage of a Dream Deferred" (Hughes), 66, 154–55
Moods (Paul Quinichette All Stars album), 136, 139–42, 199n84
Moody, James, 40, 116, 119, 126, 132–35, 198n73; Newark jazz culture and, 126
"Moody's Home" (Moody), 133, 198n75
"Moonlight in Vermont" (Blackburn), 102
Morgan, Frank, 38
Morrison, Toni, 7, 163n32, 165n54
Morrow, George, 10
Most, Sam, 136, 138
Moten, Fred, 7, 157, 166n66
"Move" (Clifford Brown's All Stars), 10–11
music: retrospective writing on, 188n80; writing and, 109–12
Muyumba, Walton, 167n1

Nagahara, Hiromu, 177n47
Nagasaki, 41
Nakamura, Nobi, 176n37
National Advisory Commission on Civil Disorders, 200n91
Navarro, Fats, 81, 83, 185n37
necropolitics, mass criminalization and racism linked to, 84–85
Newark, NJ: bebop and jazz in, 5, 21, 23, 39–42, 44, 116–20; Black music in, 118–24, 134–35; decline and renewal of, 146–47, 200n91; Great Migration in, 141, 194n8; Wing's career in, 116–17; Wing tribute in, 147–49

Newark Conservatory, 121
Newark Rebellion, 141–42
New Criticism, 94
New Jersey After Hours, 124
New Jersey Herald News, 121
New Yorker, 95–96
nicknames, as capsule history, 119
Nietzsche, Friedrich, 193n116
"Night and Day" (Porter), 87–89
"Night in Pakistan" (Araki), 177n47
Nisei. *See* Japanese Americans
Noble, Ray, 31
noise uprising, bebop as part of, 38–39, 171n53
"No 'Moonlight in Vermont,'" 102
"Nothing Yet" (Ramírez), 100–101

Ochoa Gautier, Ana María, 167n70
O'Farrill, Chico, 136, 179n62, 181n73
Olguín, Ben, 79, 183n3, 183n16
Oliver, Joe, 91
Ono, Mitsuro, 46, 49, 54, 174n9
Oquendo, Manny, 136
Orientalism (Said), 165n54
Ortega, Anthony, 38
Ory, Kid, 59
overdubbing, 174n10; Araki's experiments with, 52, 65–70; in jazz albums, 50–51

Pablito's Studio, 103
"Pablo's Roonie" (Paul Quinichette All Stars recording), 136–39, 199n80, 199n84
Pacific Northwest, bebop in, 38
Palmer, Lloyd, 93
Paredes, Américo, 41, 179n57, 179n59, 188n88
Parker, Chan, 122
Parker, Charlie "Bird," 1, 3, 21; Afro-Cuban jazz and, 136, 159–60; antinuclear stance of, 179n62; Araki's music and influence of, 61–63; critical studies of, 38–39; Darr's work with, 135; drug problems of, 35, 83–84, 144, 185n37; early bebop and, 25–28, 31, 167n1; Gillespie and, 32–33; in Los Angeles, 33–34; media coverage of, 35–37; Moody and influence of, 133; Newark jazz culture and, 126;

public bravado of, 31; Salinas and influence of, 184n27, 189n99; in Salinas's poetry, 87–89, 91–92, 102, 104–5; on substance abuse, 35; Wing's collaboration with, 40, 116, 122–24

Parker, Chaz, 81

Paul, Les, 174n10

Paul Quinichette Group (All Stars), 114–15, 135–42, 199n84

Paul Togawa Quartet, The (recording), 38

Payne, Cecil, 132

performative writing, 110

"Perpetual Emotion" (Wing song), 126–27, 197nn54–55

Petrillo, James, 29

Pettiford, Oscar, 27

Phipps, Eugene, Sr., 124, 147

Piekut, Benjamin, 49

Plamondon, Pun, 97

Plater, Bob, 181n80

Playing in the Dark (Morrison), 165n54

Pocho Che Press, 99

poetry: prose vs., 193n116; Salinas's production of, 20–21, 44, 74–81, 86–89, 98–103. *See also* jazz poetry

political activism, bebop linked to, 29–30

Pollock, Della, 110

pop music, bebop and, 8–10

Porter, Cole, 87–89

Porter, Eric, 29, 39, 167n1

Porter, Roy, 30

postmodernism, bebop in context of, 8, 162n27, 172n72

Powell, Bud, 3, 27, 40, 61–62, 83, 102, 116, 180n69, 189n99

Powell, Richie, 10

Powell, Teddy, 126

Pozo, Chano, 39, 104–6

Prado, Perez, 181n73

prison. *See* incarceration

pseudomorphosis, 110

"Quaker, The" (Wing song), 126

Quartered Notes (Salinas's jazz column), 93–97, 188n81

Quinichette, Paul, 114–15, 126, 135–42, 199n84

"Quintana / Grownup / uptown / uptempo" (Ramírez), 101

race and racism: bebop as response to, 5–6, 9–10, 19–20, 22–24, 29–30, 122–24; Black radical music and, 14–18, 22–24, 59, 165n54; competitive logic of bebop musicians and, 21, 130–32; dreaming and, 156–57; jazz criticism and, 94–97; in postwar era, 43; in recording industry, 29–30; triangulation with music and literary arts, 110–12, 165n54, 167n70; white racism, 200n91; Wing's music and influence of, 122–24

racial democracy: for Afro-Asian Americans, 5; bebop and, 118; Black experimental/radical music and, 13, 22, 45, 104, 107, 110, 131, 140; for Japanese-Americans, 5, 70; Latinx culture and, 82; Rasberry's concept of, 4, 140–41

Radano, Ronald, 7, 165n54

Ramírez, Tomás, 20, 80, 100–101

Ramsey, Guthrie P., Jr., 61, 122, 124–25, 129, 167n1, 180n69

Raney, Jimmy, 82–83

Range, Bob, 132

Rasbery, Vaughn, 4, 140–41, 173n77

Ratliff, Ben, 12, 158

recording industry: commodification of bebop by, 31–32; early bebop and, 29–30, 170n28; jazz criticism and, 95–97

Red Arc: A Call for Liberación con Salsa y Cool (album), 99, 103, 107–9, 189n99

Rediker, Marcus, 164n42

Reece, Ray, 97

Reed, Anthony, 28, 150, 162n28

re-enlightenment, bebop in context of, 8, 162n25, 173n80

relational theory, Black radical music and, 16–17, 166n59

religion, jazz and, 188n81

resistance, music as, 111–12

Resounding Afro Asia (Roberts), 119–20

rhythm: in bebop, 124–26, 129–30; drummers' perceptions of, 198n75, 202n111; Paul Quinichette Group use of, 138–42
Rhythm Dons, 120
Rich, Buddy, 41, 71, 136
Richards, Johnny (Juan Cascales), 38
"Riffs I" (Salinas), 101–2
Rivera Garza, Cristina, 77
Roach, Max, 10, 27, 59, 83
Roberts, Matana, 7
Roberts, T. Carlis, 119, 165n54
Robertson, Marta, 57
Rodney, Red, 83
Rodriguez, Willie, 136
Rogers, Shorty, 83
Roosevelt, Franklin Delano, 56
Rosenberg, Jon, 103–4
Ross, Arnold, 25
Ruff, Willie, 181n80
Russell, Ross, 86
Rustin-Paschal, Nichole, 12, 167n1

Said, Edward, 165n54
Salas, Abel, 100
Salesses, Matthew, 131–32
Salinas, Raúl R.: Araki and, 40, 83; bebop in writings of, 75, 92–93, 102; Black radical music and, 3, 13–16, 75–76, 79–84, 150; dreaming and work, 153; drug use and distribution by, 43, 75, 79, 83–84, 97–98; Ho's collaboration with, 103–9; incarceration of, 40, 43, 75–77, 84, 90–99; jazz clubs and, 184n22; jazz criticism by, 93–97, 193n120; jazz poetry by, 99–103; Kirk and, 189n99; life and work of, 20–21, 23, 39, 41–42; migration to California, 82–83; musicking in poetry of, 86–89, 121; poetry by, 20–21, 44, 74–75, 81–84, 90–99, 103–9; political consciousness of, 97–99; temporality in writings of, 86–87; Wing and, 40–41, 149–50; writing and teaching career of, 99. *See also specific works*
"Salt Peanuts" (Gillespie), 31
Sandoval, Rene, 38

Santa Anita Racetrack, internment camp at, 55–56
Saying Something (Monson), 167n1
Schultz, Anna, 167n70
Scoleri, Carmen, 93, 188n81
Seattle, bebop in, 38
segregation, 4; jazz clubs and, 184n22; in Los Angeles, 34
"Sentimental Viajes" (Ramírez), 101
"Serenade in Blue" (Wing's interpretation of), 132
Shadow and the Act, The (Muyumba), 167n1
Shearing, George, 83
"Sheik of Araby, The" (Bechet recording), 174n10
Shepp, Archie, 189n97
Simmons, John, 126–30, 197nn53–54
Simms, C. Alan, 143
Sinatra, Frank, 59
Skeete-Laessig, Yoland, 141
slavery: cultural impact of, 16–18; in Salinas's poetry, 90–92
Sloan, Nate, 158
Small Acts (Gilroy), 64
Smith, Billie, 121
"Solidarité" (Salinas), 107–9
Solis, Gabriel, 65, 180n64
Something Else by Johnny Richards (album), 38
"Song for Roland Kirk" (Salinas & Ho), 189n99
"Sonny's Blues" (Baldwin), 14, 35, 120, 159
sono-racialization, 165n54
Sorey, Tyshawn, 7, 117, 125–26, 158, 205n23
South Africa, bebop in, 39
South of the Border (Parker album), 159–60
Spalding, Esperanza, 7
"Sparrow's Last Jump" (Grennard), 35
Spears, Louie, 93
Special International Program, 42–43
Spivak, Gayatri Chakravorty, 166n60
Stacey, David, 177n47
Stairway to the Stars (television show), 122
Stanyek, Jason, 49

Steintor Variety Theater (Berlin), 39
stereotypes: of Asian masculinity, 131–32; of Black masculinity, 14–15, 21, 130–32; of Latinx masculinity, 81–84; media stereotypes of bebop, 34–37
Sterne, Jonathan, 165n54
Stitt, Sonny, 83, 102
Stoever, Jennifer, 165n54, 167n70
stories, dreaming and, 109–12
Stowe, David, 39
substance abuse, stereotypes about bebop and, 34–37
"subterranean elefantes in flames" (Ramírez), 101
Sullivan, Maxine, 177n47
Summerlin, Ed, 188n81
surveillance capitalism, mass criminalization and racism linked to, 84–85
Sy Oliver Orchestra, 116

"Take the A Train" (Ellington), 54
Taylor, Yuval, 174n10
Tejano jazz, 80–81
"Tejazz" (Salinas composition), 100–101
Tetsu Bessho and the Nisei Serenaders, 71, 181n78
theory, as action, 8, 162n28
Theurer, Michiko, 117
Thompson, Sir Charles, 114, 136, 138–39
timbral diversity, Campbell's exploration of, 53–54
Time magazine, 34, 95, 171n43
Toads, Nat, 124
Tokyo Boogie-Woogie, 177n47
"Tokyo Riff, The" (Araki), 177n47
Tomlinson, Barbara, 147–48
Tongson, Karen, 12
Torin, Sid, 32
"Tribute to a Native Son, A" (Newark tribute to Wink), 147–49
"Trip through the Mind Jail, A" (Salinas), 20–21, 74–75, 77–81, 98–99, 112–13, 183n3, 189n99
Tristano, Lennie, 51, 102, 174n10
Tucker, Sherrie, 167n1

"Turkish Mambo" (Tristano recording), 51
Turner, Richard Brent, 167n1
"Two Brothers" (Araki), 66–67

Ulanov, Barry, 35, 51, 174n11
Un Trip through the Mind Jail y Otras Excursiones (Salinas), 99, 112–13
US foreign policy, jazz music and, 42–43, 122, 173n77
US State Department, jazz ambassador tours, 122, 141

Vaughan, Sarah, 27, 40, 116
V-Discs, 29–30
Victor Gay Bop, Araki's work with, 61
Victor Hot Club (Tokyo), Araki's performances at, 60–61, 177n47
Victory Grill (club), 42, 184n22
Vietnam War, 41, 108
Volodine, Antoine, 77
"Volunteered Slavery" (Kirk), 189n99
Von Eschen, Penny, 42–43, 141

Wang, Jackie, 84
War Relocation Authority, 55–56
Washington, Kenny, 125, 164n40
Watanabe, Hiromi, 177n47
Weathers, Roscoe, 38
Weglyn, Michi, 55–56
West, Harold "Doc," 197n53
What Is This Thing Called Jazz? (Porter), 167n1
"What Makes 'Jazz' the Revolutionary Music" (Ho), 189n97
White, Frances "Chickie," 71
whiteness: anxiety over Black music and, 36, 130–32, 171nn52–53; as cultural ideal, 16; government protection of, 4; postwar evolution of, 28–29
"Wiggle Wag" (Moody), 133
Williams, James Gordon, 53–54, 163n33
Williams, Martin, 93–94
Williams, Mary Lou, 27–28, 32, 167n1, 188n81
Wilson, Nancy, 95

Wing, Harold ("Chink Williams"): August collaboration with, 196n35; Black radical music and, 3, 13, 15–16; dreaming and work of, 153; drug problems of, 145; "The Evolution of Jazz," 200n97; Garner's collaboration with, 126–30, 196n50, 197nn52–53, 198n57; life and work of, 21, 23, 39, 41, 44, 116–51; Moody's collaboration with, 132–35, 198n75, 199n81; music education for, 120–24, 143–44, 195n28; Newark culture and, 116–19, 142–44, 181n80, 194n2; Newark renewal and, 146–47; Newark tribute to, 147–49; Paul Quinichette Group recordings, 114–15, 135–42; Salinas and, 40–41; songwriting by, 121–24, 144–47, 200n97, 201n99, 201n106, 202n114

Woloch, Alex, 12
Wong, Deborah, 65
Wright, Florence, 122
writing, dreams and, 109–12

Xicanindio poetry and journalism, 3, 20–21, 40, 44, 99; jazz and, 100–103, 189n99; as resistance, 111–12

Yoshida, Etsuzo, 46, 49, 52–53
Yoshida, George, 176n37, 177n47
Young, Gus, 120
Young, Lester, 25–26, 33, 102

Zapata, Richard "Chuy," 184n27

www.ingramcontent.com/pod-product-compliance
Lightning Source LLC
Chambersburg PA
CBHW070840160426
43192CB00012B/2257